THE LIFE AND POEMS OF A CUBAN SLAVE

AFRO-LATIN@ DIASPORAS

Series Editors: Juan Flores, Natasha Gordon-Chipembere, and Miriam Jimenez Roman

The *Afro-Latin@ Diasporas* book Series publishes scholarly and creative writing on the African diasporic experience in Latin America, the Caribbean, and the United States. The series includes books which address all aspects of Afro-Latin@ life and cultural expression throughout the hemisphere, with a strong focus on Afro-Latin@s in the United States. This series is the first of its kind to combine such a broad range of topics, including religion, race, transnational identity, history, literature, music and the arts, social and cultural theory, biography, class and economic relations, gender, sexuality, sociology, politics, and migration.

Published:

The Development of Yoruba Candomble Communities in Salvador, Bahia 1835–1986
Miguel Alonso

The Life and Poems of a Cuban Slave: Juan Francisco Manzano 1797–1854
Edited by Edward J. Mullen

The Life and Poems of a Cuban Slave

Juan Francisco Manzano
1797–1854

Edited by

Edward J. Mullen

First published in 2014 by
PALGRAVE MACMILLAN®
in the United States—a division of St. Martin's Press LLC,
175 Fifth Avenue, New York, NY 10010.

Where this book is distributed in the UK, Europe and the rest of the world,
this is by Palgrave Macmillan, a division of Macmillan Publishers Limited,
registered in England, company number 785998, of Houndmills,
Basingstoke, Hampshire RG21 6XS.

Palgrave Macmillan is the global academic imprint of the above companies
and has companies and representatives throughout the world.

Palgrave® and Macmillan® are registered trademarks in the United States,
the United Kingdom, Europe and other countries.

ISBN: 978-1-137-48136-8

Library of Congress Cataloging-in-Publication Data

Manzano, Juan Francisco, 1797–1854.
    The life and poems of a Cuban slave / Juan Francisco Manzano,
1797–1854 ; edited by Edward J. Mullen.—Second Edition.
        pages cm
    Includes bibliographical references and index.
    ISBN 978–1–137–48136–8 (hardback : alk. paper)
        1. Slavery—Cuba—History—Sources. 2. Manzano, Juan Francisco,
1797–1854. I. Mullen, Edward J., 1942– editor of compilation. II. Title.

HT1076.M3 2014
306.3′62097291—dc23   2014024384

A catalogue record of the book is available from the British Library.

Design by Newgen Knowledge Works (P) Ltd., Chennai, India.

First edition: December 2014

10 9 8 7 6 5 4 3 2 1

Contents

Preface to the Second Edition

This book was first printed in 1981 under the aegis of the Shoe String Press. The original impetus for *The Life and Poems of a Cuban Slave* was to call attention to the importance of texts authored by African descended Americans in the New World that had been neglected or unavailable to the general reading public. All research, I suppose, depends upon a mutual set of discoveries. I discovered the existence of Juan Francisco Manzano's remarkable autobiography through the earlier breakthrough scholarship of G. R. Coulthard, the author of the classic *Race and Colour in Caribbean Literature* (London: Oxford Press, 1962) and Richard L. Jackson's *The Black Image in Latin American Literature* (Albuquerque: The University of New Mexico Press, 1976). Both these scholars were pioneers in the then emerging field of Afro-Hispanic Studies. Their scholarship was, in turn, indebted to a long tradition of cross-national exchange between Afro-Cubans and African Americans dating back to the era of slavery, and particularly after the U.S. intervention into the Cuban War of Independence in 1898. References to Juan Francisco Manzano were made in the early twentieth century by the bibliographer Arthur A. Schomburg, who cited him in his classic *A Bibliographical Checklist of American Negro Poetry* (Charles F. Hartman: New York, 1916), and in the early commentary published by V. B. Spratlin in *The Journal of Negro History* (Volume 19, No.1, January 1934).

Much has changed in Manzano studies since this book was first edited in the absence, I may add, of access to Roberto Friol's *Suite para Francisco Manzano* (*Suite for Juan Francisco Manzano* (1977)), which contains vital documentation about Manzano's biography and work. There have been no fewer than two translations of Manzano's autobiography into English (the first by Evelyn Picon Garfield in 1996, the second by Lloyd King in 1990), one in French (by Alain Yacou in 2004) and an adaptation in verse for children, *The Poet Slave of Cuba: A Biography of Juan Francisco Manzano* by Margarita Engle

(New York: Henry Holt, 2006). This, in addition to major books by Gera Burton, Jerome Branche, William Luis, and Ifeoma Nwankdwo. These studies have been further illuminated by a series of important essays by scholars such as Joselyn Almeida, Adrina J. Bergero, Anna Brickhouse, Robert Richmond Ellis, Fernanda Macchi, Marilyn Miller, and Fionnghuala Sweeney, among others. Important compilations, too, of Manzano's work have appeared as well, such as Abdeslam Azougarh's *Juan Francisco Manzano: Esclavo poeta en la Isla de Cuba* (Valencia: Episteme, 2000), and William Luis's *Juan Francisco Manzano. Autobiografía del esclavo poeta y otros escritos* (Madrid: Iberoamerican, 2007). The latter may be arguably considered the definitive study of the multiple transmissions of the slave-poet's voice. It offers an analysis of the various versions of Manzano's slave autobiography, the one written by the slave and those transcribed by writers and scholars. It also reproduces and annotates an unpublished nineteenth-century notebook copied by Nicholás Azcárate and contains a more accurate transcription of Manzano's handwritten autobiography, which is housed in the Bibloteca National José Martí.

Parallel to the scholarship on Manzano has been a growing awareness of the role played by his first translator, Richard Robert Madden. Madden's *Poems by a Slave in the Island of Cuba* has been included, for example, in *Documenting the South*, a digital publishing initiative that provides Internet access to text images and audio files related to southern history, literature, and culture and published under the auspices of the University of North Carolina, Chapel Hill. The text has also been included in *Sabin Americana: 1500–1926,* an online collection of books, pamphlets, serials, and other works about the Americas from the time of their discovery to the early 1900s. Although these digitalized versions of Madden's nineteenth-century work are extremely useful, they do not provide the historical context necessary to understand the complex traffic of the work of Manzano among the Caribbean, Europe, and the larger Americas. The new introductory essay to this edition builds upon my previously published "Juan Francisco Manzano: Building a Tradition," which was included in *Afro-Cuban Literature: Critical Junctures*, and published by Greenwood Press in 1998.

The present edition of Richard Robert Madden's *Poems by a Slave in the Island of Cuba, Recently Liberated; translated from the Spanish by R. R. Madden, M.D. with the History of the Early Life of the Negro Poet, Written by Himself; To Which Are Prefixed Two Pieces of Descriptive of Cuban Slavery and the Slave-Traffic* (London: Thomas Ward and Co., 1840) reproduces the London 1840 edition in its entirety. Original spelling and punctuation have been maintained throughout. Only obvious errors of punctuation and spelling have been corrected. Glosses have been supplied to clarify literary, historic, and geographic allusions. We have supplied as well the original Spanish-language versions of three of Manzano's poems that appear in the text. These are from *Parnaso cubano,* edited by Antonio López Prieto (Habana; Miguel de Villa, 1881), 253–55.

Acknowledgments

I wish to express gratitude to the British Museum and Library for facilitating access to the original 1840 edition, to the American Council of Learned Societies, and to the University of Missouri Columbia Research Council, which supported the first edition of this book. I am profoundly grateful to Pippa Letsky who assisted in the editing of this book and is responsible for the index. Special thanks is due to Brenda Klemme for her gracious help in the preparation of the manuscript and to Mike Aperauch and Jeff LaSala of Palgrave Macmillan for their help and patience in the production stage of this book.

An earlier version of the Introduction appeared in Chapter 5, "Juan Francisco Manzano: Building a Tradition," of my book, *Afro-Cuban Literature: Critical Junctures* (Westport CT. Greenwood.1998) and is reprinted with the permission of ABC CLIO.

A final word of gratitude is due to those writers and scholars (past and present) whose scholarship on Juan Francisco Manzano and Richard Robert Madden truly made this study possible.

Introduction

The Background

Cuba, the largest island in the Caribbean, has long played an important role in the literary imagination of the Western world. Viewed by many as the locus of authentic blackness, it gave rise to Afro-Cubanism, a movement in Caribbean arts and letters that stemmed from a rediscovery of the region's African heritage during the 1920s and to some extent paralleled the Harlem Renaissance in the United States.[1] There has been a cultural dialog between the United States and Cuba for centuries. A significant part of this interchange has related to questions of racial identity rooted in a long-standing tradition of cultural exchange, specifically focusing on African-based traditions. In contrast to Latin American debates on race, which have been profoundly influenced by conceptual paradigms of cultural identity anchored in myths of racial harmony and syncretism, polemics in the more racially polarized United States have produced a more forceful and open discussion of race.

Slavery and its literary portrayal constitute an important conceptual link in the development of hemispheric American studies as well as the emergence of an authentic Afro-Cuban aesthetic; they undergird the emergence of a unique black voice in Cuban literature. The history of Afro-Cubanism might be logically viewed as a metaphor for the emergence of Cuba as a nation-state.

Although since the period of discovery and colonization there have been writers of African ancestry in almost every region of Spanish America, the demographic distribution of the black diaspora has had an obvious relation to the cultivation and development of black literature.[2] One is at once struck by the fact that far more slaves from the sub-Saharan region were brought to Cuba and Brazil than to other Spanish and Portuguese territories in Latin America. Although the Portuguese began shipping slaves to Brazil as early as 1538, the Spanish did not resort to the large-scale importation of slaves until the mid-eighteenth century. However, according to some censuses, approximately 119,000 blacks were taken to Cuba between 1774 and 1807, which amounted to almost half of the entire Spanish American black population.[3] It is logical, then, that the Antilles in general and Cuba in particular should be the locus for the emergence of a body of literature dealing with the black experience in Spanish America.

Although the high-water mark of interest in black folklore, music, and writing in the Caribbean appears to be the 20-year span between the two world wars (a period roughly corresponding to the Harlem Renaissance in the United States), this flowering of black literary expression was but a logical outgrowth of a preexisting structure of literary expression relating to the large black and mulatto population. As José Juan Arrom has pointed out, the influence of black writers is evident in Cuba as early as 1608.[4] It was during the nineteenth century, however, that the first substantial body of work by and about blacks emerged. Apart from collections of folk songs by blacks,[5] virtually all works about Cuba's black population were the products of white Creole intellectuals and not Afro-Cubans. There was, however, one important exception to this phenomenon: the solitary figure of Juan Francisco Manzano (1797–1854), one of the few freed slaves to achieve literary prominence in nineteenth-century Cuban letters. In order to understand the uniqueness of Manzano, some comments about the island's socioeconomic development are in order.

Unlike the Spanish-speaking countries in the continental portion of Latin America, Cuba (like Puerto Rico) was a Spanish colony until 1898. The transformation of Cuba into a major producer of sugar, which began in the late eighteenth century, led to the massive importation of African slaves well into the nineteenth century. According to José Luciano Franco, "the number of African slaves who arrived as illegal aliens on the island after 1820 was greater than the total number of slaves who had landed in Cuba in the three centuries before."[6] As a consequence, essays and imaginative interpretations of the black condition became one of the defining characteristics of nineteenth-century Cuban literature. As Lorna Williams aptly notes, the relationship of Cuba's Creole intellectuals to the island's black population has always been problematic. Thus, although writers such as Félix Varela, José Antonio Saco, and Francisco Arango y Parreño argued in various degrees for an end to the slave trade, their attitudes toward the slaves themselves were rooted in the fear that the island's black population would eventually engulf the whites.

The literary response to the Cuban dilemma took many forms, the most often studied being a series of antislavery narratives that describe the horrors of the slave trade and offer detailed portraits of the mistreatment of blacks. The best known of these texts are Manzano's *Autobiography* (1835, 1839), Anselmo Suárez y Romero's *Francisco el ingenio; o, Las delicias del campo, novela cubana* (*The Plantation and the Delights of the Country Life*, 1839), Gertrudis Gómez de Avellaneda's *Sab* (1841), Antonio Zambrana's *El negro Francisco* (*Black Francisco*, 1875), Cirilo Villaverde's *Cecilia Valdés* (1882), Martín Morúa Delgado's *Sofía* (1891), and Francisco Calcagno's *Romualdo, uno de tantos* (*Romualdo, One of Many*, 1891). Manzano's *Autobiography* is not only the earliest antislavery narrative but also, with the exception of Martín Morúa Delgado's *Sofía*, the only such to be written by a person of African ancestry. As William Luis notes, the antislavery narrative was linked to a project to abolish slavery in Cuba; therefore the "antislavery works reflect a historical and literary counter-discourse which directly challenged the colonial slavery systems."[7] Thus, black subjects were incorporated into Cuban literary discourse as a function of their ability to achieve literary, economic, and political freedom from Spanish colonial rule.

The locus of much of the literary activity relating to the question of slavery was the home of Domingo del Monte (1804–1853), a Creole intellectual and maecenas to the principal antislavery writers of the period: Cirilo Villaverde, Felix Tanco y Bosmeniel, Ramón del Palma, Anselmo Suárez y Romero, José Antonio Echeverría, and Manuel González del Valle. Although Del Monte was an enlightened humanist and as such was appalled at the brutalizing effects of slavery, he nonetheless viewed blacks as different and intellectually inferior.[8] The literary activities of Del Monte and his cohorts with reference to Afro-Cubans was linked to a larger project. Williams put it this way:

> Consequently, the literary production of the Del Monte group may be regarded as the cultural equivalent of the Spanish American thrust for political independence with which it coincides....Hence the dualistic portraits of slaves in which the narratives abound. Since slaves could so readily embody the competing claims for social equality and political autonomy, the literary recuperation of what was politically repressed became simultaneously an anticolonialist gesture and an affirmation of being.[9]

Such "gestures," however superficially well intended, often led to the appropriation of the narrative strategies of the romantic novel that produced stereotypical portraits of black characters. Gómez de

Avellaneda's *Sab* and Suárez y Romero's *Francisco* are classic examples of this kind of writing, which, as G. R. Coulthard indicates, were to form the foundation for later portrayals of Afro-Cubans in the 1920s.[10]

The Life of Manzano

If ever there was a good example of life imitating art, the story of Juan Francisco Manzano must surely be it. Born into the double prison of slavery and Spanish colonial rule, he managed to produce the only extant slave narrative in Spanish American letters, in addition to a considerable amount of poetry and one five-act play. Tortured as a young man and falsely imprisoned as an adult, he (ironically) outlived both his masters and his literary benefactors. From his autobiographical sketch, secondary sources, and especially the painstaking archival research of Roberto Friol, we have been able to construct the following portrait of his life.[11]

Manzano was born in February 1797 in Havana, to Torbio Castro, a harpist, and María del Pilar, a house servant to the Marquesa Jústiz de Santa Ana (1733–1803). The latter, a member of Creole aristocracy, was herself a poet, having composed a poem to the Spanish emperor Charles III on the occasion of the fall of Havana to the British. Lorna Williams offers the following insightful observation concerning this paradoxical literary bond: "Because the British siege of Havana was the event that inaugurated the large-scale entry of African-born slaves into Cuba, Manzano's literary kinship with Doña Beatriz de Jústiz evokes the idea that Cuba's unprecedented dependence on slave labor was equally worthy of condemnation. In this light, the *Autobiography* itself becomes the slave's equivalent of the Marchioness Jústiz's poem to Charles III."[12] Because his parents were house (rather than field) slaves, Manzano's life until approximately the age of 11 was one of relative privilege. He indicates in the *Autobiography* that at the age of 6, he was sent to school at the home of his baptismal godmother, Trinidad de Zayas. As Friol is also quick to point out, Manzano was not black—that is, of pure African ancestry—but rather a light-skinned mulatto. Friol notes, "Tanto fenotípica como genotípicamente éste era un mestizo" ("He was both phenotypically and genotypically a mestizo").[13] Friol's use of the term *mestizo,* which in postrevolutionary Cuban critical discourse refers to both biological and cultural fusion, is instructive; it points to a conceptual bridge between nineteenth-century concepts of race and nationalism, and twentieth-century portrayals of blacks as an integral part of Cuban cultural identity. It is not accidental, then, that the figure of Manzano was to be systematically rediscovered at certain nodal moments in Cuban history, during which the construction of a sense of people hood, no matter how empirically false, became central to specific political and ideological agendas. Both Jerome Branche and Ifeoma Kiddoe Nwankwo have studied Manzano's sense of racial self and his efforts to distance himself from Blacks as a function of anti-Black racism among his potential readers.[14] Because of the circumstances of his birth (both his color and the status of his parents), Manzano occupied a curious intermediate space in the social strata of nineteenth-century colonial Cuba. He and other mulattoes were mediating elements between the African slave work force, the white Creole leisure class, and the representatives of the Spanish crown. As such, they played an important but little studied role in the maintenance of the island's economic and social infrastructure.[15] As artisans, tailors, cooks, and musicians, they drove the economic engine that would lead to Cuban independence. Afro-Cubans contributed as well to the arts and letters. As Carlos Trelles has noted, between 1815 and 1937 black Cubans published some 402 books, pamphlets, and newspapers.[16]

Sonia Labrador-Rodríguez has pointed out that Manzano was not the only Afro-Cuban poet who wrote as a slave but must be considered in tandem with such writers as Ambrosio Echemendía, José del Carmen Díaz, Manuel Roblejo, and Juan Antonio Frías. More importantly, as she notes with particular insight, Manzano's position as a literate slave not only contributed to the textual ambiguities of the *Autobiography* but also explains why the power that knowledge gave him was viewed as a potential threat "para los blancos, tanto criollos como peninsulares" ("for whites, whether Creoles or Spaniards").[17]

In spite of his privileged status, Manzano was still a slave and therefore was considered property. Thus, on the death of his first mistress in 1803 he was first apprenticed as a tailor in Havana under the care of his godmother, finally passing on to the service of María de la Concepción, La Marquesa de Prado Ameno, the second daughter of his first mistress. His period of service to the latter would constitute the chronological grid for the *Autobiography*. It was marked by repeated acts of cruelty. He finally fled to Havana, sometime between 1814 and 1817.

Manzano was largely self-taught, and it is difficult to pinpoint just when he became literate. It was, as in most slave societies, illegal in Cuba for slaves to learn to read and write. On the subject of his literacy,

Manzano himself is ambivalent. As noted, in the early pages of the *Autobiography* he claims to have been sent to school before he was 10, but elsewhere states that he was still illiterate at 16.[18] Labrador-Rodríguez has located in the *Autobiography* three key moments in which the act of learning to read (translate: the will to freedom via creativity) is first encouraged then almost simultaneously repressed, a process that accounts for the slave's heightened consciousness of the primacy of the written word.[19] Based on what little is known of Manzano's life, it is probably logical to assume that he first achieved full literacy while in the service of Nicolás Cárdenas y Manzano (the son of his second mistress), where he taught himself to write by tracing his master's penmanship. From copying the latter's writing he then proceeded to copy the verse of Juan Batista Arriaza y Supervilla (1770–1837), a popular neoclassic poet who would become his primary literary model.[20]

After his escape from the Marchioness de Prado Ameno, he obtained permission to work independently in Havana. By 1821 he had returned to the city of Matanzas, and while in the service of Don Tello Manilla he published a 15-page booklet, *Poesías líricas*. Although his first published verses appeared during a period when existing laws concerning censorship had been relaxed, their publication was not without problems. As Thomas Bremer reminds us:

> But even so, a volume of poetry would not merely have been "accepted" by a publisher, but rather, someone would have had to pay for its printing. In addition, it was absolutely impossible for a slave—legally a subject without any rights at all—to have his own works published, no matter to which genre they belonged. In any case, even if we assume that Manzano could finance the printing of his poetry himself, special permission from the colonial government would have had to be granted. It is not clear who arranged for this publication, nor for those in Cuban papers and reviews of the time.[21]

This first publication was followed in 1830 by another collection of verse, *Flores pasageras* (Fleeting Flowers) [*sic*]. Although his poetry (more specifically, critical reactions to it) will be discussed in more detail later in this essay, it is important to note that Manzano calls to mind the first African American poet, Phillis Wheatley, whose *Poems on Various Subjects, Religious and Moral,* published in London in 1773, also required the intervention and approval of a mediating white voice. As Henry Louis Gates notes, "writing, especially after the printing press became so widespread, was taken to be the *visible* sign of reason. Blacks were 'reasonable,' and hence 'men,' if—and only if—they demonstrated the mastery of the 'arts and sciences,' the eighteenth century's formula for writing."²²

The year 1835 was a pivotal year for Manzano. On March 2, 1835, he married María del Rosario, a mulatto pianist, and later that year began, at the request of Domingo del Monte, to compose his autobiography. At the time of its composition, he was still a slave, a fact made very evident in a letter he wrote to his patron in June 1835:

Mi querido y Sor Dn. Domingo: reciví la apresiable de smd. fecha 15 del corriente y, sorprendido de que en ella me dise smd. que ase tres o cuatro meses me pidio la historia, no puedo menos de manifestarle que no he tenido tal abiso con tanta antisipasión, pues en el dia mismo que reciví la de 22 me puse a recorrer el espasio que llena la carrera de mi vida, y cuando pude, me puse a escrivir crellendo que me bastaria un real de papel, pero teniendo escrito algo mas aun que saltando a veces por cuatro, a aun por cinco años, ne he llegado todabia a 1820, pero espero concluir pronto siñendome unicamente a los sucesos mas interesantes: he estado mas de cuatro ocaciones por no seguirla, un cuadro de tantas calamidades, no parese singun abultado protocolo de embusterias, y mas desde tan tierna edad los crueles azotes me asian conoser mi umilde condision; me abochorna el contarlo. y no se como demostrar los hechos dejando la parte mas terrible en el tintero, y ojala tubiera otros hechos con que llenar la historia de mi vida sin recordar el esesivo rigor con que me ha tratado mi antigua ama, obligandome o poniendome en la forsosa nesesidad a apelar a una ariesgada fuga para aliviar mi triste cuerpo de las continuas mortificasiones que no podia ya sufrir mas. asi idos preparando para bera a una debil criatura rodando en los mas graves padesimientos entregado a diversos mayorales siendo sin la menor ponderasion el blanco de los infortunios. temo desmereser en su apresio un siento por siento, pero acuerdese smd. cuando lea que yo soy esclavo y que el esclavo es un ser muerto ante su señor, y no preida en su apresio lo que he ganado: consideradme un martir y allareis que los infinitos azotes que ha mutilado mis carnes aun no formadas, jamas embiliseran a vuestro afectisimo sierve que fiádo en la prudensia que oscaraclcriza se atreve a chistar una palabra sobre esta materia, y mas cuando vive quien me ha dado tan largo que genir.²³

(Dear Senor Dr. Del Monte: I received your good letter of June 15 and was surprised to learn that you had asked me to write the story of my life three or four months ago. I must tell you that I didn't learn of this request until recently. In fact the very day I received your letter dated the 22nd, I started to think about the events of my life. When I was able to, I wrote my ideas down, thinking I would use but one *real*'s worth of paper. However, when I finally got something down on paper [even skipping four or five years] I still hadn't gotten to 1820, but I hope to finish soon by sticking to only the most interesting events. About four times I was ready to give up; a portrait filled with so many calamities seems to be nothing more than a massive record of deceits. Moreover, I'm ashamed to tell this story since a boyhood filled with cruel lashings made me aware of my humble position in life, and I'm not certain how to clearly state my case if I omit the worse part. I only wish that there were other facts to fill the story of my life without recalling the excessive rigor with which my former mistress treated me, thus forcing me into the risky position of running away in order to save my poor body from the continuous mortifications that I could no longer endure.... Remember, sir, when you read this letter, that I am a slave, and that a slave is nothing in the eyes of his master.... Consider me a martyr and you will find that the endless whippings that mutilated my young body will never make me think badly of you, and trusting in you I dare to speak about what has happened to me even though the person responsible for my suffering is still alive.)

In 1836, by now a well-known figure to the Del Monte coterie, Manzano read his famous sonnet "Treinta años" ("Thirty Years") to the group. The poem, which has been compared with George Moses Horton's (1797–1883) "On Liberty and Slavery," had been composed that year, the same year in which Manzano was freed.[24] The most famous translation is that of Richard Robert Madden, who modified the original to add additional pathos by stressing the biblical image of bondage—a common technique among abolitionist writers. The same process of reconstruction would be used by Madden during his translation of the *Autobiography*.

> When I think on the course I have run,
> From my childhood itself to this day,
> I tremble, and fain would I shun,
> The remembrance its terrors array.
> I marvel at struggles endured,
> With a destiny frightful as mine,
> At the strength for such efforts: assured
> Tho' I am, 'tis in vain to repine.
> I have known this sad life thirty years,
> And to me, thirty years it has been
> Of suff'ring, of sorrow and tears,
> Ev'ry day of its bondage I've seen.
> But 'tis nothing the past—or the pains,
> Hitherto I have struggled to bear,
> When I think, oh, my God! On the chains,
> That I know I'm yet destined to wear.[25]

Cintio Vitier cites a letter of Del Monte to José Luis Alfonso, the Marquis de Montelo, that fixes 1836 as the year in which Manzano was freed.[26] In 1839 Manzano completed his autobiography, which was corrected by Suárez y Romero (1818–1878) and then given to Madden, with a portfolio of other abolitionist writings.

Manzano contributed sporadically to a number of literary magazines, such as *El Album, El Aguinaldo Habanero,* and *La Moda o Recreo de las Bellas Damas.*[27] In 1841 he wrote a play, a five-act tragedy titled *Zafira,* which he dedicated to Valdés Machuca.[28] In 1844 he was imprisoned by the colonial authorities for having participated in an alleged conspiracy; he was found innocent and released in 1845. He published little thereafter until his death in 1854.

The Poetry

Although it was Manzano's *Autobiography* that would eventually earn his entrance into the literary canon, he self-defined himself as a poet and it was his verse, written decades before his self-portrait that helped gain his manumission. Marilyn Miller put it this way: "For while Manzano was induced to write his autobiography, he himself maintained that it was *poetry* that sustained him as a writer and as an individual."[29] It was some of his poetry, too, translated by the French abolitionist Victor Schoelcher in a series of New World antislavery documents, *Abolition de l'esclavage; examen du préjugé contre la couleur des africains et des sang-melés* (Paris: Paguerre, 1840) that helped introduce his work into the complex transatlantic dialog about slavery. It was not unremarkable that the earliest commentary about him should be written by Del Monte. As early as 1845 he called attention to Manzano in a controversial essay, "Paralelo entre Plácido y Manzano" ("Similarities between Plácido and Manzano"), which was published in the *Liceo de la Habana* in 1859. In comparing Manzano to the better-known poet Gabriel de la Concepción Valdés, Del Monte stressed two points: the importance of Manzano's status as a slave (which made him a more authentic commodity for the antislavery coterie), and his "blackness." Manzano's morphological markers of blackness validated and authenticated his work, in a curious inversion of the earlier techniques of authentication, one that required written commentary by whites. Del Monte's text reads:

> Plácido nunca fué exclavo; nació libre: era hijo de blanca y de mulato, y por supuesto su color era casi blanco. No tuvo por lo mismo que

luchar en su vida, como Manzano que era casi negro, como hijo de
negra y de mulato, y esclavo de nacimiento, con los obstáculos insu-
perables de su condición y su color, para desarrollar las dotes naturales
de su imaginación, que era realmente poética. Logró más instruc-
ción literaria que Manzano, y en sus versos, por lo comun rotundos
y armoniosos, no se encuentran las incorrecciones gramaticales y las
faltas de prosodia que en las muy sentidos y melancólicas del pobre
esclavo. Plácido se complacia en cantar las pompas y los triunfos de
los grandes de la tierra con una magnilocuencia digna de los poetas
clásicos de España: Manzano no sabe repetir en su lira otro tema que
el de las angustias de una vida azarosa y llena de peripecias terribles;
pero yo prefiero los cantos tristes del esclavo á los del mulato libre,
porque noto más profundo sentimiento de humanidad en los prim-
eros, porque brillan por su frescura y originalidad nativas, porque
los principios de mi estética y de mi filosofía se avienen más con el
lamento arrancado del corazón del oprimido que con el concierto
estrepitoso de un poeta, de quien con razón decia nuestro estóico y
malogrado Milanés en 1838:

> Y ¿qué es mirar á este vate
> Ser escabel del magnate
> Cuando el festin,
> Cantar sin rubor ni seso
> Y disputar algun hueso
> Con el mastin?
>   1845[30]

(Plácido never was a slave; he was born free; he was the son of a white
woman and a mulatto, and was therefore almost white. He didn't have
to fight in his life like Manzano who was almost completely black,
the son of a black woman and a mulatto, and therefore a slave from
birth with the insurmountable obstacles of his condition and his color
to overcome in order to develop the natural talents of his imagination, which was truly poetic. He succeeded in getting more literary
training than Manzano, and his poetry, in general, is more sonorous
and harmonious and has fewer errors of grammar and prosody than
that found in the deeply felt and melancholy verses of the poor slave.
Plácido is content to sing of the pomp and triumph of the world's
great figures with a grandiloquence worthy of Spain's classic poets.
Manzano only knows how to repeat with his lyre the theme of an
unlucky life filled with anguish and terrible turns of fate. I, however,
prefer the sad songs of the slave to those of the free mulatto because I
find in his verses a greater sense of profound human feeling; they shine
with a natural freshness and originality. This is due, no doubt, to the
fact that my philosophy and aesthetic principles are more in accord
with the lamentations torn from the heart of the oppressed than with

the clamorous concerts of a poet, of whom our stoic and unfortunate
Milanes wrote in 1838:

And why look at this poet
the footstool of the great
    When during the festival
he sings without shame nor sense
and shares bones
    with a dog?)

Manzano's reception by the conservative, pro-Spanish literary historian Emilio Martín González del Valle is also instructive. Although
written in 1874, but not published until 1884, González del Valle's
La poesía lírica en Cuba (Lyric Poetry in Cuba) conceptualizes Cuban
literature as a branch of Spanish peninsular letters. Although he considers Manzano to be "the best" of the black poets, he neutralizes
this very argument by granting him such status based on "su color
y, pelo rizo, y a su erudición de esclavo" ("his color, his kinky hair,
and his erudition as slave"). Manzano was the object of a relatively
detailed bio-bibliographic note in Antonio López Prieto's *Parnaso
cubano (Cuban Parnassus)*, which anthologized five of his poems, and
he was also mentioned in Aurelio Mitjans's *Historia de la literatura
cubana (History of Cuban Literature)*. Both critics seemed to be more
concerned with his status as a slave than his stature as a poet.[31] Even
at the height of the Afro-Cuban movement, which coincided with
the first Spanish edition of his autobiography, few, with the exception
of Ramón Guirao, refered to Manzano as a poet. Guirao's earliest
commentary, in fact, amounts to little more than a recasting of Del
Monte's earlier formulation.

During the 1970s, under the influence of Addison Gayle's *The
Black Aesthetic* (1971), Manzano's reputation as a poet fared no better. Miriam DeCosta conflated his reputation with that of Plácido,
concluding that they both illustrate "the defects of the period—a
period of imitation." Similarly, Richard Jackson metaphorically chided
Manzano for ignoring his African heritage. It would be during the
1980s and 1990s—a *reconstructionist phase*, to borrow a term from
Houston Baker—that Manzano was rediscovered as a poet. With few
exceptions, this rediscovery appears to have been a rewriting of earlier formulations, which by and large posited Manzano's poetry as
derivative and void of any real merit. Such observations are hardly
surprising, considering that not until the publication of Friol's *Suite
para Juan Francisco Manzano* in 1977 would most of Manzano's
verse even be available to scholars in any meaningful form. One result

of this textual void was the analysis of poems that in fact Manzano never wrote. Thus, Susan Willis offers a brilliant Marxist reading of "To Cuba"—a poem written, ironically, by Richard Robert Madden whose role in reinventing Manzano will be discussed later in this essay.[32]

The comments of Sylvia Molloy are instructive—less for their conclusions, I might add, than for their intertextuality with a critical discourse that has consistently denied the ability of black-based texts to signify at a level of creative abstraction:

> What strikes the modern reader about Manzano's poetry, however, is its desperately conventional, measured and ultimately *correct* style. It is mediocre Neoclassicism at its very worst, which, if one thinks of it, was to be expected. Manzano himself declares that his model was Arriaza, the contemporary Spanish poet who translated Boileau; Del Monte, an ardent Neoclassicist, helped Manzano edit his poetry; and Neoclassicism, after all, was very much the fashion of the day. Besides being the style Manzano read, heard and memorized, it was, I suspect, a style that afforded him comfort precisely because of its readymade formalism, its handy clichés, its lofty abstraction, its reassuring meters. Manzano's avowed liking for *pie forzado*—the prefixed "mold" of the poem (verse and rhyme) determining the writing itself—confirms, I believe, this suspicion.[33]

In a notable contradiction of critics who undervalue Manzano's creative potential, Antonio Vera-León notes that Manzano's writing—which he recognizes as a reciprocal endeavor between the poet and his patrons (translate: editors)—represents a step in the formation of national, autochthonous literature that borrows from the black vernacular to achieve freedom from the master grammar of urban, peninsular Spain. Thus, he reads the hypothetical origins of "Treinta años" as an involuntary parody of a canonical model in which slavery replaces courtly love as the structuring principle:

> La tradición literaria "blanca" metropolitana es celebrada en el texto de Manzano y simultáneamente desfigurada por la escritura "imperfecta" del esclavo, llena de faltas de ortografía, "contaminada" por la relación estrecha que su texto establece entre la escritura y la oralidad vernácula.

> (The urban "white" literary tradition is celebrated in Manzano's text and simultaneously disfigured by the "imperfect" writing of the slave, filled with errors in orthography and "contaminated" by the tight

relationship that his text establishes between writing and the orality of the vernacular.)[34]

An important step in the critical reevaluation of Manzano's poetic oeuvre was William Luis's discovery of 20 of his poems copied by Nicolás Azcárate (1828–1894) in a notebook in 1852. Luis's inventory of seven of the poems that have never been published strikes the reader as unremarkable: The seven unpublished poems and their related themes, in the order in which they appear, are as follows: 1) "El hortelano" portrays a gardener who is a slave to love; 2) "Al besar una flor de maravilla" equates a flower with the poetic voice's lover; 3) "Desesperación" condemns a world in which there is no hope; 4) "A la muerte" refers to the poet's confrontation with death; 5) "La esclava ausente" alludes to a female slave who thinks of herself as her master's equal; 6) "Memorias del bien pasado" depicts Ortelio's current misfortune and pain; and 7) "La visión del poeta compuesta en un Ingenio de fabrica azucar" [sic] describes the harsh reality of working in a sugar mill and the need to dream in order to escape from it.[35]

Two of the texts, "La esclava ausente" ("The Absent Slave") and "La visión del poeta compuesta en un Ingenio de fabrica azúcar" ("The Vision of a Poet Composed on a Sugar Plantation"), deal directly with the theme of slavery and are therefore something of an anomaly in Manzano's poetry. In the first poem, Luis notes, Manzano thematizes the injustices of the slave system by adopting the voice of a female slave, a technique that allows him to commingle metaphorically the dual notions of love and liberty. The second text is considerably longer (52 stanzas) and describes the horrors of slavery on a sugar plantation. It is a poem "about the inhumane treatment of slaves and the need to escape, at least in dreams, from the unbearable circumstances in which they live."[36] What is significant is that underneath the rhetorical neoclassical veneer, which seems at times to smother Manzano's voice, lurks, as Luis suggests, a political message articulated by a poetic voice not often associated with Cuba's most famous slave-poet.

Luis was not alone in recognizing some degree of psychological complexity in Manzano's verse. Rex Hauser, for example, noted similarities in Manzano's "Un sueño" ("A Dream") and the "Primero Sueño" ("First Dream"), by Sor Juana Inés de la Cruz (1648–1695), the foremost lyric poet and feminist of the colonial period. Although Hauser was primarily concerned with the linking notion of flight—a poetic trope that was a commonplace in neoclassical poetry—he appropriately remarked that Manzano's poem "is a deeply meaningful reflection on the condition of the slave in colonial American society."[37] Robert Richmond Ellis in a more radical reading of the poem concludes that it is "a dream of racial solidarity and of love between men and as such it stands as a counterpoint to the racist and masculinist brutality of the *Autobiogafía*."[38]

Reading Manzano's Autobiography

In spite of his early reputation as a poet, and as we have seen, Manzano's brief *Autobiography* was ultimately responsible for his recognition as a writer of stature. With the exception of the members of the Del Monte group, it was virtually unknown in the nineteenth century and was not available in complete printed form in Spanish until 1937; further, it was not until the 1960s that either the *Autobiography* or the other works of Manzano were the object of any broad-based critical debate. G. R. Coulthard's classic *Race and Colour in Caribbean Literature* finally reawakened interest in Manzano. In his discussion of Francisco Calcagno's *Poetas de color* (*Poets of Color*, 1878), Coulthard noted the inclusion of the *Autobiography*, stressing in particular Manzano's status as a slave: "The deepest impressions left by this autobiographical sketch are of the arbitrariness and meanness of the masters, and the total denial of any kind of rights to the slave."[39]

A fact that makes the *Autobiography* even more fascinating is Coulthard's revelation that it was translated into English in 1840 by British abolitionist Richard Robert Madden, well before the first Spanish edition appeared: "Manzano's story had a curious history as it was first published in 1840 in an English translation, in the same volume as several of his poems also translated into English... The book also contained poems by Madden himself, which deal with the horrors of slavery, very much in the tone of Suárez y Romero's *Francisco*—scenes of the brutal treatment of slaves on the plantations and a picture of the cynical and callous attitude of the slave-owners."[40] The translation and its relationship to abolitionism will be discussed in considerable detail later in this essay.

The curious philological odyssey of the *Autobiography* shows to what a large extent the voices of others (patrons, editors, translators, and critics) have played in the construction of various versions of the same slave's story. Marilyn Miller put it this way: "Ironically, then, the first version of Manzano's remarkable 'autobiography' does not bear that title or even its own name. It was staged by mentors and handlers hailing from both sides of the Atlantic who commissioned, edited, corrected, extracted, translated, and otherwise manipulated his life story, publishing it, at least, initially, in a country and language not his own."[41] Using as corroborating evidence two letters that Manzano wrote to Domingo del Monte on June 25 and September 25, 1835, one can hypothesize that the first draft was written before Manzano was manumitted in 1836.[42] In 1839, Suárez y Romero copied and corrected the Manzano original before giving it to Madden, who translated and published part of the text in 1840. Nicolás Azcárate, another member of the Del Monte coterie, prepared a notebook on the life of Manzano, which was entitled *Obras completas de Juan Francisco Manzano esclavo en la Isla de Cuba, The Complete Works of Juan Francisco Manzano, Slave on the Island of Cuba,* 1852, which in turn contains further emendations aimed at casting a discourse in more normative Spanish. Azcárate's copy of the Suárez y Romero version may have been used by Francisco Calcagno, who anthologized fragments of the life of Manzano in his *Poetas de color (Poets of Color, 1868, 1878, 1879, 1887).*[43] Calcagno (1826–1903) played an important role in Cuban literary transnational historiography and had strong ties with the Cuban exile community. He wrote the first dictionary of Cuban literature, *Diccionario biográfico cubano(Dictionary of Cuban Biography* 1878, 1886), which was published in conjunction with Néstor Ponce de León, an important member of the Cuban émigré community in New York. From 1854 until 1859 he lived in the United States where he most likely read many of the primary sources that he would later incorporate into *Poetas de color.* In 1855, in collaboration with Cirilo Villaverde, he helped collect money to assist Leopoldo Turla, one of the contributors to *El Laúd del Desterrado (The Lyre of Exile,* 1858).

   Poetas de color is made up primarily of biographical notes on four Afro-Cuban poets with the greatest emphasis given to the canonical black poets of the period: Gabriel de la Concepción Valdés, "Plácido" (1809–1844) and Juan Francisco Manzano. Although most of the book is devoted to these writers, the brief biographical sketches of Antonio Medina, Augustín Baldomero Rodríguez, and Ambrosio Echemendía are of considerable importance, as they represent virtually the only attempt to preserve and evaluate the writings of lesser-known Afro-Cubans during the nineteenth century. *Poetas de color* strikes the modern reader as a decidedly unusual book: haphazard in its organization and balance, it is also a veritable bibliographic treasure chest, replete with citations to North American and European sources. Neither an anthology proper nor a work of literary criticism, it may be best described as a combination of antislavery rhetoric, quotations from the authors anthologized, and reprints of translations of and commentary on their works, together with a lengthy appendix of supporting material. Calcagno was particularly attracted to Manzano, and he intercalated fragments of the latter's *Autobiografía* within his own commentary on slavery. Calcagno's extract of key passages of the autobiographical text (those related to torture and the mistreatment of slaves) clearly reflects the intervention of an editorial voice that aimed to create the image of a literate slave. Calcagno's commentary, however, betrays his strong ties with the plantation class. Thus in his glosses he refuted or attempted to correct statements of Manzano about treatment received at the hands of his masters, thus effectively rendering emotionally neutral parts of the original. Juan Francisco Manzano's autobiography was the first and only slave narrative written in Spanish America and Calcagno's decision to anthologize key portions of the text was responsible for the first printed version of the text in Spanish, an extraordinary accomplishment that in itself makes *Poetas de color* a primary source book for Manzano scholarship. Calcagno worked both as an editor and as a literary historian as he was familiar with an early translation of Manzano's book done by the British abolitionist Richard Robert Madden, which had been published in London in 1840. The Madden translation was shown to Calcagno by the poet and political activist José Antonio Echevarría (1815–1885).

In 1841, selections of the Madden translation were published in London in the *Christian Observer,* in what was putatively a review of *Poems by a Slave.* The editors, however, had created yet another version of the autobiography, one specifically designed to support the journal's abolitionist agenda. Consistent with the well-established protocols of the slave narrative, "authentication" was the first order of business: "The authenticity of the work is the first point to ascertain. For this, Dr. Madden...vouches." Not only did the editors reprint sizable portions of the Madden original, but it is what they elected to reproduce (virtually every scene involving physical or emotional trauma) that is significant. In addition to the traditional authenticating machinery of the slave-narrative genre, this mini-anthology of Madden's translation was divided into two parts, each shaped by an editorial voice that focused on one of the two most prominent conventions of the genre: descriptions of the cruelties inflicted on the slave, and listings of the barriers against literacy. Thus, the editors wrote: "We now return from this digression to our Cuban slave-poet, first extracting some graphic sketches of his life as described by his own pen. We shall herein see the grievous injustice and cruelty to which a slave is exposed even under the most favorable circumstances; the will, the caprice, the suspicions, however unfounded, of his employer, being sufficient to condemn him to the severest usage."[44] Thus, just as Madden's book brackets Manzano's voice between a considerable corpus of extrafictional materials, the editors of the *Christian Observer* performed much the same task, albeit with a slightly different ideological agenda in mind.

In 1937, at the height of the Afro-Cuban vogue and approximately 100 years after its composition, a Spanish edition of Manzano's *Autobiography* finally appeared.[45] The editor, José L. Franco, again corrected the style of the Manzano original, producing yet another version of the base text. The preface to the Franco edition was written by Emilio Roig de Leuchsenring, chronicler of the city of Havana; it reads in part:

> Inédita, hasta ahora, en castellano, dicha *Autobiografía,* fué escrita en 1839 a instancias del insigne humanista, poeta, historiador y *Mecenas* de las letras, en Cuba, Domingo del Monte, amigo y protector de Manzano. Se componía, primitivamente, según parece, de dos partes, pues aunque en la nota que aparece en la portada del cuaderno manuscrito se dice que no se escribió la segunda parte, Francisco Calcagno en su obra *Poetas de color,* afirma: "Sabemos sin embargo que sí se escribió y que entregada por Anselmo Suárez al poeta Ramón de Palma para ponerla en limpio y arreglar la ortografía, se extravió en manos de éste," agregando que "en eso concuerdan también José A. Echevarría y el traductor Madden."
>
> De dicha primera parte, única que ha llegado hasta nosotros, sólo se han publicado antes de ahora breves extractos en el referido libro de Calcagno. El original, a la muerte de Domingo del Monte, pasó a ser propiedad de su hijo, Leonardo del Monte y Aldama, adquiriéndolo después Vidal Morales y Morales. Por último, con la biblioteca de éste, fué comprado por la Biblioteca Nacional, donde hoy se guarda y ha sido copiado escrupulosamente para la presente edición.[46]

(Unpublished in Spanish until now, the *Autobiography* was written in 1839 at the behest of the distinguished Cuban humanist, poet, historiographer, and patron of letters Domingo del Monte, friend and protector of Manzano. It apparently originally consisted of two parts. Although a note on the frontispiece of the manuscript says that the second part was not written, Francisco Calcagno in *Poets of Color* states: "We know, however, that it was written and given by Anselmo Suárez to the poet Ramón de Palma for corrections of style and orthography and that it was lost by the latter." He [Calcagno] adds: "José A. Echevarría and the translator Madden concur on this point."

Only brief extracts of the aforementioned first part have been published in Calcagno's book. Upon the death of Domingo del Monte, the original copy became the property of his son, Leonardo del Monte y Aldama, and was later acquired by Vidal Morales y Morales. Finally it was acquired by the National Library, where today it is kept and has been carefully copied for the present edition.)

In the wake of the Cuban revolution, interest in Manzano's work was rekindled. Thus, in 1962 the Cuban National Cultural Council reissued Manzano's drama *Zafira,* which had been first published in 1842; and in 1972 the Cuban Book Institute followed suit, with the republication of the *Autobiography,* together with his letters to Domingo del Monte and his poetry. In 1975, Ivan A. Schulman prepared a modernized edition of the *Autobiography* based on the 1937 Franco text but incorporating further emendations. Yet another English translation was published by Lloyd King in 1990, under the title *The Autobiography of a Cuban Slave.*

William Luis, Sylvia Molloy, and Lorna Williams have all noted that such attempts at mediation have altered, however subtly, the original authorial voice. In his introduction to the bilingual edition of the Autobiography, Ivan Schulman, for example, broaches the question of his corrections: "The original lacks the most elementary notions of punctuation and syntax, for which reason we took in 1975 the liberty of modernizing the text. Though there are some who would object to the modifications because they distort the original, whose defects are the marks of slavery, the modern reader of either Spanish or English would find the original Spanish or its direct translation a chore to read."[47] In 2000 the Spanish hispanist Abdeslam Azougarth published *Juan Francisco Manzano. esclavo poeta en la isla de Cuba* (Madrid: Ediciones Episteme) that contains yet another version of the text in which the editor attempts to convey more authentically the voice of Manzano through more carefully controlled editorial intervention. It would be William Luis's 2007 edition of the notebook of Nicolás Azcárate (to which we have referred before), *Juan Francisco Manzano. Autobiografía del esclavo poeta y otros escritos* (Madrid:Iberoamerican, 2007), which would present scholars with a carefully crafted reconstruction of the original manuscript. This meticulous work of philological scholarship allows the reader to experience as much as possible the sense and meaning of the original. In 2006, the Cuban American novelist Margarita Engle adopted the story of Manzano in a book of verse for children, which she entitled *The Poet Slave of Cuba. A Biography of Juan Francisco Manzano* published by Henry Holt, a mainstream American publisher.

Thus, just as the original text was marred by curious lapses of memory, ellipses, and temporal dislocations, its literary genealogy is nonetheless clear. All attempts to re-create accurately the circumstances of its creation, the author's hypothetical true motivations for writing, and the text's first journey from Spanish to English are, after all, open to question. The hypothetical original—the manuscript from which Suárez y Romero copied—is located in the Biblioteca José Martí in Havana. Friol indicates that in it are 52 pages of manuscript, divided by Manzano into 18 paragraphs and blocks. He further observes that Manzano's written prose contains deviations from standard Spanish, a fact noted by virtually all those who have studied his work. For example, Susan Willis observes that the lack of "sentence divisions gives the narrative a hurried and unreflected appearance." Thomas Bremer concludes that "Manzano's practice of writing without any structuring through paragraphs contributes...to the authenticity of the work." Sylvia Molloy finds the original Spanish text to be a not particularly "harmonious piece: unsystematic in its spelling, arbitrary in its punctuation, nonchalant in its syntax, this text is, quite obviously, *different.*" This virtual obsession with the obvious belies, I believe, another critical agenda: the deliberate emphasis upon the aspects of Manzano's language that link him with the nonscribal oral traditions of his African ancestors. As Lorna Williams aptly notes, deviations from normative Spanish were quite common in nineteenth-century Cuba, even among educated Cubans.[48] Before the invention of the typewriter in the late nineteenth century, of course, all texts were handwritten, and typesetters routinely created paragraph divisions, normalized punctuation, and corrected errors in spelling. Virtually all writers were subjected to some form of editorial control, as a function of the emergent technology of printing, which at the time was extremely labor-intensive. If Manzano had not been a slave, such extensive commentary about his nonstandard Spanish would, I believe, seem quite unnecessary.

In dealing with the autobiography in general and the slave narrative in particular, the critic is at once confronted with a set of problems unique in the analysis of literature. One of the first difficulties that the reader of a slave narrative faces is the question of its accuracy, its relation to truth.[49] Here, however, the general theoretical problem of analyzing literature is carried a step further. The predicament can be evoked by paraphrasing the Soviet semiotician Jurig Lotman, according to whom any literary discourse is a secondary modeling of the world, ultimately based upon the primary modeling system, which is language. Hence, literary art is, in a sense, twice removed from reality, inasmuch as it uses an already existing linguistic model of the world to construct yet another model.[50] The problem of this constant distancing from reality is further complicated in the slave narrative because the reader (audience) is never certain whether he or she is dealing with fact or fiction. As the impact of a persuasive discourse on any hypothetical audience is a direct function of the reader's perception of the accuracy of the document, the question of authenticity has always played a central role in this genre.

Manzano's first translator was particularly aware of this problem and consequently provided rather detailed information about the authenticity of the text in his preface to *Poems by a Slave*. This device was characteristic of eighteenth-century North American slave narratives; they were generally prefaced by introductory remarks wherein a respected white person confirmed the moral character of the author and the truthfulness of the facts.[51] As an abolitionist, Madden was obviously familiar with this approach. His preface, in part, reads:

> The author of the Poems I have attempted to translate, is now living at the Havana, and gains his livelihood by hiring himself out as an occasional servant. His name, for obvious reasons, I think it advisable not to publish, but to leave no doubt of the authenticity of these Poems, I have deposited the originals in the Spanish language in the hands of the secretary of the "British and Foreign Anti-Slavery Society." It was written in two parts—the second part fell into the hands of persons connected with his former master, and I fear it is not likely to be restored to the person to whom I am indebted for the first portion of this manuscript. As far, however, as this portion goes, I have no hesitation in saying, it is the most perfect picture of Cuban slavery that ever has been given to the world and so full and faithful in its details, that it is difficult to imagine, that the portion which has been suppressed, can throw any greater light on the evils of this system, than the first part had done. (iii–v)[52]

Manzano's *Autobiography* is a brief (some 40 pages), first-person narration of his life until approximately the age of 20, when he escaped from a sadistic master to seek sanctuary in Havana. The fragmentation the reader senses may be explained in part by the truncated nature of the text itself. As only the first part was preserved, the discourse as a whole lacks a feeling of completeness, a characteristic of the North American slave narrative, which followed a firmly established set of conventions. It may be broadly divided, from the perspectives of theme and tone, into two sections. Thus, the first six pages describe a period of plentitude and offer a brief genealogy and a portrait of the subject's life as a young boy. Quite unlike, however, the North American slave narrative, which almost invariably began with the sentence "I was born,"[53] Manzano's narrative voice focused on the lineage of his parents, María del Pilar and Torbio Castro, and their privileged position within the social order, thus establishing one of the thematic tensions: the narrator's phenotype and intellectual difference from other black slaves. The book begins with a sketch of Manzano's early life as the pampered son of his mistress's lady-in-waiting. We learn, for example, that he was sent to school by his mistress, learned to recite by memory the sermons of the celebrated mystic and Renaissance preacher Luis de Granada (1504–1588), and was well instructed in matters of the church. When he was 11 and subsequent to the death of his mistress, Manzano's parents were sent to the estate of Molino and he to the home of his godparents in Havana, where he was treated like a white child and was not allowed to associate with the children of other blacks.

There is a sudden shift in both tone and style when Manzano enters into the service of the Marquesa de Prado Ameno. It is at this juncture, the narrator indicates, that his "true" story begins, and it is this second narrative division that constitutes most of the written text. The transition from plentitude to a living hell is accomplished with neither rhetorical transition nor explanation. The entire thematic rupture, in a curious way, may be read as a metaphor for the way in which Manzano chose to textualize his lived experience. Fragmented, punctuated with lapses in memory and temporal dislocations, Manzano's written recollections stand in sharp contrast to the formulaic diction of his verse. Miriam DeCosta-Willis described this transition in the following way: "What he calls... 'the true history of my life' began with a primal experience—his entombment in a dark coal chute... [T]he metaphor of his life was a fall—a fall from grace, a precipitous downward descent... into an invisible non-being."[54] It is not coincidental either that this nodal moment took place during the critical period of adolescent emancipation and was located spatially away from the nurturing urban setting of Havana, on the grounds of the plantation estate, El Molino, a physical space that would become virtually synonymous with torture. Thus, the urban/rural axis becomes one of the structuring principles linking together and dramatizing episodes that otherwise appear to lack narrative cohesion.

The narrator's description of his first experience of physical abuse can be read as a virtual paradigm of his lived experience; it is presented with a remarkable richness of psychological detail, a fact that has received scant attention. The act of writing about abuse—most particularly from the point of view of the abused—is conditioned with special pitfalls, as portrayals of physical and mental disintegration simultaneously evoke fascination and horror. The reader is struck by the fact that there appears to be no causal relationship between the actions of the slave and the punishments he receives. Thus, the entire cycle of punishment/forgiveness—which is repeated with a predictable regularity—begins with disarming innocence. We are told that for a miniscule act of mischief, Manzano was locked up in a coal cellar. The event itself is recounted, as Susan Willis has noted, with a high degree of semantic parataxis, which to no small degree accounts for its remarkable psychological verisimilitude.[55] In reordering his memories Manzano not only stressed the disfigurement of the body but also registered a fascination with the state of his moods, experienced as beyond his control, capriciously controlled by the whims of his mistress, who had him brutally treated for the slightest offense (real or imagined). During his confinement in the coal pit, his fears rather quickly coalesced into a web of unnamed evils, ghostly apparitions, and thoughts of death—a sort of momentary descent into psychosis. As the narrator admits, at about the age of 13 or 14 he became chronically "melancholy."

The *Autobiography,* at a primary level of organization, is structured around recollections of moments of both physical and psychological trauma.[56] There are no fewer than ten incidents that lead to moments of abuse. What makes the recording of these moments so extraordinary is that although they are repetitive, they are interlaced with periods of relative calm, a reflection no doubt of the obviously bipolar personality of Manzano's owner. This feature is mirrored in no small part in the narrator's voice, shifting as it does between passivity and rage, happiness and despair, and illness and health. His memories are a veritable catalog of infirmities: a fever of unknown origin, weeping cranial lesions, clinical depressions, pulmonary edemas, and dysentery. Precisely because the narrator's voice orders these events nonsequentially, the resultant story engages the modern reader. The narrative climaxes with Manzano's escape to Havana after learning that the Marquesa had arranged to have him sent to the Molino estate for punishment because he had taken a bath without permission:

> I remembered at that moment the fate of one of my uncles, who in a case like mine, took the same determination of escaping to Havana, to

Don Nicolas, Don Manuel, and the Senor Marques and was brought back again like a wild beast—but for all that I resolved to venture on my escape, and in case of detection, to suffer for something. I waited till twelve o'clock. That night everybody retired early, it being very cold and rainy. I saddled the horse for the first time in my life, put on the bridle, but with such trembling that I hardly knew what I was about, after that I knelt down, said a prayer, and mounted the horse. When I was going away, I heard the sound of a voice saying, "God bless you, make haste." I thought that nobody saw me, but as I know afterwards, I was seen by several of the negroes, but nobody offered any impediment to my flight.[57]

Although it is a brief and somewhat fragmented work, Manzano's *Autobiography* is the only document written by a slave during the period, and consequently it must be considered an important source of information concerning slave life. In this sense the book is somewhat similar to such novels as *Sab, Francisco,* and especially *Cecilia Valdés,* which depicted the types and customs of various social or provincial milieus. The distinction is, of course, one of degree. In Manzano's *Autobiography* the description of customs and social background is incidental and subordinate to the book's implicit goal: the depiction of the narrator's personal anguish in a world in which he is unable to control his own destiny. Manzano becomes both the first-person narrator of his own personal story and also the projection and emblem of an entire class of individuals victimized by racism and colonial oppression. Thus, although the text is extraordinarily brief and has the deceptive appearance of being less sophisticated in a literary sense, it is paradoxically a more complex work than the others.

Balanced as it is on the razor's edge between fact and fiction, social document and literary saga, Manzano's *Autobiography* has had a wide range of readings. Manzano's critical interpreters disagree on rather fundamental issues, such as the structuring principles that the author elected to in plotting his story. Bremer feels the text "can be easily divided into a chronological series of various segments and episodes." Willis notes a similar pattern of linear sequentially in the narrative but posits that at its deepest level of structure, "the narrative is based on a series of discontinuous events, each of which is crystallized in a moment of torture." She further attributes Manzano's disregard for standard literary convention to a separation of the narrator from a hypothetical audience. Friol stresses as well the text's lack of narrative symmetry, which he concludes contributes to its uniqueness and vitality as a memorial act. Molloy appears to follow, to some extent, the same line of argumentation when she concludes that the *Autobiography*'s originality, "the stubborn, uncontrolled energy that is possibly its greatest achievement," emanates precisely from the author's lack of a master image.[58]

Sonia Labrador-Rodríguez approaches the text from a slightly different critical focus, one more informed by culturist theory. She notes that Manzano's decision to write was not only contingent on his will to gain freedom but was also motivated by a desire to establish a dialog with a literate public, a sector of the social strata to which he felt he belonged by virtue of his own literacy. Thus, she surmises, Manzano as narrator elected three principal strategies: the rejection of diachrony in favor of the privileging of events (that is, moments of torture), the distancing of the subject from the condition of slavery, and finally, the projection of the writing subject as an intellectual.[59]

On the other hand, Martha Cobb, Miriam DeCosta-Willis, and Luis A. Jiménez all call attention to structural and thematic similarities between Manzano's discourse and the generic conventions of the North American slave narrative.[60] Each to varying degrees explicitly compares Manzano's text with *Narrative of the Life of Frederick Douglass, an American Slave, Written by Himself* (1845) and thus places in the foreground the interconnectedness of diasporic literature. The parallels between the Cuban work and Douglass's text in fact are quite striking.

Both books are buttressed by considerable supporting materials (prefaces, letters, appendixes) that plainly reflect the intervention of abolitionists in their printing. Both appear to be informed by a similar alienating vision of society, and they are rather closely parallel in terms of their structures (organizational patterns). Both begin with the narrator's account of his genealogy, and both describe a "loss of innocence," when the narrators are catapulted from the protected world of childhood to experience the full rigors of slavery. There are, too, similar realizations of the alternatives to slavery, which lead to dramatic escapes. The presence of similar stylistic devices, recurrent imagery, and careful selection of events to maintain a narrative momentum ultimately link these works; however—and perhaps more importantly—both narratives project a similar portrait of psychological and physical torment, one firmly rooted in the alien/exile theme that has characterized much of black literature from the early times to the present.

All of this leads to the question of possible mutual influence. Bearing in mind that Madden, Manzano's first translator, was an ardent abolitionist and was no doubt thoroughly familiar with the

North American slave narrative, it would not seem unreasonable to assume that he discussed this popular and highly influential form with Del Monte and the other members of his *tertulia*. That Madden read several of these accounts to this same circle is also within the range of possibility.[61] Madden's knowledge of the slave narrative no doubt played a role as well in his ultimate selection of the Manzano text over the longer, sentimental novel *Francisco,* by Anselmo Suárez y Romero.[62]

The Madden Translation

The history and genesis of the Madden translation first attracted the attention primarily of scholars of Spanish and Anglophone literatures but more recently it has moved into the realm of transatlantic and transnational hemispheric studies, evincing as it does a curious literary "triangle trade" between Great Britain, Cuba, Continental Europe, and the United States during the nineteenth century centered around the abolitionist cause.[63] Fionnghuala Sweeny categorizes Manzano's "Autobiography as both a 'networked text' and a 'borderline text'" and stresses its importance as an independent Atlantic document: "The work can be regarded as something of a joint production, with both author (Manzano) and editor (Madden) making a substantial contribution to the work's final form."[64] Marilyn Miller, in an essay comparing Manzano with Alexander von Humboldt, suggests "that we also examine their writings within a network of circulation, one that implicates not only a Cuban poet and a German scientific traveler, but also the Cuban man of letters Domingo del Monte and the Irish diplomat Richard Robert Madden, as well as the tangential figures as Scottish abolitionist David Turnbull and Victor Schoelcher."[65] Anna Brickhouse further locates "the circulation of Manzano's narrative as a complex site of transatlantic and transamerican negotiations over the geography of slavery and U.S. expansionism."[66] Joselyn Almeida suggests that the Madden translation provided British abolitionists with the cultural capital necessary to "ensure a future beyond 1840 given the realignment of geopolitical and economic power in the Atlantic."[67] If one considers the fact that the English version had been extant for almost 100 years before the publication of the Spanish text by José L. Franco in 1937, it is legitimate to consider Madden's translation as a work of both diasporic and hemispheric American literature in the broadest and most universal sense of the term. The singular English translation of Juan Francisco Manzano's poetry and prose is inextricably linked to the career of Richard Robert Madden, an Irish physician who was employed by the British Colonial Office from 1833 to 1839 in Jamaica and Cuba. A prolific writer and humanitarian, Madden produced in his lifetime no fewer than 40 volumes of writings, on topics ranging from literature to medicine. The youngest son of Edward Madden, a silk manufacturer, Richard was born in Dublin, Ireland, on August 22, 1798. He was educated at private schools in Dublin and studied medicine in Paris, Naples, and London. Much of his early life was spent traveling on the Continent. After a sojourn in the Middle East between 1824 and 1827, he returned to England and married Harriet Elmslie, the daughter of a Jamaican planter, in 1828. He practiced as a surgeon for about five years before accepting a position in 1833 as a special magistrate to administer the statute abolishing slavery in the colonies.[68] It is not clear exactly how Madden became involved in the British abolitionist movement. The only information concerning this aspect of his life and work is offered by comments his son, Thomas More Madden, made in 1891:

> The agitation for the abolition of negro slavery was then in full swing; and into this movement Dr. Madden threw himself with all the ardour of his nature, the leading characteristic of which was an intense love of justice and a hatred of oppression in whatever clime or on whatever race it might be exercised. Accordingly he became an active member of the Anti-Slavery Society, and was thus brought into intimate contact with men like Wilberforce, Sturge, Clarkeson, Bright and the other leaders of that great movement by which the shackles of slavery were ultimately riven from millions of suffering human beings in every part of the world, whose only crime was that of race and colour. On the passing of the law for the abolition of slavery in the West Indies, in 1833 Dr. Madden resolved on abandoning his professional prospects with the object of personally assisting in the carrying out of that great work of humanity. Accordingly, through the willing assistance of Sir F. Buxton and his other colleagues in the Anti-Slavery Society, he was appointed by the Government to the office of Special Magistrate in Jamaica, and embarked from Falmouth for that island on the 5th October 1833.[69]

Madden's stay in Jamaica was brief and unpleasant. He resigned his position in November 1834, finding it impossible to cope with the openly hostile colonial government, and returned to Great Britain by way of the United States that same year. In 1835 Madden was asked by Sir Thomas Buxton to assist him in a campaign to end the Spanish involvement in the Atlantic slave trade and was in 1836 appointed superintendent of liberated Africans. In this capacity he served as a judge in one of the mixed courts established in 1835 under a supplementary slave treaty with Spain; the courts had jurisdiction over the cases of captured slave ships.

Madden's reputation as an abolitionist, which had preceded him to Havana, caused a furor. Deeply suspicious of the British, who had emancipated their slaves, the reactionary Spanish captain-general of Havana wrote: "Dr. Madden is a dangerous man from whatever point of view he is considered, and living in this Island he will have far too many opportunities to disseminate seditious ideas directly or indirectly, which not even my constant vigilance can prevent."[70] There were continuous clashes between Madden and the Cuban authorities during his stay in Havana, but the Spanish government was unsuccessful in its attempts to have him removed from office. Madden's *Memoirs* contain the following account of the animosity:

> Dr. Madden's unsparing exposure of the atrocities which were daily brought officially under his notice in connexion with slavery in Cuba—necessarily brought him into conflict with the Spanish authorities by whom that infamous system was connived at and fostered. By them, therefore, and by the great slave-trading interest of the island, he was assailed with an intensity of hatred which had no effect whatever in altering the line of conduct which he deemed it his duty to pursue, and in which he was sustained by the righteousness of his cause, as well as by the approval of the Government by whom he had been sent out to Cuba. Thus, in reply to one of the attacks of the Spanish authorities, by whom his removal was demanded, we find the following letter from Viscount Palmerston to M. Aguilar, Spanish Minister at London:—"Foreign Office, 15th May 1837. The undersigned must express his regret that the zeal and perseverance in the performance of a public duty, which have obtained for Dr. Madden the approbation of his own Government, should not have equally secured him that of the Government of Cuba....Dr. Madden has given indisputable proof of that anxiety and assiduity in the discharge of difficult duties, without which he would not be fit for the appointment he holds. [Signed] Palmerston."[71]

During his stay in Havana Madden did not limit his criticism to the Spanish colonial government: he charged the U.S. consul in Havana, Nicholas Trist, with aiding U.S. ships engaged in the Cuban slave trade. The details of the complicity appeared in Madden's pamphlet *A Letter to W. E. Channing, D.D. on the Subject of the Abuse of the Flag of the United States, in the Island of Cuba, and the Advantage Taken of Its Protection in Promoting the Slave Trade.*[72]

Madden reported his findings to the General Anti-Slavery Convention in London. Madden's report at once calls to mind the important links between the British and the U.S. abolitionist movements during the nineteenth century. Both movements were rooted in two important phenomena, the natural-rights philosophies of the eighteenth century and the rise of evangelical religion based on the teachings of the New Testament. The formal and personal links between the two movements were very close during their respective developments.[73]

The significance of Madden's translation of a Cuban slave narrative may be explained by the position that the British abolitionists took after 1838, the year that saw the termination of the apprenticeship system—the last vestige of slavery in the British colonies. Given the fact that by 1838 British abolitionists had achieved all they could within the framework of their own political system, they became more concerned with slavery as a worldwide issue. In particular, literature became an important vehicle for abolitionist views.[74] American abolitionists were particularly eager to see the British involved, recognizing the importance that Great Britain exercised over public opinion in America.

A notice of Madden's participation in the convention was included in an essay published in London in the *Eclectic Review*:

> Among the finest and most valuable proceedings of the convention was the reading of an admirable paper by Dr. Madden on the state of slavery in the island of Cuba, which has justly been called "the centre of the slave system," and which, as to the actual horrors of slavery there, is still to the public a *terra incognita*. Dr. Madden has been for three years the official Protector of imported Africans at Havanna, a post which he has filled with the justice and the firmness belonging to an Englishman. He has had ample opportunities of observation, and has with rare courage and fidelity detailed what he knows. We applaud not his fidelity only, but his courage also, because he is about to return to Cuba and to face the men whom he has exposed. The paper, which will of course be published in the proceedings of the convention is in course of translation into the Spanish language, and is designed for extensive circulation in the Spanish dominions.[75]

Madden's translation of Cuban materials, which without his intervention would probably now be virtually forgotten by both Hispanic and English readers, had a curious history in the abolitionist literary circles of the day. As Madden did not publish Manzano's full name, a number of American writers, among them Amelia E. Barr and William

Wells Brown, confused Manzano with the better known mulatto poet Plácido (Gabriel de la Concepción Valdés, 1809–1844); curious hybrid biographical sketches of the writers resulted.[76] All this goes to point out the complexities of the abolitionist literary network of the times and the links that existed among Britain, the United States, and Cuba. In this connection, it is also important that many of the most significant American slave narratives were frequently reprinted in England (such as *Narrative of the Life of Frederick Douglass, The Autobiography of the Reverand Josiah Henson*, and John Brown's *Slave Life in Georgia*). It is equally interesting that Lewis Alexis Chamerozow had served as the secretary of the British and Foreign Anti-Slavery Society before editing the narrative of John Brown, that the British abolitionist Sir George Stephen had corresponded with Harriet Beecher Stowe, and finally that many of the most prominent authors of slave narratives (including Douglass and Henson) spent extensive periods in England.

Paradoxically, Madden's translation of the Manzano *Autobiography*, an extremely problematic endeavor from its inception, has led modern readers to understand the original more fully. Virtually all critics who have written about Manzano have taken note of it. The most detailed comparisons of the Spanish and English versions were made by William Luis and Sylvia Molloy, respectively. Luis noted that a parallel reading reveals serious discrepancies, besides the fact that the English version is considerably more polished: minor mistranslations of lexical features, frequent omission of names and dates, and perhaps more importantly a rearrangement and tightening in the sequencing of the episodes of torture. Such editorial interventions, which conformed to the expectations (both rhetorical and structural) of a mid-Victorian abolitionist readership, Luis correctly claims, muted the voice of the original narrator, effectively suppressing an important psychological dimension of the text.[77]

Molloy, whose comparative focus is slightly different, carefully assessed what Madden omitted from the original, in order to identify points of "resistance" in Manzano's story. She noted the suppression of the author's name, the reordering of events, and, perhaps most significant, the loss of the alternation of pain and joy, the subtextual bipolarity that suffuses the original with such powerful psychological depth. For Molloy, however, "more revealing are other passages suppressed by Madden, those dealing more directly with Manzano's person—his urges, his appetites."[78] The relationship between the body and Manzano's peculiar rise to literacy offers Molloy a productive avenue for opening up a text that seems to be closed. Reading

Madden's translation—less as a translation than as an abolitionist reconstruction, a recasting of a slave's discourse—allows the twentieth-century reader a glimpse, however fleeting, into an extremely complicated process of literary construction.

From all that has been said thus far it becomes clear that the Manzano *Autobiography,* standing as it does as a singular document in Afro-Cuban literature, cannot be dismissed facilely. Although it is not a long work, it is complex, resulting as it did from so many factors at work in Cuban colonial society. Although earlier critics chose to view the text almost exclusively in terms of the narrator's conditioned attitudes toward society, of his basic passivity and desire to aspire to a white, rather than a black, world, more recent readings suggest a far more nuanced text. Thus, more recent critical assessments of Manzano's *Autobiography* view it more properly as a foundational document in Afro-Cuban literary discourse. Richard Jackson put it this way:

> The search for Black identity in Hispanic literature began with Juan Francisco Manzano, and it is appropriate to begin this discussion with him. His legacy lives on in the writing of his Afro-Cuban compatriots and other twentieth-century Black Hispanic writers who have not forgotten the past.... Writing became one of the obsessions of his life. The autobiography he left us, even with its contradictions, is a remarkable account of a survivor of slavery who willed himself the knowledge to be able to write about it, which was in itself a heroic act. He was dependent on the prudence of white sponsors for protection but took the chance in the hope that telling his story would help him attain the freedom he so desperately desired.[79]

Whatever their attitudes toward the text in terms of its literary sophistication, most readers will agree that it is indeed a "memorable discourse," and that the genius of Manzano lies in his having found a literary voice in which to express a profound crisis in nineteenth-century Cuban society. Whether one regards the *Autobiography* as a literary work or a historical document, it is a remarkable expression of human experience.

Notes

1. See Edward J. Mullen, *Afro-Cuban Literature: Critical Junctures* (Westport, CT: Greenwood, 1998).
2. See William W. Megenney, "The Black in Hispanic-Caribbean and Brazilian Poetry: A Comparative Perspective," *Revista Interamericana Review* 5 (1975): 47–66.

3. Philip D. Curtin, *The Atlantic Slave Trade (A Census)* (Madison: University of Wisconsin Press, 1969), 46.

4. José Juan Arrom, "La poesía afrocubana," *Revista Iberoamericana* 4 (1942): 379–411.

5. See, for example, *El cancionero del esclavo: Colección de poesías laureadas y recomendadas por el jurado en el certamen convocado por la sociedad abolicionista española* (Madrid: La sociedad abolicionista española, 1866).

6. Cited in Lorna Williams, *The Representation of Slavery in Cuban Fiction* (Columbia: University of Missouri Press, 1994), 9.

7. William Luis, *Literary Bondage: Slavery in Cuban Narrative* (Austin: University of Texas Press, 1990), 27.

8. See Jerome Branche, *"Mulato entre negros (y blancos)*: Writing, Race, the Antislavery Question, and Juan Francisco Manzano's *Autobiografía," Bulletin of Latin American Research* 20.1 (2001): 63–87, which questions the tradition of ascribing benevolence to the abolitionist tradition.

9. Williams, *Representation of Slavery,* 18–19.

10. G. R. Coulthard, *Race and Colour in Caribbean Literature* (London: Oxford University Press, 1962), 12–13.

11. See Roberto Friol, *Suite para Juan Francisco Manzano* (Havana: Editorial Arte y Literatura, 1977).

12. Williams, *Representation of Slavery,* 48.

13. Friol, *Suite,* 153.

14. See Branche, *"Mulato entre negros,"* as well as Ifeoma Kiddoe Nwankwo, *Black Cosmopolitanism: Racial Consciousness and Transnational Identity in the Nineteenth-Century Americas* (Philadelphia: University of Pennsylvania Press, 2005): 187–255.

15. For an excellent discussion of the social structure and daily life of Afro-Cubans during the mid-nineteenth century, see Adriana J. Bergero, "Escritura, vida cotidiana y resignificaciones en La Habana de Juan Francisco Manzano," *Afro-Hispanic Review* 24.2 (2005): 7–32.

16. Carlos M. Trelles, "Bibliografía de autores de raza de color de Cuba," *Cuba Contemporáneo* 43 (1927): 31.

17. Sonia Labrador-Rodríguez, "La intelectualidad negra en Cuba en el siglo XIX: El caso de Manzano," *Revista Iberoamericana* 62 (1996): 23.

18. Lorna Williams in particular notes this inconsistency (*Representation of Slavery,* 46).

19. Labrador-Rodríguez, "La intelectualidad negra," 20–21.

20. See Sylvia Molloy, "From Serf to Self: The Autobiography of Juan Francisco Manzano," *MLN* 104.2 (1989): 412–13.

21. Thomas Bremer, "The Slave Who Wrote Poetry: Comments on the Literary Works and the Autobiography of Juan Francisco Manzano," in *Slavery in the Americas,* ed. Wolfgang Binder (Würzburg: Königshausen and Neumann, 1993), 490.

22. Henry Louis Gates, "Editor's Introduction," in *"Race," Writing and Difference*, ed. Henry Louis Gates (Chicago: University of Chicago Press, 1986), 8.

23. Cited in *Obras de Juan Francisco Manzano*, ed. Israel M. Moliner (Havana: Instituto del Libro Cubano, 1972), 85–86.

24. See Martha Cobb, *Harlem, Haiti, and Havana: A Comparative Study of Langston Hughes, Jacques Roumain, and Nicolás Guillén* (Washington, DC: Three Continents Press, 1979), 28.

25. Cited in Edward J. Mullen, ed., *The Life and Poems of a Cuban Slave: Juan Francisco Manzano, 1797–1854* (Hamden, CT: Archon Books, 1981), 115. Also see Marilyn G. Miller, "Reading Juan Francisco Manzano in the Wake of Alexander von Humbolt," *Atlantic Studies* 7.2 (2010): 180–81.

26. Cintio Vitier, "Dos poetas cubanos: Plácido y Manzano," *Bohemia* 14 (1973): 20.

27. For detailed comment on Manzano's publishing history, see Antonio López Prieto's important bio-bibliographic essay "Juan Francisco Manzano" in his *Parnaso cubano: Colección de poesías selectas de autores cubanas desde Zequeira a nuestros días* (Havana: Miguel de Villa, 1881), 251–52.

28. See José Juan Arrom, *Historia de la literatura dramática cubana* (New Haven, CT: Yale University Press, 1944), 52–53, as well as Marilyn Miller, "Imitation and Improvisation in Juan Francisco Manzano's *Zafira*," *Colonial Latin America Reviews* 17.1 (2008): 49–71.

29. See Miller, "Imitation and Improvisation," 50 as well as her "Rebeldía narrativa, resistencia poética y expesión 'libre' en Juan francicsco Manzano," *Revista Iberoamericana* 71.1 (2005): 417–36. Also of importance is the edition of Abdeslam Azougarh, *Juan Francisco Manzano: esclavo poeta en la isla de cuba* (Valencia: Episteme, 2000) especially "La poesía," 33–52; and A. Lewis Galanes, *Poesías de J. F. Manzano, esclavo en la isla de Cuba* (Madrid: Betania, 1991), in which she reprints 13 poems transcribed by the English Quaker B. B. Wiffen. William Luis's *Juan Francisco Manzano. Autobiografía del esclavo poeta y otros escritos* (Madrid: Iberoamerica, 2007) presents the most complete annotated version of Manzano's poems. See "Poesías," 135–99.

30. Cited in Francisco Calcagno, *Poetas de color* (Havana: Imp. Militar de la V. Soler y Compañía, 1878), 45–46.

31. Emilio Martín González del Valle, *La poesía lírica en Cuba* (Barcelona: Tipo-Lit. de Celestino Verdaguer, 1884), 171; Prieto, *Parnaso cubano*, 252; Aurelio Mitjans, *Historia de la literatura cubana* (1890; reprint, Madrid: Editorial América, 1918), 187–88.

32. Miriam DeCosta, "Social Lyricism and the Caribbean Poet/Rebel," *CLA Journal* 15.4 (1972): 442; Richard L. Jackson, *The Black Image in Latin American Literature* (Albuquerque: University of

New Mexico Press, 1976), 94 (Jackson seems to have altered this position in his *Black Writers and the Hispanic Canon* [New York: Twayne Publishers, 1997], especially 24); Susan Willis, "Crushed Geraniums: Juan Francisco Manzano and the Language of Poetry," in *The Slave's Narrative,* ed. Charles T. Davis and Henry Louis Gates Jr (New York: Oxford University Press, 1985), 199–224 (especially 213–17).

33. Molloy, "From Serf to Self," 414.
34. Antonio Vera-León, "Juan Francisco Manzano: El estilo bárbaro de la nación," *Hispamérica* 20.60 (1991): 7–8.
35. William Luis, "Nicolás Azcárate's Antislavery Notebook and the Unpublished Poems of the Slave Juan Francisco Manzano," *Revista de Estudios Hispánicos* 28.3 (1994): 335. Also see Luis, *Autobiografía del esclavo poeta,* "Azcárte, abolicionista y difusor de la cultura cubana," 20–30.
36. Luis, "Nicolás Azcarate's Antislavery Notebook," 339.
37. Rex Hauser, "Two New World Dreamers: Manzano and Sor Juana," *Afro-Hispanic Review* 12.2 (1993): 3.
38. Robert Richmond Ellis, "Reading through the Veil of Juan Francisco Manzano: From Homoerotic Violence to the Dream of a Homoracial Bond," *PMLA* 113.3 (1998): 443.
39. Coulthard, *Race and Colour,* 19.
40. Ibid., 20.
41. Miller, "Reading Juan Francisco Manzano in the Wake of Alexandar von Humbolt," 175. For a detailed account of the various versions of the *Autobiography,* see Luis, *Juan Francisco Manzano Autobiografía del esclavo poeta y ostros escritos,* 30–58.
42. Friol, *Suite,* 29.
43. See Edward J. Mullen, "Francisco Calcagno and the Afro-Cuban Literary Canon, *PALARA* 12 (2008): 29–37.
44. "Review of New Publications," *Christian Observer* 41 (1841): 44, 48.
45. José L. Franco, ed., *Autobiografía, cartas y versos de Juan Fco. Manzano* (Havana: Municipio de la Habana, 1937).
46. Ibid., n.p.
47. *The Autobiography of a Slave/Autobiografía de un esclavo,* ed. Ivan A. Schulman and trans. Evelyn Picon Garfield (Detroit: Wayne State University Press, 1996), 28.
48. Willis, "Crushed Geraniums," 206; Bremer, "Slave Who Wrote Poetry," 495; Molloy, "From Serf to Self," 394; Williams, *Representation of Slavery,* 25.
49. For an interesting discussion of these problems, see John W. Blassingame, *Slave Testimony: Two Centuries of Letters, Speeches, Interviews, and Autobiographies* (Baton Rouge: Louisiana State University Press, 1977), xvii–lxv.
50. See Daniel Laferriere, "Making Room for Semiotics," *Academe: Bulletin of the AAUP* 65 (1979): 434–40.

51. See Frances Smith Foster, *Witnessing Slavery* (Westport, CT: Greenwood Press, 1979). See also the important essay by Barbara Foley, "History, Fiction and the Ground Between: The Use of the Documentary Made in Black Literature," *PMLA* 95 (1980): 389–403.

52. Mullen, *Life and Poems of a Cuban Slave,* 21.

53. See James Olney, "'I Was Born': Slave Narratives, Their Status as Autobiography and as Literature," in *The Slave's Narrative,* ed. Charles Davis and Henry Louis Gates, 148–75. Oxford: Oxford University Press, 1985.

54. Miriam DeCosta-Willis, "Self and Society in the Afro-Cuban Slave Narrative," *Latin American Literary Review* 26.32 (1988): 9.

55. Willis, "Crushed Geraniums," 207.

56. See Robert Richmond Ellis, "Reading through the Veil of Juan Francisco Manzano," who claims that the autobiography "can also be read as silent testimony to a kind of abuse largely unacknowledged by historians of slavery and critics of slave narratives: the sexual violation of male slaves" (422). Also of interest with reference to the discourse of torture is Julio Ramos, "The Law Is Other: Literature and the Constitution of the Juridical Subject in Nineteenth Century Cuba," *Annals of Scholarship* 11.1–2 (1996): 1–35; and Elaine Scarry, *The Body in Pain: The Making and the Unmaking of the World* (Oxford and New York: Oxford University Press, 1985).

57. Mullen, *Life and Poems of a Cuban Slave,* 106.

58. Bremer, "Slave Who Wrote Poetry," 493; Willis, "Crushed Geraniums," 206; Friol, *Suite,* 47; Molloy, "From Serf to Self," 417.

59. Labrador-Rodríguez, "La intelectualidad negra," 16.

60. See Martha Cobb, "The Slave Narrative and the Black Literary Tradition," in *The Art of Slave Narrative: Original Essays in Criticism and Theory,* ed. John Sekora and Darwin Turner (Macomb: Western Illinois University Press, 1982), 36–44; DeCosta-Willis, "Self and Society," 6–15; Luis A. Jiménez, "Nineteenth Century Autobiography in the Afro-Americas: Frederick Douglass and Juan Francisco Manzano," *Afro-Hispanic Review* 14.2 (1995): 47–52.

61. See Jackson, *Black Writers,* 25, for commentary on this point. Gera Burton reproduces a letter in *Ambivalence and the Postcolonial Subject: The Strategic Alliance of Juan Franciso Manzano and Richard Robert Madden* (New York: Peter Lang, 2004), 95, which confirms that Manzano frequently visited him during his tenure in Havana.

62. See César Leante, "Dos obras antiesclavistas cubanas," *Cuadernos Americanos* 207 (1976): 175–89.

63. See Fernanda Macchi, "Juan Francisco Manzano el discurso abolicionista: Una lectura enmarcada," *Revista Iberoanericana* 217–218 (2007): 63–77, and her "Richard Robert Madden y el origen de las indias," *Afro-Hispanic Review* 27.2 (2008): 71–90, for a discussion

of the links between Madden's writing and the ideological goals of Anglophone abolitionism.

64. Fionnghuala Sweeney, "Atlantic Countercultures and the Networked Text: Juan Francisco Manzano, R. R. Madden and the Cuban Slave Narrative," *Forum for Modern Language Studies* 40.4 (2004): 402.

65. Marilyn Miller, "Reading Juan Francisco Manzano in the Wake of Alexander von Humbolt," 165.

66. Anna Brickhouse, "Manzano, Madden, 'El Negro Mártir,' and the Revisionist Geographies of Abolitionism" in *American Literary Geographies: Spatial Practice and Cultural Production, 1500–1900*, ed. Martin Brückner and Hsuan L. Hsu (Newark: University of Delaware Press, 2007), 232–33.

67. Joselyn Almeida, "Translating a Slave's Life: Richard Robert Madden and the Post-Abolition Trafficking of Juan Manzano's Poems by a Slave in the Island of Cuba," in *Circulations: Romanticism and the Black Atlantic*, ed. Paul Youngquist and Frances Botkin (October 2011): 2. Web.

68. See David R. Murray, "Richard Robert Madden: His Career as a Slavery Abolitionist," *Studies* 61 (1972): 43–44.

69. Cited in Richard Robert Madden, preface to *The Memoirs (Chiefly Autobiographical) from 1798 to 1886 of Richard Robert Madden; M.D., F.R.C.S.*, ed. Thomas More Madden (London: Ward and Downey, 1891).

70. Cited in Murray, "Richard Robert Madden," 49.

71. Madden, *Memoirs*, 80.

72. Richard Robert Madden, *A Letter to W. E. Channing, D.D. on the Subject of the Abuse of the Flag of the United States, in the Island of Cuba, and the Advantage Taken of Its Protection in Promoting the Slave Trade* (Boston: Ticknor, 1839). A review of the pamphlet appeared in the *Boston Christian Examiner* 27 (January 1840): 410–11: "The name of Mr. Trist has been frequently in the newspapers of late, with many disgraceful additions; but until we read this pamphlet of Dr. Madden we knew no sure ground of belief as to the justness of their application. . . . He brings against the Consul serious charges of misconduct, and substantiated by documentary evidence of apparently unquestionable authority."

73. See Howard R. Temperly, "British and American Abolitionists," in *The Antislavery Vanguard: New Essays on the Abolitionists*, ed. Martin Duberman (Princeton: Princeton University Press, 1965), 337–58.

74. For example, the following resolution was proposed and unanimously adopted by the General Anti-Slavery Convention: "That while the literature of Great Britain exercises so vast an influence over the public opinion of America, we deem it the duty of British abolitionists. . . through. . . leading religious, political, and literary periodicals. . . to spread before the American public evidence of the deep indignation of the civilized world against a slave-holding republic"

(cited in "The Proceedings of the General Anti-Slavery Convention held in London, 1840," *Eclectic Review* 8 [1841]: 233).

75. Ibid., 236.
76. See Frederick S. Stimson, *Cuba's Romantic Poet: The Story of Plácido* (Chapel Hill: University of North Carolina Press, 1964), 99–102. Also see "Notes to the Text" in Floyd J. Miller's edition of Martin R. Delany's *Blake or the Huts of America* (Boston: Beacon Press, 1970), which contains an interesting note on Plácido, whom Delany refers to in the aforementioned novel (319).
77. See Luis, *Literary Bondage,* 92–98.
78. Molloy, "From Serf to Self," 407. See also Julio Ramos, "Cuerpo, lengua, subjectividad," *Revista de Crítica Literaria* 19.38 (1993): 225–37.
79. Jackson, *Black Writers,* 20–21.

POEMS,

WRITTEN IN SLAVERY

&c. &c. &c.

POEMS

by

A SLAVE IN THE ISLAND OF CUBA,

RECENTLY LIBERATED;

TRANSLATED FROM THE SPANISH,

by

R. R. MADDEN, M.D.

WITH THE HISTORY OF THE

EARLY LIFE OF THE NEGRO POET,

WRITTEN BY HIMSELF

TO WHICH ARE PREFIXED

TWO PIECES DESCRIPTIVE OF

CUBAN SLAVERY AND THE SLAVE-TRAFFIC,

By R. R. M.

LONDON:

THOMAS WARD AND CO.,

27, PATERNOSTER ROW;

AND MAY BE HAD AT THE OFFICE OF THE BRITISH AND FOREIGN
ANTI-SLAVERY SOCIETY. 27, NEW BROAD STREET.

1840.

To

JOSEPH STURGE,

The Howard of Our Days,

The Friend and Faithful Follower

of

THOMAS CLARKSON,

This Little Work

Is Dedicated by His Friend,

R. R. MADDEN

London, Oct. 21st, 1840.

PREFACE

A Collection of Poems written by a slave recently liberated in the Island of Cuba, was presented to me in the year 1838, by a gentleman at Havana,[1] a Creole, highly distinguished, not only in Cuba, but in Spain, for his literary attainments. Some of these pieces had fortunately found their way to Havana, and attracted the attention of the literary people there, while the poor author was in slavery in the neighbourhood of Matanzas.[2] The gentleman to whom I have alluded, with the assistance of a few friends, of pursuits similar to his own—(for literature, even at the Havana, has its humanizing influence,) redeemed this poor fellow from slavery, and enabled him to publish such of his Poems, as were of a publishable kind in a country like Cuba, where slavery is under the especial protection, and knowledge under the ban of the censors of the press.

A few of those pieces which were unpublished or unpublishable in Cuba, I have endeavoured to put into English verse; and to the best of my ability, have tried to render, so as to give the sense of the writer (sometimes purposely obscured in the original) as plainly as the spirit of the latter, and the circumstances under which these pieces were written, would admit of. I am sensible I have not done justice to these Poems, but I trust I have done enough to vindicate in some degree the character of negro intellect, at least the attempt affords me an opportunity of recording my conviction, that the blessings of education and good government are only wanting to make the natives of Africa, intellectually and morally, equal to the people of any nation on the surface of the globe.

To form any just opinion of the merit of these pieces, it is necessary to consider the circumstances under which they were written, and how are these circumstances to be estimated by one ignorant of the nature of Cuban slavery? I had at first thought it would have been necessary to have prefixed some notice both of the trade in slaves, and the system of slavery in that island, but I found it impossible in any reasonable limits to effect this object, and the very abundance of my materials was an obstacle to the undertaking, or rather induced me to reserve these materials without abridgment for other purposes of higher interest, more likely to benefit the cause I am desirous to promote. I determined, therefore, to give a short but faithful sketch of the Cuban slave-trade merchant and planter in verse, and the presumption of the attempt is sufficiently obvious to myself to render any apology available in a literary point of view. As portraits, however rudely sketched, of the characters I have attempted to describe, the vivid impression which the originals have made on my mind, were too strong to leave these pictures without a resemblance, which an abler artist might have better, though not perhaps more faithfully delineated. Montgomery,[3] and Hanna Moore[4] have given us the character of the slave-trade captains of former times, and Cowper[5] has admirably described the general horrors of slavery itself. But though the brigands of this trade, and the evils of this system in other colonies have been frequently depicted, I am not aware that the wealthy merchants in such high repute in the Havana who carry on this trade; and the polished cavaliers, and hospitable Creoles, who are the planters of this island, have been portrayed except by travellers, who have judged of their humanity by the courteousness of their manners, and the amenities of slavery, by their deportment at the social board.

The author of the Poems I have attempted to translate, is now living at the Havana, and gains his livelihood by hiring himself out as an occasional servant. His name, for obvious reasons, I think it advisable not to publish, but to leave no doubt of the authenticity of these Poems, I have deposited the originals in the Spanish language in the hands of the secretary of the "British and Foreign Anti-slavery Society."

He is now in his forty-second year. He was born in Cuba. His father and mother lived and died in slavery in Cuba. The former was a "pardo" negro; the latter, the offspring of an African and a mulatto union. He was about thirty-eight years of age when he obtained his liberty. The price paid for it was 800 dollars. He obtained employment as a tailor for some time after he got his freedom, subsequently, he went out to service—then tried the business of a house-painter, and was not successful—was advised to set up as a confectioner, and lost all his money in that line, and eventually, has settled down as a "chef de cuisine" in occasional service. The gentleman who was mainly instrumental in obtaining his liberation from slavery, induced him to write his history. This task he accomplished in a manner alike creditable to his talents and his integrity. It was written in two parts—the second part fell into the hands of persons connected with his former master, and I fear it is not likely to be restored to the person to whom I am indebted for the first portion of this manuscript. As far, however, as this portion goes, I have no hesitation in saying, it is the most perfect picture of Cuban slavery that ever has been given to the world, and so full and faithful in its details, that it is difficult to imagine, that the portion which has been suppressed, can throw any greater light on the evils of this system, than the first part has done. I have given a literal translation of it, and that translation, revised by a Spaniard,[6] will be found at the end of these poems. To prevent the inconvenience of frequent references to notes for the meaning of Spanish terms, in common use in relation to slavery and slave-trade topics, I have given a glossary of such words as most frequently occur in conversation, or in books on these subjects.

As to the merit of the Poems, the opinion I have expressed is shared by a very distinguished Spanish scholar, and the author of them was introduced to me by him in the following terms:— "Mi querido Amigo esta carta se la entregara a v, el poeta J. F. M. de quien hable à v, y cuyos versos y exelente ingenio han llamada la atencion, aun en esta pais de todas las personas despreocupadas y buenas."[7]

Notes

1. Domingo del Monte (1804–1853).
2. Provincial capital of Matanzas province in western Cuba.
3. James Montgomery (1771–1854), English poet and author of *The West Indies* (1809), a poem in honor of the abolition of the slave trade.
4. Hanna Moore (1745–1833), English religious writer and member of the famed "Clapham Sect."
5. William Cowper (1731–1800), poet of the Evangelical party. He wrote a number of poems on the subject of poetry.
6. Anselmo Suárez y Romero (1818–1878).
7. "My Dear Friend, this letter is brought to you by the poet J. F. M. of whom I spoke to you before and whose excellent verse and wit have caught the attention of the good people of leisure in this country."

THE
SLAVE-TRADE MERCHANT;
A POEM,

DESCRIPTIVE OF
THE CUBAN SPECULATORS IN STOLEN MEN

"Come let us lie in wait for blood, let us lay snares for the innocent without cause. Let us swallow him up alive like hell, as one that goeth down to the pit. We shall fill our houses with spoils. Cast in thy lot with us, and let us all have one purse."

Prov. 1:11–14.

BY R. R. MADDEN, M.D.

POEMS.

THE SLAVE-TRADE MERCHANT[1]

Behold, yon placid, plodding, staid old man,
His still and solemn features closely scan!
In his calm look how wisdom's light is shed,
How the grey hairs, become his honored head!
Mark how the merchants bow, as he goes by,
How men on 'Change, at his approach draw nigh,
"Highly respected," and esteemed; 'tis said,
His fame to Afric's farthest shore is spread!
Behold, his house:—if marble speak elsewhere,
"Sermons in stones" are with a vengeance here,
Whate'er the potent will of wealth can do
Or pride can wish, is offered to your view.
Those gay saloons, this banquet hall's array,
This glaring pile in all its pomp survey
The grandeur strikes—one must not look for taste—
What's gorgeous, cannot always be quite chaste.
Behold, his heart! it is not all that's fair
And smooth without, that's staunch and sound elsewhere.
E'en in the calmest breast, the lust of gold
May have its firmest seat and fastest hold,
May fix its fatal canker in the core,
Reach every feeling, taint it more and more;
Nor leave one spot of soundness where it falls,
Nor spark of pity where its lust enthralls.
Behold, his conscience! oh, what deep repose,
It slumbers on in one long deadly doze:
Why do you wonder that it thus does sleep;
That crime should prosper, or that guilt so deep,
So long unfelt should seem unscathed, in fine,
Should know no shame, and fear no law divine.

Is there a curse like that which shrines offence,
Which hardens crime and sears the moral sense,

And leaves the culprit in his guilt unshamed,
And takes him hence unchanged and unreclaimed.
Behold, the peace that's owned by him who feels
He does no wrong, or outrage when he deals
In human flesh; or yet supplies the gold
To stir the strife, whose victims you behold.

The Cuban merchant prosecutes his trade
Without a qualm, or a reproach being made;
Sits at his desk, and with composure sends
A formal order to his Gold-coast friends
For some five hundred "bultos"[2] of effects,
And bids them ship "the goods" as he directs.
That human cargo, to its full amount,
Is duly bought and shipped on his account;
Stowed to the best advantage in the hold,
And limb to limb in chains, as you behold:
On every breast, the well-known brand, J. G.
In letters bold, engraved on flesh you see.
The slaves by times are in their fetters used
To dance and sing, and forcibly amused,
To make the negroes merry when they pine,
Or seem to brood o'er some concealed design.
And when the voyage to its close draws near,
No pains are spared to make the slaves appear
In fit condition for the market stall;
Their limbs are greased, their heads are shaved, and all
These naked wretches, wasted as they are,
And marked with many a recent wound and scar,
Are landed boldly on the coast, and soon
Are penned, like cattle, in the barracone.[3]
Tricked out for sale and huddled in a mass,
Exposed to ev'ry broker who may pass,
Rudely examined, roused with the "courbash,"[4]
And walked, and run, and startled with the lash,
Or ranged in line are sold by parcel there;
Spectres of men! the pictures of despair.
Their owner comes, "the royal merchant" deigns
To view his chattels, and to count his gains.
To him, what boots it,[5] how these slaves were made,
What wrongs the poor have suffered by his trade.
To him, what boots it, if the sale is good,
How many perished in the fray of blood!
How many peaceful hamlets were attacked,
And poor defenceless villages were sacked!
How many wretched beings in each town

Maimed at the onslaught, or in flight cut down!
How many infants from the breast were torn,
And frenzied mothers dragged away forlorn!
To him, what boots it, how the ship is crammed;
How many hundreds in the hold are jammed!
How small the space! what piteous cries below!
What frightful tumult in that den of woe!
Or how the hatches when the gale comes on,
Are battened down, and ev'ry hope seems gone;
What struggling hands in vain are lifted there,
Or how the lips are parched that move in prayer,
Or mutter imprecations wild and dread,
On all around, the dying and the dead:
What cares the merchant for that crowded hold
The voyage pays, if half the slaves are sold!

What does it matter to that proud senor,
How many sick have sunk to rise no more;
How many children in the waving throng.
Crushed in the crowd, or trampled by the strong!
What boots it, in that dungeon of despair,
How many beings gasp and pant for air!
How many creatures draw infected breath,
And drag out life, aye, in the midst of death!
Yet to look down, my God, one instant there,
The shrieks and groans of that live mass to hear;
To breathe that horrid atmosphere, and dwell
But for one moment in that human hell!
It matters little, if he sell the sound,
How many sick, that might not sell, were drowned;
How many wretched creatures pined away,
Or wasted bodies made their "plash" per day?

They're only negroes—true, they count not here.
Perhaps, their cries and groans may count elsewhere,
And one on high may say for these and all,
A price was paid, and it redeemed from thrall.
If the proud "merchants who are princes" here,
Believe his word, or his commandments fear,
How can they dare to advocate this trade,
Or call the sacred scriptures to its aid.
How can they have the boldness to lay claim,
And boast their title to the christian name;
Or yet pretend to walk in reason's light,
And wage eternal war with human right.
The pen does all the business of the sword,

On Congo's shore, the Cuban merchant's word
Serves to send forth a thousand brigands bold,
"To make a prey," and fill another hold;
To ravage distant nations at his ease,
By written order, just as he may please:
"Set snares and traps to catch" his fellow-men
And "lie in wait" to link their fetters, then,
Send forth his agents to foment the strife
Of hostile tribes—and when their feuds are rife,
To waste a province to provide a prey,
Yet dare to make humanity his plea.

Is there no sacred minister of peace
To raise his voice, and bid these horrors cease?
No holy priest in all this ruthless clime,
To warn these men, or to denounce their crime?
No new Las Casas[6] to be found once more,
To leave his country for this blood-stained shore;
And tell the titled felon of his deeds,
With all the freedom the occasion needs?
Alas! no voice is raised in Cuba—save
To plead for bondage, and revile the slave,
Basely to pander to oppression's aim,
And desecrate religion's sacred name.
Yet in this moral Golgotha,[7] where round
The grave of mercy none but foes are found,
Some lone and weary pilgrim may have come,
And caused a voice to echo from this tomb.
From him, perhaps, the proud oppressors e'en
May hear the crimes, they still would strive to screen,
And find a corner of the veil they cast
O'er Cuban bondage has been raised—at last,
And some, perhaps, at length aroused may think,
With all their gold they stand on ruin's brink,
And learn, at last, to ask of their own breasts,
Why have they used their fellow-men like beasts;
Why should it be that each should thus "despise
His brother" man, and scoff "the stranger's cries"?
"Have they not all one Father who's above?
Hath not one God created them in love?
Are they not all in God's own image made,
Or were the words of life to be obeyed?"
Or held unworthy of the Lord on high,
"He that *shall* steal and sell a man shall die?"
Perhaps, fanatics only in their zeal,
May think that others, thus should speak or feel,

And none but zealots dream, that negroes' rights
Were God's own gifts, as well, as those of whites.
Perhaps, the Cuban merchants too, may think
In guilt's great chain, he's but the farthest link.
Forsooth, he sees not all the ills take place,
Nor goes in person to the human chase;
He does not hunt the negro down himself,
Of course, he only furnishes the pelf.[8]
He does not watch the blazing huts beset,
Nor slips the horde at rapine's yell, nor yet
Selects the captives from the wretched band,
Nor spears the aged with his own right hand.
The orphan's cries, the wretched mother's groans,
He does not hear; nor sees the human bones
Strewed o'er the desert bleaching in the sun,
Memorials sad, of former murders done.
He does not brand the captives for the mart,
Nor stow the cargo—'tis the captain's part;
To him the middle passage[9] only seems
A trip of pleasure that with profit teems;
Some sixty deaths or so, on board his ship,
Are bagatelles in such a gainful trip;
Nay, fifty thousand dollars he can boast,
The smallest cargo yields him from the coast.

He need not leave his counting-house, 'tis true,
Nor bid Havana and its joys adieu,
To start the hunt on Afric's burning shore,
And drench its soil with streams of human gore;
He need not part with friends and comrades here
To sever nature's dearest ties elsewhere;
Nor risk the loss of friendship with the host
Of foreign traders, when he sweeps the coast.
But this most grave and "excellent Senor,"
Is cap in hand with the official corps,
Receives the homage due to wealth that's gained,
No matter how, or where it be obtained.
His friends are too indulgent to proclaim
What deeds are coupled with his wide-spread fame.
'Tis true, he merely purchases the prey,
And kills by proxy only in the fray;
His agents simply snare the victims first
They make the war, and he defrays the cost.

Such is the merchant in his trade of blood;
The Indian savage in his fiercest mood

Is not more cruel, merciless in strife,
Ruthless in war, and reckless of man's life!
To human suffering, sympathy, and shame,
His heart is closed, and wealth is all his aim.
Behold, him now in social circles shine
Polite and courteous, bland—almost benign,
Calm as the grave, yet affable to all,
His well-taught smile has nothing to appal;
It plays like sunbeams on a marble tomb,
Or coldly glancing o'er the death-like gloom
Creeps o'er his features, as the crisping air,
On Lake Asphaltes[10] steals, and stagnates there.
Serene as summer how the Euxine[11] looks
Before the gale its slumb'ring rage provokes.
Who would imagine, while the calm is there,
What deadly work its depths might still declare?
Or think, beneath such gently swelling waves
Thousands of human beings find their graves,
But who can ponder here, and reconcile
The scowl of murder, with its merchant's smile!

Behold, his friends! observe the kindred traits,
They must resemble, for one draught pourtrays
The tribe of Cuban traders, linked in crime
Of ev'ry grade in guilt, of every clime.
Stealers of men, and shedders of man's gore;
The more they grasp, the rage for gain the more,
Contagious guilt within their circle reigns,
And all in contact with it shows its stains.
Behold, the land! regard its fertile fields,
Look on the victims of the wealth it yields:
Ask of these creatures how they came to be
Dragged from their homes, and sold in slavery?
And when you hear "the cry" of men "go up."
"Robbed of their hire," and made to drink the cup
Of grief, whose bitter anguish is above
All human woe, the wretched can approve,
Think on their wrongs, and venture to reply,
"Shall not the land yet tremble" for this cry!
God of all light and truth, in mercy cause
The men who rule these lands to fear thy laws
O'erthrow oppression, stalled in guilty state;
Raise the poor stranger, spoiled and desolate.
Reprove the despot, and redeem the slave;
For help there's none, but thine that here can save.

Thou who can'st "loose the fettered in due time,"
Break down this bondage, yet forgive its crime;
Let truth and justice, fraught with mercy still,
Prevail at last o'er every tyrant's will.

Notes

1. For a detailed discussion of this poem, see Joselyn Almeida, "Translating a Slave's Life: Richard Robert Madden and the Post-Abolition Trafficking of Juan Manzano's *Poems by a Slave in the Island of Cuba*"; Anna Brickhouse, "Manzano, Madden, 'El Negro Mártir,' and the Revisionist Geographies of Abolitionism," 217–18.
2. Package or goods.
3. Stalls.
4. A whip.
5. What does it matter that.
6. Bartolome de Las Casas (1475–1565), a Dominican friar and author of the *Brevísima relación de la destrucción de Las Indias*, a book which championed the rights of the Indians.
7. Cavalry.
8. Money, booty.
9. Journey by ship to the slave port.
10. Asphalities Lacus, the biblical salt sea between Israel and Jordan.
11. The Black Sea, the sea between Europe and Asia connected with the Aegean Sea.

THE SUGAR ESTATE;
A POEM,

ILLUSTRATIVE OF
LIFE AND DEATH IN CUBAN SLAVERY.

"Happy the bonds that hold you,
Sure they be sweeter far than liberty;
There is no blessedness but in such bondage;
Happy! thrice happy chains! such links are heavenly."

Beaumont and Fletcher.

BY R. R. MADDEN.

The Sugar Estate[1]

Canto I.

No more of rapine and its wasted plains,
Its stolen victims and unhallowed gains,
Its Christian merchants, and the brigands bold
Who wage their wars and do their work for gold.
No more horrors sick'ning to the heart,
Commercial murders and the crowded mart;
The living cargoes and the constant trace
Of pain and anguish in each shrunken face!
Far from the city and its tainted breath,
Its moral plague and atmosphere of death;
The grave of freedom, honesty, and truth,
The haunt of folly and its shoals for youth.
Its empty churches and its crowded jails,
Its grasping dealers and its human sales,
Its gambling nobles and its spendthrift crowd.
Profuse, rapacious, indolent, and proud.
Far from the shade of its impending fate,
The cry of vengeance or the curse of hate,
From all the futile pleasures of the town,
The proud Havana's infamous renown:
Its fell pursuits, its routes and revels gay,
Its ruthless deeds and never-failing play;
Its walks and gardens, and its "barracones,"
Its Tacon's[2] glories and its "bozals"[3] groans,
Its invoiced negroes and its pleasures' lures,
Its bills of lading and its light amours,
Its daily press, its amatory strains,
Its puling sonnets and its clanking chains.
Far from the deadly influence whose sway
Degrades the tyrant and the victim,—nay,
Curdles the milk of human kindness, e'en
In woman's breast, and crisps the smoothest mien.

Far from those ladies, foreigners, and all
Whose wretched negroes tremble at their call,
Their morning strife, the evening calm of theirs,
Their angry gestures and their gala airs,
Their home-spent passions and their smiling lips,
Their out-door meekness and their in-door whips,
Their tender glances and their love-sick sighs,
Their female scourgings and their household cries.

Far from the foreign merchants who compete
In style and gaudy splendor with the great;
Who feast the ladies of the slave-trade clique,
And give such charming soirées once a week;
Where shares and ventures in the odious trade,
A common subject of discourse is made:
Where dealers talk jocosely of their plans,
And playful fair ones, tap them with their fans.
And say they're naughty when they speak in sport,
Of swearing certain captors out of court,
Or when their mirth is in the highest mood,
They jest of murder, and the joke seems good.

Far from a spot where men of ev'ry clime,
By easy stages led from crime to crime,
Descend at last to guilt's extreme degree,
And steep their hands in that of slavery.
Where men are found to advocate its cause,
And laugh to scorn their country's outraged laws:
Where the unmasked Republican contends
For slave-trade interests and their guilt defends;
Brawls about freedom, grasps its glaive and brand,
And sides with bondage in a foreign land.

Far from the agents who protect this trade,
Who sell their seals and signatures to aid
Their Spanish friends, their slavers to ensure,
Deceive the cruisers and their shares secure.
Far from official dabblers in the mart,
By small degrees grown ossified at heart,
Who chop and change their slave or two at first,
And soon would deal in hundreds if they durst;
And seem to think their pound of flesh is quite
Their own, to keep or sell by legal right.
Far from these planters, strangers, or Creoles.[4]
Friends of the traffic of congenial souls;

Nobles with titles at the market rates,
Brokers in bills and bankrupts with estates;
Settlers from old Virginia and its farms;
Sharpers in exile, safe from law's alarms.

Far from the seat of government where he
Who rules the land, but reigns where none are free;
Goes thro' the solemn mockery of state,
Prohibits crime and gravely tells its fate,
While the offender pays his half doubloon,
For each "bozal," and calls the bribe a boon
For public works, a voluntary gift,
The worthy ruler can't refuse to lift.
Tho' when the guilt is dragged before his eyes,
His injured honour "lifts its head and lies."

Now for the country and the peaceful plains,
Where rural pleasure and contentment reigns,
Those happy plains where man's productive toil
Finds sweet requital in a fertile soil;
Where healthful labour's cheerful aspect glows,
And evening brings to nature sweet repose
Where grateful peasants love their masters kind,
And peace and plenty bless the simple mind.
Oh! thou most lovely of the fair Antilles,
How oft I've wished, to see thy verdant hills,
Thy beauteous meads, thy woods with fragrance rife,
Teeming at once with loveliness and life,
Thy blooming gardens, those delightful glades,
And far-famed vales, whose verdure never fades,
Thy justly prized San Marco's[5] smiling plain,
And Guines'[6] waving fields of ripening cane.

How oft I've said in weariness of mind,
When shall I leave this heartless town behind?
When shall my trammelled spirit walk abroad,
And range those fields unknown to strife and fraud?
When shall I look on nature's face serene,
And feast my eyes, on one vast view of green.
When shall I roam by Almendares[7] stream,
Of Cuba's nymphs and Naiades haply dream,
By sweet Cohima's lovely banks, or those
Of Grandé's[8] river, stray at evening's close?
When shall I hear the songs of birds once more,
And hail the time when harvest yields its store?

Behold the country! all my hopes are crowned!
Here peace and joy are surely to be found;
Here nature riots in luxuriance wild,
And smiles on earth, as on her wayward child,
And loves to sport in ev'ry shape that's strange,
And e'en uncouth, and here exults in change.
The giant ceiba rears its bulk on high,
The rustling cocoa here confronts the sky,
The lofty cedar and caoba spread
Their noble branches o'er the torrent's bed;
The light bamboo's umbrageous beauty vies
With Valambrossa's shades in Cuban eyes,
Citron and lime, and orange ever near,
Cluster together; interweaving here
Their leaves, and blending their congenial hues
And fragrant odours, fresh with morning dews!

The straggling date, the waving palm behold,
The shady mango and its fruit of gold,
The broad-leafed plantain and the sheltered walk,
The sweet banana and its crowded stalk,
The choice anona and sapota rare,
The gorgeous shaddock and the guava fair.
But high o'er all the brave palmetto reigns,
The royal palm—the pride of Cuban plains,
Its swelling column with Ionian grace
Soaring aloft and tap'ring from its base;
Where is the park, forsooth, can boast of trees
To form a noble avenue like these?
The Theban temple and the solemn line
Of granite sphynxes leading to its shrine,
Like ghosts of former sights and scenes now rise,
And seem as if, to flit before my eyes;
But here the noble avenue doth lead
To no such sacred edifice indeed,
The vista strikes—no sculptured walls surprise—
A planter's house is all that meets one's eyes.
The owner comes, a cavalier 'tis plain,
In mein and manner, grave, austere, and vain;
A youthful noble—proud and passion swayed,
And poor, perhaps—if all he owed was paid:
His slender frame and haggard looks display,
The grave signs of premature decay.
Time, less than pleasure, may, perhaps, have done
The work of havoc which these lines make known,

And left this gay and thoughtless cavalier
A wreck of man, ere age had yet drawn near.

The solemn farce of Spanish etiquette,
In town or country no one must forget;
The Condè[9] comes, he halts at distance due,
Draws himself up and takes his guest in view,
Bow number one—advancing to the door,
Bow number two—as formal as before,
Bow number three—an effort at a smile,
And greeting then in true Castillian style;
"Sir, you are welcome to my house and lands,
Whate'er I own, is quite at your command,
My whole estate at your disposal—lies,"
(And echo dwells upon that word and dies)
"Regard these slaves, I pray, sir, as your own,
No hesitation—compliment, there's none;
I'm highly flattered that you like this hall,
You must accept it, furniture, and all.
You find me here quite in a rustic way—
I love the country—and can truly say
I envy none—my time is wholly spent
In making those poor negroes here, content.
You see them yonder in that field of cane,
They have no cause, believe me, to complain;
They want for nothing, have no wish on earth,
Except for work—of which there's no great dearth,
I only wish the poor, but, fared elsewhere,
One-half so well, as all our slaves do here.
Observe—the field is not so very far—
How full of mirth and glee our negroes are!
How well they look! how pleased to work! you see
What happy creatures even slaves can be!
We spare no pains indeed to make them so,
It is, no doubt, our interest so to do,
Besides, you know, humanity itself
Has claims upon us, quite apart from pelf."
The bell for dinner gave the Condè's tongue
A respite here—but one that was not long;
His house, his style of living, and address
Were all in keeping—showy to excess.
His conversation answered to his board,
Garnish of words and dishes in accord,
Abundant sweetmeats, olios, and ragouts,
Frieandeaus, fritters, harricots, and stews,

Hock, soda-water, claret, and for guests,
Who need instruction, and have grateful breasts,
The standing topic strangers still must hear
At every planter's table, and must bear
With patience too, though one which smells of graves,
The old proverbial happiness of slaves.

'Tis not polite to contradict one's host,
On most occasions, 'tis but labour lost,
At times moreover, men's opinions here
Are fashioned by their entertainer's cheer.
The stomach has its influence we find,
And sometimes its dominion o'er the mind.
And, hence, we trav'lling gentlemen who dine
With Cuban planters, judge them by their wine;
And if they're civil, courteous, and give feasts,
We think their slaves are treated like their guests.

One might have thought so in the present case,
And after dinner, though not after grace—
I failed not duly to assure my host,
It gave me joy to hear a planter boast
Of negroes so contented with their state
And so resigned to their unhappy fate. ,
'Tis highly pleasing, Senor Count, I said,
To find that slaves are so well clothed and fed;
So lightly worked—so fond of labour too,
So very grateful, Sir, for all you do,

To make them happy, and improve their lot:
And though, I must acknowledge, I am not
A friend of bondage—here I must confess,
By your account, it does not seem to press.
But still, with great respect, it seems to me,
A man might almost set his negroes free,
Without extreme injustice to the slaves,
Or very serious mischief to the knaves;
Though here, of course, they must be far too wise
To wish to break so good a master's ties.

No one, perhaps, replied the Count, can more
The sad, but strong necessity deplore,
Of buying men to cultivate our plains,
And holding these, our fellow-men in chains.
The very name of slavery, to me

Is vile and odious to the last degree;
I know it has some evils, few indeed,
But still enough, perhaps for slander's need.
Think not, I pray, I advocate this cause,
Or speak of such a system with applause;
Sir! in the abstract it must be condemned,
It is the practice only I defend;
For "quo ad"[10] morals, nothing can be worse,
But "quo ad" sugar, 'tis the sole resource.

I always thought on principle 'twas wrong
To purchase negroes, when the gang was strong;
And prices are so ruinous of late,
A man who buys must mortgage his estate.
But while I own the system's not the best—
I feel for Cuba and her sons opprest;
Her vital interests and the vested rights,
In "bozal" negroes,—of the injured whites.
I freely grant that treaties should be kept
In certain cases, some I must except,
Where there's "a sacred privilege" at stake,
Or staple trade,—we cannot well forsake.
But treaties are like protocols at par,
Truces in love, or stratagems in war;
Compacts to drive thro',—in a coach and four,
Suspended state hostilities on shore.

But still, however, freely I object
On such like scores, I mean no disrespect
To your great nation?—nay, you need not smile,
I only think your government is vile,
And all its treaties pre-concerted feats,
To please a set of hypocrites and cheats!
A pack of wretches envious of our gains,
Who make such noise about our whips and chains:
Fools and fanatics! exaltados![11] knaves!
Rogues who would rob poor planters of their slaves!
Fiends in disguise! philanthropists who'd swear
That black is white, to bring their ends to bear;
Villians who talk of savages possest
Of human rights, by men like me opprestl
Of slaves entitled to redress for wrongs
At hands like mine:—and dare to wag their tongues
Against the sacred privilege and right
Which ev'ry law accords the skin that's white!

Are they not preachers of sedition, nay,
Do they not tamper with our slaves and say,
The blacks should rise and cut their masters' throats?
Would they not put the question to their votes,
In case they spared their owners' lives, how they
Should work the whites, while they reposed all day?
Scoundrels! to think, that men like me were born
To grind the cane, or meant to plant the corn.

Yes, cried the Condè, as he wiped his brow,
I always speak as I have spoken now,
Coolly and calmly on a subject, so
Extremely grave, and so important too.
I'm sure you see the only wish I have,
Is for the real welfare of the slave;
And must perceive the only dread I feel
Is for the negro from fanatic zeal.
You see how happy and content he seems,
His bondage here—a paradise he deems,
Compared with that from which he first was torn,
And doubtless too, in which the wretch was born;
Having no claim to freedom from his birth,
And none of course, in after life on earth,
His rights are vested in his master's hands,
And he devotes them to his fertile lands.
You see his title to a master's care,
To compensation for the wear and tear
Of thews and sinews, while his strength remains
He wants for nothing, and he sings in chains.
Where wants are few,—no wages are required,
Nor is that sort of stimulus desired,
Crack the whip, it stirs the dullest drones,
It makes them lively and it breaks no bones.
In short, take all things here into account,
You'll find, believe me, sir, no small amount
Of peace, of rural happiness, and bliss,
On all estates administered like this.
There may be some plantations, to be sure,
Where slaves have some slight hardships to endure:
Where masters happen to abuse their power,
Or agents' tempers, are perhaps, too sour,
But this, of course, is very rare, you'll find,
In fact, we're far too lenient and too kind.
The humblest slave's protected by the laws,
A syndick's[12] chosen to defend his cause.

But how the slave's to get from the estate
To seek that syndick, and to pass the gate
From which he knows full well he dare not budge,
However near the house of the said judge.
These, sir, are things the law has left in doubt,
And has not very clearly pointed out;
'Tis quite sufficient that these laws are good,
The framers of them, never understood
The laws were made to be fulfilled, of course,
But only meant to be supposed in force.

"Oh, Senor Condè," I exclaimed, "'tis clear
The master's will is law and justice here,
His word is legal evidence, his skin
Presumptive proof of right that's sure to win.
His wealth has all the influence direct
Of truth itself and pleads with full effect.
His code is one that supersedes all laws,
Convicts the royal cedulas of flaws,
And makes the mill-house bench the judgment seat,
Where drivers lay their culprits at his feet.
In all the scene there's nothing to recall
Customs remembered only to appal;
Nought to remind one now of lictor's rods;
Of captives trembling at their master's nods.
Of savage tortures or of legal crimes;
Of heathen habits or of pagan times.
'Tis sweet to think we live in christian lands
Where slaves are merely held by silken bands:
And none make victims of their prisoners more
For mere amusement, as they did of yore.
We only take their lives, for lucre's sake;
We have no Roman holidays to make;
No circus toils and terrors to abash;
We but enliven labour with the lash.

'Tis good to know your system works so well;
That slaves and planters in such friendship dwell,
That negroes hug their chains devoid of fear,
And owners use their power like angels here.
'Tis well, I say, that things are thus with you,
When all without, looks black and threatening too.

I think, sir, said the Condè, you must be
Wearied with so much riding, and I see

You're not accustomed to these roads of ours;
Our ways, indeed, are not so smooth as yours,
But still they serve for us, we make them do,
We are not fond of anything that's new.
You seem fatigued—you'll find your room prepared,
I quite regret you have so badly fared;
But since I can't prevail on you to stay,
And spend with us another lonely day,
You may depend you shall be called at four,
And find your horses saddled at the door!

End of Canto I.

Canto II.

Whoever spent a night on an estate
In time of crop, and had endured of late
Fatigue and toil, that amply might dispose
A weary trav'ller to enjoy repose,
And roused at midnight, heard the frightful bell,
The dismal conch's loud blast at change of spell,
The crack of whips, the hurried tramp of men,
The creaking mill, the driver's threats, and then
The sudden scream, the savage bloodhounds growl,
The shout prolonged, the "stokers" ceaseless howl;
All the dread noise that's requisite to keep
The jaded cattle and the slaves from sleep;
To rouse the weak, to drown the women's cries
And cause one deaf'ning uproar to uprise.
Whoever found this tumult at its height,
This Cuban Babel's strife at dead of night;
Whoever listened to these horrid sounds,
And might not deem, hell had enlarged her bounds,
Made this plantation part of her domain,
And giv'n its owner, slaves, and lust of gain.

Loathing the couch itself, whereon I lay,
With thankful breast I hailed the break of day,
And breathed more freely when I reached the door
'Twas joy to feel, I ne'er should enter more.
The waning stars were yet in the grey sky,
The morning dawn just peering forth on high
Yet all is bustle round the mill-house walls,
The slave still trembles, and the lash still falls.
The drowsy negroes haggard, spent, and worn,
Like drunken men reel past; and night and morn
Brings no repose, but one unbroken chain
Of fruitless toil, of weariness and pain.

The mayoral who oversees the band,
Before me now is standing, whip in hand,
The straw-hat slouching o'er his olive face,
Sturdy in figure, active in his pace;
Nor coat nor waistcoat incommode his breast,
He walks erect, expands his ample chest,
Displays a tawdry brooch of ample size,
Large silver buckles in each brace likewise;
A long strait sword with hilt of plated brass,
And rings and trinkets too like all his class.

What means this sword that dangles at his side?
Those blood-hounds too; what evils can betide?
A man of peace, a simple overseer,
A "mayoral," who has no cause to fear.
All in his mien and manner bears the brand
Of might unquestioned, uncontrolled command.
The bold regard, the fixed and searching glance
Of one who dealt but little in romance.

With all due awe and reverence possest,
This worthy person gravely I addrest,
Named what I wished to see, how far I came,
And all except my unimportant aim.
The man for one who held a despot's sway,
Was frank and almost civil in his way.
Freely complied with every wish exprest,
Unveiled the secrets of this shrine unblest.
And spoke of horrors here, as things well-known.
And deeds, of course, that ev'ry day were done.
Here were two hundred negroes, great and small,
The full-grown gang two hundred strong—they call
The female slaves, of ev'ry age—they own
Are short of fifty, or a fourth alone,
Of these, not one was married by a priest,
Or saw one either Sabbath-day or feast;
No sacred rite, no sacrament was known,
The pagans christened and the burial done,
The law, to its strict letter was obeyed;
The farce was over and the fees were paid.
Here, with two hundred working men, last year,
They boast they made two thousand boxes clear
Of first-class sugar—and the boast is one
That tells a tale of murder largely done.
The deaths they tell you of the slaves, are here
Some ten per cent, and sometimes twelve a year.
A fair consumption too of human life,
Where wholesale slaughter shows no martial strife.
But then, perhaps, the births were in excess;
Alas! the births each year are less and less.
Three in the last twelve months, and two of these
Had died, because the mothers did not please
To rear up slaves; and they preferred to see
Their children dead before their face, ere they
Would give their young "negritos" to the kind
Indulgent masters which they are said to find.

Jamaica bondsmen in "the good old times,"
Of our West Indian cruelties and crimes,
Were pretty hardly worked, both old and young,
Yet here is an amount of labour, wrung
From Cuban slaves, just double that of ours,
And nearly twice the sum of working hours;
For here the grasping master still must have
Just thrice the produce from each working slave.
All to the charge of British planters laid,
Compared with this—is thrown into the shade,
And yields the bad pre-eminence in crime
To Spanish guilt in ev'ry tropic clime.
What does it matter here, how many lives
Are lost in labour, while the planter thrives,
The Bozal market happily is nigh,
And there the planter finds a fresh supply:
'Tis cheaper far to buy new strength, we're told,
Than spare the spent, or husband out the old;
'Tis not a plan by which a planter saves,
To purchase females, or to rear up slaves.
But times there are, when one has listened long
And heard atrocious things, as if no wrong
Was done the ear, or offered to the heart,
That silence seems at last, a felon's part.

Tell me, Senor! I somewhat calmly said,
Where shall I find the aged negro's shed,
And see the poor old slaves of the estate,
The weak, decrepid, worn-out slaves, whose fate
It is, to feel a master's care at length,
For whom they toiled through life, and spent their strength;
How does it happen, none are to be seen
Unfit for labour, who from age, have been
Exempt from toil and hardship, at the close
Of life, and now entitled to repose?
How does it happen, that the stranger sees
No ransomed nursling on the mother's knees,
No pregnant woman, whom the law doth yield
A month's brief rest, and respite from the field.
No tender children, on the Sabbath-day
Trained to be good, poor things, or taught to pray,
No place of refuge for declining age,
In nature's course, to quit this mortal stage?

I'd always thought that "mayorals" were folks
Who never laughed or deigned to deal in jokes,

But this man laughed, as if he'd reason, then
Till his great sides with laughter shook again.
At length, somewhat composed, he coolly said,
Who could have put such nonsense in your head?
Who ever heard of negroes getting old,
Or planters suffering female slaves to fold
Their arms, and sit like Creole ladies still,
Or taking pregnant women from the mill?
You've not been long in Cuba, I suppose,
From what you say of Sabbaths and repose,
And paid not much attention, I opine,
To many matters in the planting line?
You have to learn what slaves are worth the score,
What blacks are for, and whose they are, moreo'er!
We purchase slaves to cultivate our plains,
We don't want saints or scholars to cut canes;
We buy a negro for his flesh and bone,
He must have muscle, brains, he need have none.
But where, you ask me, are the poor old slaves?
Where should they be, of course, but in their graves!
We do not send them there before their time,
But let them die, when they are past their prime.
Men who are worked by night as well as day,
Some how or other, live not to be grey
Sink from exhaustion—sicken—droop and die,
And leave the Count another batch to buy;
There's stock abundant in the slave bazaars,
Thanks to the banner of the stripes and stars![13]
You cannot think, how soon the want of sleep
Breaks down their strength, 'tis well they are so cheap,
Four hours for rest—in time of crop—for five
Or six long months, and few indeed will thrive.

With twenty hours of unremitting toil,
Twelve in the field, and eight in doors, to boil
Or grind the cane—believe me few grow old,
But life is cheap, and sugar, sir,—is gold.
You think our interest is to use our blacks
As careful owners use their costly hacks;
Our interest is to make the most we can
Of every negro in the shortest span.
As for the women, they embroil estates,
There's never peace with them, within your gates:
They're always shamming, skulking from the field,
And most abusive when their backs are wealed.

Sure to be sick when strangers pass this way,
They take advantage of us every way;
For well they know, the Condè cannot bear
The thoughts of flogging while his friends are here.
As for the talk of marriage, you must jest,
What! marry wretched negroes by a priest!
Why, sir, there's not a priest within some ten
Or twelve good leagues of the estate—and, then,
Were one to come, the Count would have to pay;
I marry all the best and cheapest way.
We have not many marriages, 'tis true,
The men are many and the females few.

We stall our negroes as we pen our sheep,
And hold them fast as good stone walls can keep
A negro gang, and ev'ry night you'll find
The "spell" released, in yonder square confined,
We have, no doubt, our runaways at times,
And flight, you know, we count the worst of crimes.
Slaves who are flogged and worked in chains by day,
Left in the stocks all night—you think would stay
On the estate as soon as they're set free,
And yet the fools again will dare to flee.
We are not always scourging—by the way,
Tuesday in common is our flogging day;
At other times we only use the whip,
To stir the drones and make the young ones skip;
Then as to food, you may be sure we give
Enough, to let the wretched creatures live:
The diet's somewhat slender, there's no doubt,
It would not do, to let them grow too stout;
Nor is it here, nor on estates around,
That fat and saucy negroes may be found.

Nay, said the speaker, in a graver tone,
You seem to hear of things but little known;
Gaze on these wretched negroes as you may,
You've heard but little of their wrongs to-day.
If I must speak still plainer, and must call
Things by their proper names, that must appal:
'Tis not the scourge, or shackel, plague or pest,
That wears the negro out—but want of rest.
Night after night in constant labour past,
Will break down nature, and its strength at last.
Day after day in toil and terror spent,

The slave will sink—and die with our consent;
The four hours' rest another victim gains,
It frees another negro from his chains;
And still we hear from planters o'er and o'er
The solemn lie, that negroes need no more.
You think, no doubt, the mayoral's to blame,
He works the negroes thus, and his the shame;
He plies the whip, and therefore he's the man
That's marked for vengeance, and deserves its ban.
I think I read what passes in your mind,
You deem our tribe the dregs of human kind;
Men who are formed by nature for this post,
To ev'ry feeling of their species lost.
How little know you of the men who fill
This wretched office, and who loathe it still
Men who have felt oppression's iron hand,
Or want has driven from their land,
And forced to take this execrable place
To get their bread; in spite of its disgrace.
Think you we have no feelings for these slaves,
And are the willing instruments of knaves,
Who drains the life's blood of the negroes core,
And leaves the guilt and odium at our door?
Think you, for us there's profit in the gain,
Wrung from the mortal agony and pain,
Of sinking strength, of sickness, and despair
We daily witness, and we must not spare?
Think you, for us there's pleasure in the groans
Of mothers, listening to the piteous moans
Of wailing infants, stretched before their eyes,
They dare not leave the hoe, to hush those cries,
Nor ask the driver for a moment's rest,
To sooth the child, that's screaming for the breast?
These sights and scenes become, no doubt, in time,
Familiar to us, and with some the crime
Finds favour even —but not much with me;
I would not care if ev'ry slave was free,
And ev'ry planter too to toil compelled,
We are their dogs, and worse than dogs are held.

Our despot does not live on his estate,
He loves the town, and there he goes the gait
Of other fools, and thinks that all grandees,
Should lead a life of luxury and ease.
He finds Havana stored with ev'ry vice,

Can feed his pampered senses or entice;
There in his squalid splendour he can move,
Exhaust the passions and imagine love;
Plume up his haughty indigence in smiles,
And waste a harvest on a harlot's wiles.

There he can find among his gay compeers,
Gamblers enough and spendthrifts of his years,
To get a "montè"[14] up, at noon or night,
And keep the game forbidden out of sight:
There he can stake a crop upon a card
God help the negroes, if his luck is hard,
For then the Count we're sure to see next day,
The gambler comes, to find fresh funds for play.

The "mayoral" is summoned to his lord,
The menial comes, uncovered to afford
A strict account of all the sugar made,
That's fit for sale and ready for the trade;
The last year's crop, he's told, will never do,
It must be doubled; or an agent new
Must take his place—and then the debts of old,
The heavy charges on the produce sold,
The merchant's twelve per cent on each advance
Have swallowed up the funds he got by chance,
Or had received in driblets from the hands
Of knaves, who made their fortunes on his lands;
He must look out, and find a man who'll make
The negroes work and keep the slave awake;
He'll not be told they can't be worked much more,
They sleep too much, and have no need of four
Or five hours' rest, his neighbors all agree
That slaves in crop can do right well with three.
Sugar he'll have, he cares not how, or by
What cruel means, he gets a new supply;
'Tis idle to remonstrate or resist,
Obey one must, or be at once dismissed.
Think you, indeed, a gamester's heart is made
Of human stuff that's moved by prayers, or swayed
By an earthly influence but one,
The lust of gold, to play for stakes unwon.
The Condè's orders are obeyed, of course,
And these, augmented rigour must enforce:
"Boca abajos,"[15] morning, noon, and night,
Unceasing torture, and unsparing might,

Murmurs arise, and driftless schemes are rife,
Of wild revenge, 'mongst men made sick of life.
And when the outburst comes, what signifies
Who is the victim—so a white man dies.

I know full well the perils of my post,
How many lives its odious tasks have cost!
You see this sword, these blood-hounds at my beck,
I count on these, to keep the slaves in check,
These are the dogs we train to hunt the blacks,
To scent their trail and come upon their tracks,
To run them down and chase the "cimarone,"[16]
And mangle those who prowl at night alone.
These are our friends and allies, it is fit
That brutes like these should be so, I admit.

Ah, Senor Mio! briefly I replied,
The words you speak are not to be denied;
You know too well your duties, it appears,
For me to question or dispute your fears,
Too well you know the torments you inflict,
For me to doubt the sufferings you depict.
Too well you've done the biddings of your lord,
To fail to be detested and abhorred;
Too much have harassed and oppressed the poor,
For me to think your system can endure.
Your fields are fair and fertile, I allow,
But no good man can say—"God speed the plough."
There's wealth unfailing in your people's toil;
'Twould wrong the poor, to cry—"God bless the soil,"
'Twere asking blood to beg that God would deign
"To give the early and the latter rain,"
One prayer indeed can hardly be supprest,
God help the slave! and pity the opprest.

R. R. M.

Notes

1. See Almeida, "Translating a Slave's Life"; Brickhouse, "Manzano, Madden," 218–20.
2. Miguel Tacón (1775–1854), colonial governor of Cuba from 1834 to 1838.
3. Recently imported slaves.
4. People of native birth but European descent.
5. A municipality in the province of Havana, Cuba.

6. A municipality in the province of Havana, Cuba.
7. A river in Cuba which empties into the Atlantic just west of Havana.
8. A vast estuary along the northern Cuban coast.
9. Count.
10. As far as.
11. Saints; exalted persons.
12. A local council appointed to protect the rights of slaves.
13. Ships flying the flag of the United States were often used to evade British antislavery laws.
14. A card game.
15. Face down.
16. A runaway slave.

LIFE OF THE NEGRO POET

WRITTEN BY HIMSELF.

*AND TRANSLATED FROM THE SPANISH
BY R. R. M.*

Life of the Negro Poet

The Senora Donna Beatrice,[1] the wife of Don Juan M—[2] took a pleasure every time she went to her beautiful estate, the Molino, to make choice of the finest Creole children about the age of ten or eleven years, and carry them to town, where she gave them instruction conformable to their new condition. Her house was always filled with these young slaves instructed in everything necessary to her service. One of the favourite young slaves was Maria M—,[3] my mother, who was greatly esteemed for her intelligence, and her occupation was to wait on the Senora Marquesa of J. in her advanced age. This lady was accustomed when she was pleased with her attendants, to give them their liberty when they were about to marry, if it were with some mechanic[4] likewise free; providing them with all things necessary, as if they had been her own children, without depriving them after their marriage of the favour and protection of her house, which extended even to their children and husbands; of which conduct there are many notable examples, amongst those who were not even born in the house. Various changes, however, taking place in the service, Maria became the chief waiting-woman of the Marquesa. In this situation she married Toribio de Castro, and in due time, I was ushered into the world.

My master took a fancy to me, and it is said I was more in his arms than in those of my mother. She had all the privileges of a slave who had acted as a dry-nurse, and also partly as a wet-nurse, media criandera; and having married one of the head slaves of the house, and given a little Creole to her mistress, I was called by this lady, "the child of her old age." I was brought up by the side of my mistress without separating from her, except at bed-time, and she never went out without taking me in her volante. With the difference of hours in respect to some, and days in regard to others, I was the contemporary of Don Miguel de C.,[5] and also of Don Manuel O'R. now Count of B.;[6] which two families lived in a splendid house, close to the Machina, separated only by doors which divided the apartments; for, in fact, it was two houses made into one.

It would be tedious to detail the particulars of my childhood, treated by my mistress with greater kindness than I deserved, and whom I was accustomed to call "my mother." At six years of age, on account, perhaps, of too much vivacity, more than anything else, I was sent to school to my godmother[7] every day at noon; and every evening I was brought to the house, that my mistress might see me, who seldom went out without seeing me, for if she did, I roared and cried, and so disturbed the house, that sometimes it was necessary to send for the whip, which nobody dared to lay on me, for not even my parents were authorised to flog me, and I knowing this, often took advantage of it. On one occasion, being very bold, my father beat me, but my mistress hearing of it, did not allow him for many days to come into her presence, until he procured the intercession of her Confessor, the father Maya, a Franciscan, and then he was forgiven; after the latter had explained to him that my Senora, as mistress, and my father, as a parent, had each their respective direction of me.

At ten years of age, I learned by heart some of the longest sermons of Father Louis, of Granada,[8] and the visitors who came to the house on Sundays, used to hear me repeat them when I came from the chapel, where I was sent with my godmother, to learn how to behave in church; because, although the service was performed every Sunday in the house, I was not permitted to be present, on account of the tricks I might have played with the other children.

I also knew my catechism well, and as much of religion as a woman could teach me. I knew how to sew tolerably, and to place the furniture in order. On one occasion, I was taken to the Opera, and received some presents for reciting what I heard, but many more for the sermons, and my parents got what I received in the drawing-room.

But passing over much of my early history, in which there was nothing but happiness, I must not omit the circumstances which happened at my baptism; on that occasion, I was dressed in the same robe in which the Senora Donna Beatrice was baptized, which was celebrated with great rejoicings, my father being skilled in music, and playing on the flute and clarionet; and my mistress desiring to solemnize that day with one of her noble traits of generosity, in part liberated my parents by "coartacion," giving them the power at any time of purchasing their liberty at the sum of three hundred dollars each; what greater happiness could be looked for at her hands.

At the age of ten, I was placed under the care of my godfather; having learned something of my father's trade, which was that of a tailor, previously, to being sent to the estate. My mother gave birth to two other children. One of them, for what reason I know not, was made free—and this one died. My father lamenting his death, saying, "if things had been otherwise, I might have been content, my two living children are slaves, and the one that was free is dead;" whereupon my generous mistress had a document prepared, in which it was declared that the next child they should have should be free; and it happened that twins were subsequently born, who are still living, and both were freed.[9] My parents now were removed to the estate of the Molino, where they were placed in charge of the house, and about this period the Marquesa died there. I was sent for in her last illness. I remember little of what happened on my arrival, except being at the bedside of my mistress with my mother, Donna Joaquina, and the priest, and that her hand rested on my shoulder, while my mother and Donna Joaquina wept a great deal, and spoke about something which I did not understand, and then that I was taken away. Soon after I went to play, and the following morning I saw her stretched on a large bed, and cried, and was carried down stairs where the other servants were mourning for their mistress; and all night long all the negroes of the estate made great lamentation, repeated the rosary, and I wept with them.

I was taken to the Havana, to my godfather, with whom I soon learned my mistress had left me; for some years I saw nothing of my father. My godfather had taken up his residence in the courtyard of the Count, in the street Inquisidor, where I was accustomed to go about the house, and to leave it when I thought proper, without knowing whether I had a master or not.

But one day, being permitted to go to the house of the Marquesa, to see my old acquaintances there, I know not what passed there, but when I was about returning to my godfather, and my dear godmother, I was not allowed to go: here I was clothed in a rich livery, with a great deal of gold lace, and what with my fine clothes, going to the theatres, to tertulias, balls, and places of amusement, I soon forgot my old quiet mode of life, and the kindness even of my godmother herself. After some time I was taken to the house of Donna Joaquina, who treated me like a white child, saw that I was properly clothed, and even combed my hair herself; and as in the time of the Marquesa de J.,[10] she allowed me not to pray with the other negro children at church—and at mealtime my plate was given to me to eat at the feet of the Senora Marquesa de P.,[11] and all this time I was far away from my father and mother.

I had already at the age of twelve years composed some verses in memory, because my godfather did not wish me to learn to write, but I dictated my verses by stealth to a young mulatto girl, of the name of Serafina, which verses were of an amatory character. From this age, I passed on without many changes in my lot to my fourteenth year; but the important part of my history began when I was about eighteen, when fortune's bitterest enmity was turned on me, as we shall see hereafter.

For the slightest crime of boyhood, it was the custom to shut me up in a place for charcoal, for four-and-twenty hours at a time. I was timid in the extreme, and my prison, which still may be seen, was so obscure, that at mid-day no object could be distinguished in it without a candle. Here after being flogged I was placed, with orders to the slaves, under threats of the greatest punishment, to abstain from giving me a drop of water. What I suffered from hunger and thirst, tormented with fear, in a place so dismal and distant from the house, and almost suffocated with the vapours arising from the common sink, that was close to my dungeon, and constantly terrified by the rats that passed over me and about me, may be easily imagined. My head was filled with frightful fancies, with all the monstrous tales I had ever heard of ghosts and apparitions, and sorcery; and often when a troop of rats would arouse me with their noise, I would imagine I was surrounded by evil spirits, and I would roar aloud and pray for mercy; and then I would be taken out and almost flayed alive, again shut up, and the key taken away, and kept in the room of my mistress, the Senora herself. On two occasions, the Senor Don Nicholas and his brother showed me compassion, introducing through an aperture in the door, a morsel of bread and some water, with the aid of a coffee-pot with a long spout. This kind of punishment was so frequent that there was not a week that I did not suffer it twice or thrice, and in the country on the estate I suffered a like martyrdom. I attributed the smallness of my stature and debility of my constitution to the life of suffering I led, from my thirteenth or fourteenth year.

My ordinary crimes were—not to hear the first time I was called; or if at the time of getting a buffet I uttered a word of complaint; and I led a life of so much misery, daily receiving blows on the face, that often made the blood spout from both my nostrils; no sooner would I hear myself called than I would begin to shiver, so that I could hardly keep on my legs, but supposing this to be only shamming on my part, frequently would I receive from a stout negro lashes in abundance.

About the age of fifteen or sixteen, I was taken to Matanzas once more, and embraced my parents and brothers.

The character, grave, and honourable of my father, and being always in his sight, caused my time to pass a little lighter than before. I did not suffer the horrible and continual scourgings, nor the blows of the hand, that an unfortunate boy is wont to suffer far away from his miserable parents; notwithstanding, my unfortunate cheeks were slapped often enough. We passed five years in Matanzas, where my employment was to sweep and clean the house as well as I could at sunrise, before any one in the house was up; this done I had to seat myself at the door of my mistress, that she might find me there when she awoke, then I had to follow her about wherever she went, like an automaton with my arms crossed. When breakfast, or the other meals were over, I had to gather up what was left, and having to put my hand to clear away the dishes, and when they rose from table I had to walk behind them. Then came the hour of sewing, I had to seat myself in sight of my mistress to sew women's dresses, to make gowns, shifts, robes, pillow-cases, to mark and to hem fine things in cambric, and mend all kinds of clothing.

At the hour of drawing, which a master taught, I was also present, stationed behind a chair, and what I saw done and heard, corrected and explained, put me in the condition of counting myself as one of the pupils of the drawing-class. One of the children, I forget which, gave me an old tablet, and a crayon; and with my face turned to the wall, the next day I sat down in a corner, and began making mouths, eyes, ears, and going on in this way, I came to perfect myself, so that I was able to copy a head so faithfully, that having finished one, my mistress observing me, showed it to the master, who said that I would turn out a great artist, and that it would be for her one day a great satisfaction that I should take the portraits of all my masters.

At night I had to go to sleep at twelve or one o'clock, some ten or twelve squares of buildings distant, where my mother lived (in the negro barracones.) Being extremely timid, it was a serious matter to me to pass to this place in the wettest nights. With these troubles, and other treatment something worse, my character became every day more grave and melancholy, and my only comfort was to fly to the arms of my mother, for my father was of a sterner nature. He used to be sleeping when my poor mother and my brother Florence waited up for me, till the hour of my arrival.

Some attacks of ague, which nearly ended my days, prevented me from accompanying my mistress to Havana. When I recovered, no one could enjoy himself in two years as I did in four months; I bathed four times a-day, and even in the night, I fished, rode on horseback, made excursions into the mountains, ascended the highest hills, eat all kinds of fruits; in short, I enjoyed all the innocent pleasures of youth. In this little epoch I grew stout and lively, but when I returned to my old mode of life, my health broke down again, and I became as I was before.

When I recovered sufficiently, my first destiny was to be a page, as well in Havana as in Matanzas; already I was used to sit up from my earliest years the greatest part of the night, in the city, either at the theatre, or at parties, or in the house of the Marquis M—H—[12] and the Senoras C.,[13] from which we went out at ten o'clock, and after supper play began, and continued till eleven or twelve; and at Matanzas, on the days appointed, and sometimes not, when they dined at the house of the Count J.,[14] or in that of Don Juan M.,[15] and generally to pass the evening in the house of the Senoras G.,[16] in which the most distinguished persons of the town met and played at trecillo, malilla, or burro.[17] While my lady played, I could not quit the side of her chair till midnight, when we usually returned to the Molino. If during the tertullia I fell asleep, or when behind the volante, if the lanthorn went out by accident, even as soon as we arrived, the mayoral, or administrador was called up, and I was put for the night in the stocks, and at day-break I was called to an account, not as a boy; and so much power has sleep over a man, four or five nights seldom passed that I did not fall into the same faults. My poor mother and brothers more than twice sat up waiting for me while I was in confinement, waiting a sorrowful morning.

She, all anxiety when I did not come, used sometimes to leave her hut, and approaching the door of the infirmary, which was in front of the place allotted to the men where the stocks were, on the lefthand side, at times would find me there; and would call to me, "Juan," and I sighing, would answer her, and then she would say outside, "Ah, my child!" and then it was she would call on her husband in his grave— for at this time my father was dead.

Three times I remember the repetition of this scene, at other times I used to meet my mother seeking me—once above all, a memorable time to me—when the event which follows happened:—

We were returning from the town late one night, when the volante was going very fast, and I was seated as usual, with one hand holding the bar, and having the lanthorn in the other, I fell asleep, and it fell out of my hand; on awaking, I missed the lanthorn, and jumped down to get it, but such was my terror, I was unable to come up with the volante. I followed, well knowing what was to come, but when I came close to the house, I was seized by Don Sylvester, the young mayoral. Leading me to the stocks, we met my mother, who giving way to the impulses of her heart, came up to complete my misfortunes. On seeing me, she attempted to inquire what I had done, but the mayoral ordered her to be silent, and treated her as one raising a disturbance. Without regard to her entreaties, and being irritated at being called up at that hour, he raised his hand, and struck my mother with the whip. I felt the blow in my own heart! To utter a loud cry, and from a downcast boy, with the timidity of one as meek as a lamb to become all at once like a raging lion, was a thing of moment—with all my strength I fell on him with teeth and hands and it may be imagined how many cuffs, kicks, and blows were given in the struggle that ensued.

My mother and myself were carried off and shut up in the same place; the two twin children were brought to her, while Florence and Fernando were left weeping alone in the hut. Scarcely it dawned, when the mayoral, with two negroes acting under him, took hold of me and my mother, and led us as victims to the place of sacrifice. I suffered more punishment than was ordered in consequence of my attack on the mayoral. But who can describe the powers of the laws of nature on mothers? the fault of my mother was, that seeing they were going to kill me, as she thought, she inquired what I had done, and this was sufficient to receive a blow and to be further chastised. At beholding my mother in this situation, for the first time in her life, (she being exempted from work) stripped by the negroes and thrown down to be scourged, overwhelmed with grief and trembling, I asked them to have pity on her for God's sake; but at the sound of the first lash, infuriated like a tiger, I flew at the mayoral, and was near losing my life in his hands; but let us throw a veil over the rest of this doleful scene.

I said before, that I was like my mistress's lap-dog, since it was my duty to follow her wherever she went, except to her own private rooms, for then I remained outside to prevent any body from going in, receiving any messages, and keeping silence when she was there. One afternoon, I followed her into the garden, where I was set to gather up flowers and transplant some little roots, when the gardener was employed in his occupation there. At the time of leaving the garden, I took unconsciously, a small leaf, one alone of geranium, thinking only of making verses; I was following, with this little leaf in my hand, two or three yards behind my mistress, so absent in my mind that I was squeezing the leaf with my fingers to give it greater fragrancy. At the entrance of the anti-chamber she turned back, I made room for her, but the smell attracted her attention; full of anger, on a sudden and in a quick tone she asked me "What have you got in your hands?" Motionless and trembling, I dropt the remains of the leaf, and, as if it was a whole plant, for this crime I was struck on the face, and delivered to the care of the overseer, Don Lucas Rodriguez. It was about six o'clock in the afternoon, and in the middle of winter. The volante was ready to go to town, and I was to ride behind; but alas! I was little aware what was to come in the next hour! Instead of riding in the volante, I was taken to the stocks, which were in a building, formerly an infirmary, and now used for a prison, and for depositing the bodies of the dead till the hour of interment. My feet were put in the stocks, where shivering with cold, without any covering, they shut me in. What a frightful night I passed there! My fancy saw the dead rising and walking about the room, and scrambling up to a window above the river and near a cataract, I listened to its roar, which seemed to me like the howling of a legion of ghosts. Scarcely day-light appeared, when I heard the unbolting of the door; a negro came in followed by the overseer wrapt in his cloak; they took me out and put me on a board fixed on a kind of fork, where I saw a bundle of rods. The overseer, from under a handkerchief over his mouth, roared out, "tie him fast;" when my hands were tied behind like a criminal, and my feet secured in an aperture of the board. Oh, my God! Let me not speak of this frightful scene! When I recovered I found myself in the arms of my mother, bathed in tears, and disconsolate, who, at the request of Don Jaime Florido,[18] left me and retired. When my mistress rose next morning, her first care was to inquire whether I was treated as I deserved; and the servant who was waiting on her called me; and she asked, if I would dare to take any more leaves of her geranium? As I could not answer, I was near undergoing the same punishment, but thought to say, no. About eleven o'clock, I became dangerously ill: three days I was in this state. My mother used to come to see me in the night- time, when she thought my mistress out. At the sixth day I was out of danger, and could walk about. I met my mother one day, who said to me, "Juan, I have got the money to purchase your liberty; as your father is dead, you must act as a father to your brothers; they shall not chastise you any more." My only answer was a flood of tears; she went away, and I to my business; but the result of my mother's visit was disappointment; the money was not paid, and I daily expected the time of my liberty, but that time was not destined for many a long year to come.

Some time after, it happened that a carrier brought to the house some chickens, some capons, and a letter, and as I was always on guard like a sentinel, it was my misfortune to receive them; leaving the fowls outside, I took the letter to my mistress who after reading it, ordered me to take them to Don Juan Mato their steward, to whom I delivered what I received. Two weeks after this, I was called to an account for one capon missing, I said without hesitating, that I received three capons, and two chickens, which I delivered. Nothing more was said of the matter, but the following day I saw the mayoral coming along towards the house, who after talking with my mistress for some time, went away again. I served the breakfast, and when I was going to take the first morsel, taking advantage of the moment to eat something, my mistress ordered me to go to the mayoral's house, and tell him—I do not remember what. With sad forebodings, and an oppressed heart, being accustomed to deliver myself up on such occasions, away I went trembling. When I arrived at the door, I saw the mayoral of the Molino, and the mayoral of the Ingenio, together. I delivered my message to the first, who said, "Come in man," I obeyed, and was going to repeat it again, when Senor Dominguez, the mayoral of the Ingenio, took hold of my arm, saying, "it is to me, to whom you are sent;" took out of his pocket a thin rope, tied my hands behind me as a criminal, mounted his horse, and commanded me to run quick before him, to avoid either my mother or my brothers seeing me. Scarcely had I run a mile before the horse, stumbling at every step, when two dogs that were following us, fell upon me; one taking hold of the left side of my face pierced it through, and the other lacerated my left thigh and leg in a shocking manner, which wounds are open yet, notwithstanding it happened twenty-four years ago. The mayoral alighted on the moment, and separated me from their graps, but my blood flowed profusely, particularly from my leg—he then pulled me by the rope, making use at the same time, of the most disgusting language; this pull partly dislocated my right arm, which at times pains me yet. Getting up, I walked as well as I could, till we arrived at the Ingenio. They put a rope round my neck, bound up my wounds, and put me in the stocks. At night, all the people of the estate were assembled together and arranged in a line, I was put in the middle of them, the mayoral and six negroes surrounded me, and at the word "upon him," they threw me down; two of them held my hands, two my legs, and the other sat upon my back. They then asked me about the missing capon, and I did not know what to say. Twenty-five lashes were laid on me, they then asked me again to tell the truth. I was perplexed: at last, thinking to escape further punishment, I said, "I stole it." "What have you done with the money?" was the next question, and this was another trying point. "I bought a hat." "Where is it?" "I bought a pair of shoes." "No such thing," and I said so many things to escape punishment, but all to no purpose. Nine successive nights the same scene was repeated, and every night I told a thousand lies. After the whipping, I was sent to look after the cattle and work in the fields. Every morning my mistress was informed of what I said the previous night.

At the end of ten days, the cause of my punishment being known, Dionisio Copandonga, who was the carrier who brought the fowls, went to the mayoral, and said that the missed capon was eaten by the steward Don Manuel Pipa, and which capon was left behind in a mistake; the cook Simona was examined and confirmed the account.

I do not know whether my mistress was made acquainted with this transaction; but certain it is, that since that moment, my punishment ceased, my fetters were taken off, and my work eased, and a coarse linen dress was put on me. But the same day an accident happened, which contributed much towards my mistress forgiving me.

After helping to load sugar, I was sent to pile blocks of wood in one of the buildings; while so employed, all of a sudden the roof with a loud crash gave way, burying under its ruins the negro Andres Criollo; I escaped unhurt through a back door. The alarm given, all the people came to the rescue of poor Andres, who with great difficulty and labour was taken from under the ruins, with his skull broken, and he died in the Molino a few hours after. Early next morning, as I was piling the refuse of sugar canes, there arrived the then Master Pancho, and now Don F., followed by my second brother, who was in his service, and who intimated to me that his master was coming to take me back to the house. This was owing to my brother, who hearing of the accident and my narrow escape, begged earnestly of his young master to intercede with his mother on my behalf, which he easily obtained. I was presented to my mistress, who for the first time received me with kindness. But my heart was so oppressed, that neither her kindness nor eating, or drinking could comfort me; I had no comfort except in weeping: my mistress observing it, and to prevent my crying so much, and the same time being so very drowsy, ordered me to move about, and clean all the furniture, tables, chairs, drawers, &c. All

my liveliness disappeared, and as my brother was greatly attached to me, he became melancholy himself; he tried, however, to cheer me up, but always finished our conversations in tears: for this reason, also, my mistress would not let me wait upon her, nor ride in the volante to town; and at last appointed me to the service of young Master Pancho; they bought me a hat and a pair of shoes, a new thing for me, and my master allowed me to bathe, to take a walk in the afternoon, and to go fishing, and hunting with Senor.

Besides the events just related, there happened two other circumstances resembling each other; one while at Havana, and the other at Matanzas, and which I think worth relating, before I begin to speak of my passing to the service of Don Nicolas de C.[19] on my return to Havana. The first of these events happened when the new coin of our C. M. King Ferdinand the Seventh, began to circulate. Don Nicolas gave me a peseta of the old coin one night; next morning there came at the door a beggar, my mistress gave me a peseta of the new coin for him, which calling my attention, and having the other in my pocket, one is as much worth as the other, muttered I to myself, and changing the pesetas, I gave to the beggar the old one; after I went to my usual place in the antichamber, I sat down in the corner, and taking the new coin out of my pocket, began like a monkey turning it over and over again, when escaping through my fingers it fell down on the floor, making a rattling noise; at its sound my mistress came out of her chamber, made me pick it up; she looked at it, and her face reddened, she bid me go into her chamber, sit in a corner, and wait there; of course, my peseta remained in her possession, she recognized it as the same she gave me for the beggar two minutes before; with such proofs my fate was decided. My mistress was busy going in and out, till at last she sat down to write; soon after the carrier of the Ingenio, who happened to be there at the time with his drove of mules, came into the chamber with a bundle containing a coarse hemp dress, and while he was unfolding it, he dropt a new rope, drawing near me at the same time; trembling, and suspecting his intentions, I sprang up on a sudden, and escaping through another door, ran for protection to Don Nicolas; in the way, I met the young lady Concha, who kindly said to me, "go to my papa." The Marquis was always very kind to me. I used to sleep in his room, and whenever he was afflicted with headache, I gave him warm water, held his head and attended on him till he recovered. When I arrived at his room, which was in an instant, and he saw me at his feet, "What have you done now?" said he; in my confusion I related my case so confusedly, that he understanding that I stole the peseta, said in an angry tone, "You knave, why did you steal the peseta?" "No, sir," I replied, "your son Nicolasito gave it to me." "When?" "Last night," said I: we then went to the Senorito's room, who looking at the peseta, said that he did not give it to me. In truth, I was so frightened and confused, that I could not state the particulars sufficiently clear, on account of the presence of the carrier; and the name of the Ingenio, with its new mayoral, Don Simon Diaz, so inspired me with horror, that all conspired to confuse a boy of sixteen years only as I was. The Marquis interceded for me, and for all that, I was shut up in a dungeon four whole days, without any food, except what my brother could introduce through a little opening at the bottom of the door, and that was little. At the fifth day I was taken out, dressed with a coarse linen dress and tied with a rope. They were going to send me with the baggage of the family, and the other servants, my brother among them, to Matanzas: when the hour arrived, and they were leading me away, I met at the door Donna Beatriz, at present a nun in the Convent of the Ursulinas who interceded for me, that the rope might be taken off, which was done;

we embarked in a schooner for Matanzas, where we arrived at the end of two days.

While on board, and before coming on shore, I changed the coarse dress for the one my brother, unseen, had provided for me; as soon as we landed, my brother and I instead of going with the rest of the servants to present ourselves to Don Juan Gomez, who had instructions about us from the family, but being ignorant of it, and desirous to see our mother, we left the rest of the servants, and went to the Molino, where after presenting ourselves to the mayoral, and telling him that the rest of the servants were coming. We ran at full speed towards my mother's house; but we scarcely arrived and had time to embrace her, when the Creole, Santiago, greatly agitated and full of anger, called me out, saying, "come with me," not suspecting the secret instructions he had, I refused to go with him, and my mother asking me what have I done, but without giving me time to explain myself, very abruptly took hold of my arm, tied me with a rope, and led me towards the Ingenio Saint Miguel, where we arrived about eleven o'clock, fasting all this time. The mayoral read the letter sent to him from Havana, and then put me in fetters; twenty-five lashes in the morning and as many more in the evening for the term of nine days, was the order of the letter. The mayoral questioned me about the peseta, I told him plainly and truly the fact, and for the first time, this savage man showed pity; he did not put in execution his orders, but sent me to work with the rest of the negroes; here I remained two weeks, when my mistress again sent for me.

The second event happened at Matanzas. My mistress sent me to get change of a gold doubloon at Don Juan de Torres, when I returned, she told me to put the change on a card-table, some time after she took it and put it into her pocket. As it was my business to dust all the furniture every half-hour, whether it was dusty or not, when I came to this card-table, and put down one-half of it, down fell a peseta, which it seems got between the joints; at the sound of it she came from the next room, and asked me about it, I told her how it came there, she then counted her change, and missed the peseta, which she took without saying a word the rest of the day; but next day about ten o'clock, the mayoral of the Ingenio came, who fastened my arms behind me, and ordered me to go before his horse; telling me, at the same time, that my mistress suspected that I put the peseta myself between the joints of the table on purpose to keep it. This mayoral, whose name I do not remember, stopped before a tavern, dismounted, went in, and ordered breakfast for both; untied my arms, and kindly told me to make myself easy and not be afraid. While I was eating, he was conversing with a man, and I heard him say, "his father besought of him to pity me, he had some children of his own." After breakfast he mounted his horse, and made me ride behind him on the horse. When we arrived at the Ingenio, he invited me to dine with him, and at night put me under the care of an old negro woman; I remained in this way nine days, when I was sent for by my mistress. At the period I speak of my father was then living, and used to question me about these things, and advising me to tell always the truth, and to be honest and faithful. As this was the first time that I had been at the Ingenio, and considering the good treatment I experienced, I think it was owing to my mistress's secret instructions.

The second time that I was at Matanzas, there never passed a day without bringing some trouble to me; no, I cannot relate the incredible hardships of my life, a life full of sorrows! My heart sickened through sufferings, once after having received many blows on the face, and that happened almost daily; my mistress said, "I will make an end of you before you are of age;" these words left such an impression on my mind, that I asked my mother the meaning of them, who quite astonished, and after making me repeat them twice over, said, "my son, God is more powerful than the devil." She said no more about it; but this and some hints I received from the old servants of the house, began to unfold the true meaning of her expressions. On another occasion, going to be chastised, for I do not remember what trifle, a gentleman, always kind to me, interceded for me: but my mistress said to him, "mind, Senor, this boy will be one day worse than Rousseau and Voltaire, remember my words." These strange names, and the way that my mistress expressed herself made me very anxious to know what sort of bad people they were; but when I found out, that they were enemies of God, I became more uneasy, for since my infancy I was taught to love and fear God, and my trust in him was such, that I employed always part of the night praying God to lighten my sufferings, and to preserve me from mischief on the following day, and if I did anything wrong I attributed it to my lukewarmness in prayers, or that I might have forgotten to pray; and I firmly believe that my prayers were heard, and to this I attribute the preservation of my life once, on occasion of my running away from Matanzas to Havana, as I will relate hereafter.

Although oppressed with so many sufferings, sometimes I gave way to the impulses of my naturally cheerful character. Whenever I went to Senor Estorino's house, I used to draw decorations on paper, figures on cards or pasteboard, and scenes from Chinese shades, then making frames of wild canes, for puppet shows, with a pen-knife, the puppets seemed to dance by themselves. I painted also portraits of the sons of Don Felix Llano, Don Manuel and Don Felixe Puebla, Don Francisco Madruga, and many others; to see all this, there used to come several boys of the town, and on these occasions, I used to do my best to enliven these entertainments.

Some time after this, we went to Havana, where I was appointed to the service of young Don Nicolas, who esteemed me not as a slave, but as a son, notwithstanding his youth. In his company the sadness of my soul began to disappear, but soon after I contracted a disease in my chest with a spasmodic cough, of which with the assistance of Doctor Francisco Lubian, and with time and youth, I was perfectly cured. As I said before, I was now kindly treated, and never was without money in my pocket. My business was to take care of his wardrobe, to clean his shoes, and wait upon him: he only forbad me going out by myself, to go to the kitchen, and to have any intercourse with loose characters; and as he himself though young, was very circumspect, so he wished every body about him to be; I never received any reprimand from him, and I loved him very much. As soon as day dawned, I used to get up, prepare his table, arm-chair and books, and I adapted myself so well to his customs, and manners that I began to give myself up to study. From his book of rhetoric I learnt by heart a lesson every day, which I used to recite like a parrot, without knowing the meaning; but being tired of it, I determined to do something more useful, and that was to learn to write: but here was a difficulty, I did not know how to begin, nor did I know how to mend a pen, and I would not touch any of my master's; however, I bought ink, pens, and penknife, and some very fine paper; then taking some of the bits of written paper thrown away by my master, I put a piece of them between one of my fine sheets, and traced the characters underneath, in order to accustom my hand to make letters; with this stratagem, at the end of a month I could write almost the same hand as my master's. Extremely pleased with myself, I employed the hours from five to ten every evening, exercising my hand to write, and in daytime I used to copy the inscriptions at the bottom of pictures hung in the walls; by these means, I could imitate the best hand-writing. My master was told how I employed the evenings, and once he surprised me with all my writing apparatus, but he only advised me to drop that pastime, as not adapted to my situation in life, and that it would be more useful to me to employ my time in needle-work, a business that indeed at the same time I did not neglect. In vain was I forbidden to write, for when everybody went to bed, I used to light a piece of candle, and when at my leisure I copied the best verses, thinking that if I could imitate these, I would become a poet. Once, some of my sonnets fell into one of my friend's hands, and Doctor Coronado was the first to foretell, that I would be a great poet, notwithstanding all opposition; he was told how I had taught myself to write, and he encouraged me, saying, that many of the great poets began in the same way.

At this time my master was near contracting an alliance with Senorita Donna Teresa de H.,[20] and I was the messenger between them, an office very productive, since I had plenty of money given to me, so much that I did not know what to do with it; I bought a handsome inkstand, a rule, and a good provision of pens, ink, and paper; the rest of my money I sent to my mother. We went to Guanajay[21] on a visit to Count de G.,[22] where my future young mistress resided. As the first needle-work my mistress made was dressmaking, under the care of Senora Domingo, her dressmaker; I learned to make fine dresses, and I had the honour to make some dresses for my future mistress, in recompense for which I experienced all sorts of kindness; and when they were married I was their page, and as I was so punctual in my attendance on them, I was treated more kindly from day to day. But this happiness lasted only about three years, when my former mistress of Matanzas, hearing reports so favorable of me, resolved to take me into her own service again. At this time I was so punctual in attending sick people, though only eighteen years old, that whenever there was a person ill in the family, they asked permission of my mistress to let me attend upon them. One of them was Don Jose Maria P.[23] who was very ill; I prepared for him his bath, administered the doctor's prescription in due time, helped him to rise from his bed, watched the whole of the night, with paper and ink before me, and put down, for the guidance of the doctor, the time that he slept, whether composedly or not, how many times he awoke, how many he coughed, if he snored &c.; I was much praised for this by the doctors, Don Andres Terriltes, Don Nicolas Gutierres, and others. While I was attending this gentleman, my former mistress arrived, and intimated very kindly to me her intention to take me back. I listened to her sorrowfully, for my heart became oppressed at the thoughts of returning to those places so memorable and so sad to me. I was obliged to follow her to her sister's, the Countess of B.[24] where she was on a visit for a few days; she forbade me to bid farewell to my young masters, but I stole away unperceived, and went to take leave of them. Don Nicolas, who since his childhood was very partial to me, took leave of me weeping, as also his lady, both loading me with presents; the Senora gave me some Holland handkerchiefs and two gold doubloons; Don Nicolas all my clothes, including two new coats, and a gold doubloon besides.

I left them so downcast and with such sad forebodings that early next morning I ventured to ask paper and ink, in order to advertise for a new master. This quite astonished my mistress, and saying that she took me back for my own sake, and that I had better stop with her till she made some other arrangements, and when she turned her back I was sorry for having given her this uneasiness. At dinner-time, she mentioned my boldness to her sister the Countess, and, with an angry tone, said to me before all the company, "this is the return you intend to make for all the care I took in your education; did I ever put my hands on you?" I was very near saying, yes, many a time, but thought better to say, no. She then asked me if I remembered her mama? and at my answering, yes; she said, "I occupy her place, mind that," here the conversation dropt. After prayers in the afternoon, I was sent for by the Countess and Donna Maria Pizarro, who both tried to persuade me to desist from my intention. I plainly told them, that I was afraid of my mistress's fiery temper; this conversation ended by the Countess advising me to stop with my mistress till she thought proper to give me my liberty.

Some time after this we left for Matanzas, stopping at the Molino. Here they pointed out to me my new duties, and I acquitted myself so much to their satisfaction, that in a short time I was the head servant of the house. During all this time, after superintending the business of the house, and after breakfast, I used to employ myself at needle-work. At the end of about two weeks after we were in town, it happened that one morning oversleeping myself, a cock found his way into my room, which was close to that of my mistress; the cock crew, I do not know how many times, I only heard him once, I started from my bed, and went about my business, and were it not for the interference of Don Tomas Gener, who, at my request, kindly interceded for me, I should not have escaped being sent to the Molino.

When I was about nineteen years of age, I had some pride in acquitting myself of my duties, so much to the satisfaction of my mistress, and never waited to be ordered twice; at this time I could not bear to be scolded for trifles; but the propensity to humble the self-love of those who are in the good graces of their masters, is a contagious disease in all rich families. Such was the case with a person, who without any cause or provocation on my part, began to treat me badly, calling me bad names, all of which I suffered, till he called my mother out of her name: then I retorted on him a similar expression, he gave me a blow, which I could not avoid, and I returned it. My mistress was out, and I was to go after her at the house of the Senora. When we returned, she was told of what happened; I excused myself, saying, that I could not suffer my mother to be called so bad a name; "So," said she, "if he repeats it again, you will not respect my house?" At the third day we went to breakfast to the Molino: meanwhile I was uneasy, I had before me all the vicissitudes of my life, and was apprehensive of what was to come. Soon after our arrival, I saw the mayoral coming towards the house; I escaped through the garden, and hid myself: in the afternoon I went to town, to the Count of G.,[25] who gave me shelter and protection; I was still uneasy, I wept bitterly when I remembered the kindness I was treated with by the other masters in Havana. Scarcely was I there five days, when for a trifling fault they sent for a commissary of police, who secured me with a rope, and took me to the public prison in the middle of the day; at four o'clock, there came a white man from the country, who demanded me, and I was delivered to him; he put on me the coarse linen dress, he tied my arms with a rope, and led me towards the Molino, which I desired never to see again, after having been so well treated by my former masters, being now also somewhat elated with the praises bestowed on my abilities, and a little proud of my acquaintance in the city with persons that knew how to reward services. At the Molino, Don Saturnino Carrias, the mayoral at this time, examined me, I told the truth, and he sent me to work at the fields without any chastisement or fetters. I was there about nine days, when my mistress coming to the Molino to breakfast, sent for me, gave me a fine suit of clothes, and took me to town again in the volante. I was known at this time under the name of the Chinito, or the little Mulatto of the Marquesa.

About this time I went to the house of the lady of Senor Apodaca, a grandee of Havana, where they were making some preparations for his reception. Senor Aparicio, a painter and decorator, was employed in painting some emblems allusive to a rose, as the name of the lady was Rosa; I helped the painter, and he gave me ten dollars for my work, and having by way of amusement painted some garlands, he saw that I might be useful to him, and asked my mistress to lend me to him, but she would not consent; at the conclusion of his work he gave me two dollars more, which money I kept with the intention to spend it at Havana. My mistress found out that the servants met together in a barn after midnight, to play at cards till the morning. The first thing she did on the following morning was to search my pockets, and finding that I had more money than she gave me, took me for an accomplice in their game; and notwithstanding my telling her how I came in possession of the money, she kept it, and sent me to the Molino, where I was received by the mayoral, and treated kindly, the same as before; at the end of three or four days my mistress sent for me, and I returned to town.

Some time past on without any novelty, when my mother died suddenly. I was made acquainted with this accident soon afterwards, when my mistress gave me three dollars to have prayers said for her. A few days after she gave me leave to go to the Molino, to see what my mother had left. The mayoral gave me the key of the house, where I only found a very large old box empty: as there was a secret in it, which I knew, I pulled the spring, and found there some trinkets of pure gold, but the most worthy were three ancient bracelets, near two inches broad and very thick, two strings of beads, one of gold, the other coral and gold: I found also a bundle of papers, in which were some accounts of debts due to us, one of 200 and odd dollars, another of 400, payable by my mistress, and some others for small sums. When I was born, my grandfather gave me a young mare, of a fine breed: she gave five colts, which my father purposed should be given to my brothers; after that she gave three more, making altogether eight colts. I returned to my mistress, and gave an account of what I found. At the end of five or six days, I asked her if she had examined the bills; she answered calmly, "not yet;" and I went to inform the Creole, Rosa Brindiz, who had the care of my sister, María del Rosario. Rosa was continually urging me not to lose any opportunity of asking my mistress about it, as she wanted my sister's share, to repay herself the expenses of nursing and keeping her, and as I was the eldest, it was my duty, she said, to look after the money. Teased by her, I ventured to mention it again to my mistress; but what was my astonishment, when instead of money, she said "You are in a great hurry for your inheritance, do you not know that I am the lawful heir of my slaves? if you speak to me again about it, I will send you where you will never see the sun nor the moon again; go and clean the furniture." The following day I made Rosa acquainted with this answer, and some days after she came herself to speak to my mistress, with whom she was a long time: when she came out I gave her two of the three bracelets, and all the beads. My mistress, who was always watching me, came near us, and intimated to Rosa, that she disliked her to have any communication with me, or any of the servants, and Rosa went away, and never came there any more.

As for me, from the moment that I lost my hopes, I ceased to be a faithful slave; from an humble, submissive being, I turned the most discontented of mankind: I wished to have wings to fly from that place, and to go to Havana; and from that day my only thoughts were in planning how to escape and run away. Some days after I sold to a silver-smith the other bracelet, and for which he gave me seven dollars, and some reals; I gave the dollars to a priest, for prayers to be said for my poor mother. It was not long before my mistress knew of it, through the priest; she asked me where I had the money from, I told her; she wanted to know the name of the silversmith, I said I did not know; she flew into a passion. "You will know then for what you are born, you cannot dispose of any thing without my consent." She then sent me to the Molino for the third time. Don Saturnino, the mayoral, inquired what I had done, I told him, very peevishly and weeping, for I did not care for the consequences at that moment, but he pitied me, untied my arms, and sent me to his kitchen, with orders not to stir from there. At the end of ten days, he said to me, "As your mistress is coming tomorrow to breakfast here, to save appearances, I will put on you the fetters, and send you to work; but if she inquires whether you have been whipped, you must say, yes." Next morning, about nine, she sent for me, gave me a new suit of clothes; and when I went to him to deliver the coarse ones, with an angry tone, he said to me, "Now, mind what you are about; in less than two months you have been sent to me three times, and I have treated you kindly, endeavour to do your best not to come here again, if you do, you shall be treated severely; go to your mistress, go, and beware." I went to my mistress, and threw myself at her feet, she bade me get up, and ordered a good breakfast for me; but I could not eat anything, my heart was uneasy; Havana, with all the happy days I enjoyed there, was continually in my mind, and my only wish was to go there. My mistress observed with wonder my not eating breakfast, particularly of some nice stew she ordered for me: the truth is, that she could not do without me for a length of time, and this was the reason that my journeys to the Molino never exceeded nine or ten days; and although she struck me so often, and degraded me, calling me always the worst of all the Creoles born in the Molino. I was still attached to her, and shall never forget the care she had taken on my education.

After this she treated me with more kindness; she allowed me to go a fishing, which was my most pleasant amusement. Next morning my mistress went to the house of the Senora Gomez, where they played at cards, and it was my duty to stand behind her chair all the time; if she was a winner I carried home the money bag, and when I delivered it to her she put her hand into it and gave me some. She was much pleased, when she saw me making myself a pair of trousers, which I learned myself; for since the idea of freedom took possession of my mind, I endeavored to learn every thing useful to me; I invented many fancy things in my leisure hours, though these were few, I took sheets of paper, and doubling them in different shapes and forms, I turned them in various shapes as flowers, pineapples, shells, fans, epaulettes, and many more things, for which I was praised by everybody. As my mistress treated me with a little more kindness, I insensibly began to be more calm, my heart more composed, and to forget her late harsh behavior towards me. I began to be as comfortable as ever; in a word, I thought myself already free, and waited only to be of age; this hope encouraged me to learn many useful things, so that if I should not be a slave I should earn an honest livelihood. At this time I wrote a great many sonnets. Poetry requires an object, but I had none to enflame my breast, this was the cause of my verses being nothing else than poor imitations. I was very anxious to read every book or paper that fell in my way, either at home or in the streets, and if I met with any poetry I learnt it by heart, in consequence of this, I could recite many things in poetry. Besides, when my mistress had company at dinner, and that was almost every day, she had always some poet invited who recited verses and composed sonnets extempore; I had in a corner of the room some ink in an egg-shell and a pen, and while the company applauded and filled their glasses with wine away I went to my corner, and wrote as many verses as I could remember.

Three or four months after this, as my mistress was unwell, she was advised to go to the bathing town of Madruga[26] to bathe; with her complaint she turned cross and peevish; she reproached my having disposed of my mother's trinkets, having five brothers, and that that was a robbery, and that if I was put in possession of the inheritance, I soon would lose it in gambling, and she was continually threatening me with the Molino and with Don Saturnino, whose last words were imprinted on my heart, and I had no wish to pay him another visit. With the belief that if I could go to Havana I would have my liberty, I inquired the distance, and was told twelve leagues, which I could not reach on foot in one night; I then dropt for the present that idea, waiting for a better opportunity. It was my custom to clean myself and change twice a week, and one day before dressing I went to bathe in a bath, thirty yards distant; while in the bath my mistress called me, in an instant I dressed myself and was before her, "What were you doing in the bath? Who gave you liberty to go? Why did you go?" were her angry inquiries, and with her fist she made my nostrils bleed profusely; all this happened at the street-door, and before all the people, but what confused me more was, that there lived opposite a young mulatto girl, of my own age, the first who inspired me with love, a thing I did not feel before; or rather I loved her as a sister, and our intercourse was kept up by some little presents from one to another, and I told her that I was free. About ten o'clock, my mistress ordered my shoes to be taken off and my head shaved, after which I was commanded to carry water for the use of the house, with a large barrel upon my head; the brook was distant thirty yards with a declivity towards it from the side of the house; I went, filled the barrel, and with some help I put it upon my head, I was returning up the little hill, when my foot missed, and down I went upon my knee, the barrel falling a little forward came rolling down, struck against my chest, and both tumbled in the brook. My mistress said, "that is a trick of your's to evade work," she threatened me with the Molino and Don Saturnino, which name had a magic effect on me, and I began to think seriously about escaping to Havana. The following morning when all the people were at church, a free servant called me aside, and in a whisper, said to me, "my friend, if you suffer it is your fault; you are treated worse than the meanest slave; make your escape, and present yourself before the Captain-General at Havana, state your ill treatment to him, and he will do you justice;" at the same time showing me the road to Havana.

At eleven o'clock, I saw Don Saturnino arrive at the house; from this moment my heart beat violently, my blood was agitated, and I could not rest, I trembled like a leaf, my only comfort at that moment was the solitude of my room, there I went; and there I heard the servants talking together, one was inquiring of the other the reason of the coming of Don Saturnino. "Why," said the other, "to take away Juan F." This was more than I could endure, a general trembling took possession of my limbs, and my head ached very much. I fancied myself already in the hands of Don Saturnino, leading me away tied like the greatest criminal—from this moment I determined on my escape. I left my room with this determination, when I met again the same servant, who said to me, "Man take out that horse from the stable, and leave him outside, for fear that when Don Saturnino may want him in the night, you will make too much noise, and will disturb your mistress—here are the spurs, take them, and there is the saddle, and so you will know where to find every thing." And then he gave me such a look as quite convinced me that, he advised me to take the opportunity, and not lose it. I was hesitating, yet I did not like to leave behind me my brothers, and then I was afraid to travel a whole night through roads unknown to me, and alone, and in danger of falling in with any commissary of police; but what was my surprise, when after supper, as I was sitting on a bench by myself, meditating about what to do, Don Saturnino came to me and asked, "Where do you sleep?" I pointed to him the place and he went away; this entirely determined me to make my escape—he might have made the inquiry with a good intention, but I could not consider it but with great suspicion. I remembered at that moment the fate of one of my uncles, who in a case like mine, took the same determination of escaping to Havana, to Don Nicolas, Don Manuel, and the Senor Marques and was brought back again like a wild beast—but for all that I resolved to venture on my escape, and in case of detection, to suffer for something. I waited till twelve o'clock. That night everybody retired early, it being very cold and rainy. I saddled the horse for the first time in my life, put on the bridle, but with such trembling that I hardly knew what I was about, after that I knelt down, said a prayer, and mounted the horse. When I was going away, I heard the sound of a voice saying, "God bless you, make haste." I thought that nobody saw me, but as I knew afterwards, I was seen by several of the negroes, but nobody offered any impediment to my flight.

JUAN—.

Notes

1. Doña Beatriz de Jústiz, Marquesa de Santa Ana.
2. Don Juan Manzano.
3. María del Pilar Manzano.
4. Artisan.
5. Don Miguel Cárdenas y Manzano.
6. Don Manuel O'Reilly, Conde de Buenavista.
7. Trinidad de Zayas.
8. Luis de Granada (1504–1588), ascetic writer, mystic, and celebrated preacher of the Renaissance.
9. The Spanish text indicates that only the female twin survived.
10. Marquesa de Jústiz.
11. Marquesa de Prado Ameno.
12. Marqués de Monte Hermoso.
13. Las Señoras Beatas de Cárdenas.
14. Conde de Jibacoa.
15. Don Juan Manuel O'Farrell.
16. Las Señoras Gómez.
17. Card games.
18. Don Jaime Florit.
19. Don Nicolás de Cárdenas.
20. Doña Teresa de Herrera.
21. A city in the Cuban province of Pinar del Rio.
22. Conde de Jibacoa.
23. José Maria de Peñalver.
24. Condesa de Buenavista.
25. Conde de Jibacoa.
26. A suburb of Havana.

POEMS,
WRITTEN IN SLAVERY,
BY JUAN————

AND TRANSLATED FROM THE SPANISH,

BY R. R. M.

TO DEATH

Oh, thou dread scourge and terror of our race,
While thy strong hand bows down the proudest head,
Filling the earth with cries in every place,
And grief and wailing o'er the silent dead.

Hear one poor Christian's humble prayer to thee,
And speak in words that one may hear and live;
I only beg thou wilt not ask of me,
This gift of life, that God was pleased to give.

While passion's spell is on my heart—nor yet
While angry feelings rankle in my breast—
Nor while remembrance ever is beset
With wrongs that men despair to see redressed.

Oh, yet not while I feel this bosom rise,
With tender transports when the partner dear
Of all my cares, with bright and beaming eyes
Smiles in my face—and Eden's joys seem here.

But let it be, when thou dost see me yield,
Give my whole heart and soul to God above.
To him who gave me life, nay more, revealed
The truths of life eternal and of love.

TO CALUMNY

Silence, audacious wickedness which aims
At honour's breast, or strikes with driftless breath,
The lightest word that's spoken thus defames,
And where it falls, inflicts a moral death.

If with malign, deliberate intent,
The shaft is sped, the bow that vibrates yet,
One day will hurt the hand by which 'tis bent,
And leave a wound its malice justly met.

For once the winged arrow is sent forth,
Who then may tell where, when, or how 'twill fall?
Or, who may pluck its barb from wounded worth,
And send it back, and swiftly too withal.

RELIGION.

AN ODE.

Yes, tho' in gloom and sadness I may rise,
One blessed strain can soothe my troubled soul,
No sooner wakened than with streaming eyes,
Upward I look, and there I seek my goal.
Soaring in spirit o'er the things of earth,
The spark imprisoned bursts its bonds of clay;
I feel delight above all human mirth,
And wrapt in love, I live but then to pray;

To thee, dear Father!—mighty and supreme!
Immense! eternal! infinite! and blest!
Oh, how the grandeur of the theme doth seem
T'enlarge my thoughts, and to inflame my breast.
Hail, blessed faith! thou only hope and trust,
Solace most sweet, and stay of hope most sure;
Thou sole support and shield of the opprest,
The weak, the wronged, the wretched, and the poor.

In thee, all trouble is absorbed and lost;
In ev'ry breath of thine there's vital air;
Whose mild and genial influence, the just
Rejoice to find, the wretched e'en may share.
For thee, when darkness brooded o'er the land,
A remnant, faithful to the law they feared,
Still wept and sighed—'till mercy's hour at hand,
The mighty standard of the cross was reared.

Then in the depths of fear, as by a spell,
The voice of hope was heard, the tidings glad,
Of truth eternal, far and wide were spread,
And demons trembled as their idols fell;
But soon the foe of truth and justice came,
Far worse there's none than tyranny can prove,
That fitting agent of a spirit's aim,
Indocile ever to the God of love.

But vain was all that monster's rage renewed,
Thousands of martyrs fell beneath its sway;
Still in that cradle purpled with their blood,
The infant faith waxed stronger every day.
Now the triumphant gospel is our guide,
Our sure conductor to eternal light:

The future vast; the heavenly portals hide
Their joys no longer from our spirit's sight.

'Tis thou, O God, by faith who dost reveal
Mysterious wonders to our senses weak:
When thou dost speak to hearts that deeply feel,
And humbly hear when thou dost deign to speak.
Oh, when the mantle of thy peace descends,
How the soul then exults in her attire!
The garb of grace to ev'ry thought extends,
And wraps reflection in seraphic fire.

In thee, I find all purity and peace,
All truth and goodness, wisdom far above
All worldly wisdom, might beyond increase,
And yet surpassing these, unbounded love.
Oh, that its light were shed on those whose deeds
Belie the doctrines of the church they claim;
Whose impious tongues profane their father's creeds,
And sanction wrong, e'en in religion's name.

Oh, God of mercy, throned in glory high,
O'er earth and all its miseries, look down!
Behold the wretched, hear the captives' cry,
And call thy exiled children round thy throne!
There would I fain in contemplation gaze,
On thy eternal beauty, and would make
Of love one lasting canticle of praise,
And ev'ry theme but that, henceforth forsake.

THIRTY YEARS.[1]

When I think on the course I have run,
From my childhood itself to this day,
I tremble, and fain would I shun,
The remembrance its terrors array.

I marvel at struggles endured,
With a destiny frightful as mine,
At the strength for such efforts—assured
Tho' I am, 'tis in vain to repine.

I have known this sad life thirty years,
And to me, thirty years it has been
Of suff'ring, of sorrow and tears,
Ev'ry day of its bondage I've seen.

But 'tis nothing the past—or the pains,
Hitherto I have struggled to bear,
When I think, oh, my God! on the chains,
That I know I'm yet destined to wear.

[1] According to Francisco Calcagno (*Poetas de color* [Habana: Imp. Militar de la V. de Soler y Compañia, 1878], p. 42) the poem that was first read in 1836 was published in *El Aguinaldo Habanero* in 1837 under the title of "Mis treinta años." Martha Cobb, in *Harlem, Haiti and Havana*, compared the poem to a text by George Moses Horton (1797–1883): "The above poem, ten verses long, bears an interesting resemblance in theme and tone to a much shorter work by the Cuban slave poet Juan Francisco Manzano....In Havana, Juan Manzano, by then past the prime of his life, at last achieved freedom. Paralleling the life of Horton in the apparent effects of freedom on his poetic career, Manzano stopped writing and publishing, with the result that little else was heard of him after he became a free man" [p. 28]. Also see Luis, *Juan Franciso Manzano*, 137–38, note 8.

THE CUCUYA;[1] OR FIRE-FLY.

The fire-fly is heedlessly wandering about
Through field and through forest is winging his route,
As free as the butterfly sporting in air,
From flower to flower, it flits here and there:
Now glowing with beautiful phosphoric light,
Then paling its lustre and waning in night:
It bears no effulgence in rivalry near,
But shrouds ev'ry gleam as the dawn doth appear.

It sparkles alone in the soft summer's eve,
Itself, though unseen, by the track it doth leave,
The youth of the village at night-fall pursue
O'er hill and o'er dale, as it comes into view;
Now shining before them, now lost to their eyes,
The sparkle they catch at, just twinkles and dies;
And the mead is one moment all spangled with fire,
And the next, every sparklet is sure to expire.

On the leaf of the orange awhile it disports,
When the blossom is there, to its cup it resorts,
And still the more brightly and dazzling it shines,
It baffles its tiny pursuers' designs.
But see the sweet maiden, the innocent child,
The pride of the village—as fair as the wild
And beautiful flowers she twines in her hair—
How light is her step, and how joyous her air!

And oft as one looks on such brightness and bloom,
On such beauty as her's, one might envy the doom
Of a captive "Cucuya," that's destined like this,
To be touched by her hand, and revived by her kiss;
Imprisoned itself, by a mistress so kind,
It hardly can seem, to be closely confined,
And a prisoner thus tenderly treated in fine,
By a keeper so gentle, might cease to repine.

In the cage which her delicate hands have prepared,
The captive "Cucuya" is shining unscared,

---

[1] Antonio López Prieto indicates in his *Parnaso cubano* (Habana: M. de Villa, 1881), p. 252, that the poem was first published in *El Aguinaldo Habanera*, number 6, in 1837. The title in Spanish is "La Cocuyera." Also see Luis, *Juan Franciso Manzano*, 135, note 1.

Suspended before her, with others as bright,
In beauty's own bondage revealing their light.
But this amongst all is her favourite one,
And she bears it at dusk to her alcove alone,
'Tis fed by her hand on the cane that's most choice,
And in secret it gleams, at the sound of her voice.

Thus cherished, the honey of Hybla would now
Scarce tempt the "Cucuya" her care to forego;
And daily it seems to grow brighter and gain
Increasing effulgence, forgetting its pain.
Oh! beautiful maiden, may heaven accord,
Thy care of the captive, its fitting reward;
And never may fortune the fetters remove,
Of a heart that is thine in the bondage of love.

THE CLOCK THAT GAINS.[1]

The Clock's too fast they say;
But what matter, how it gains!
Time will not pass away
Any faster for its pains.

The tiny hands may race
Round the circle, they may range,
The Sun has but one pace,
And his course he cannot change.

The beams that daily shine
On the dial, err not so,
For they're ruled by laws divine,
And they vary not, we know.

But tho' the Clock is fast,
Yet the moments I must say,
More slowly never passed,
Than they seemed to pass today.

[1] Antonio López Prieto indicates in his *Parnaso cubano*, p. 252, that the poem was first published in *El Aguinaldo Habanera*, number 6, in 1837. The title in Spanish is "El relox adelantado." Also see Luis, *Juan Franciso Manzano*, 169, note 182.

THE DREAM[1]

"Addressed to My Younger Brother"

Thou knowest, dear Florence, my sufferings of old,
The struggles maintained with oppression for years,
We shared them together, and each was consoled
With the whispers of love that were mingled with tears.

But now, far apart, this sad pleasure is gone,
We mingle our sighs and our sorrows no more;
The course is a new one that each has to run,
And dreary the prospect for either in store.

But in slumber, our spirits, at least, shall commune,
Behold, how they meet in the visions of sleep;
In dreams that recall early days, like the one
In my brother's remembrance, I fondly would keep.

For solitude pining, in anguish of late
The heights of Quintana I sought, for repose,
And there of seclusion enamoured, the weight
Of my cares was forgotten, I felt not my woes.

Exhausted and weary, the spell of the place
Soon weighed down my eyelids, and slumber then stole
So softly o'er nature, it left not a trace
Of trouble or sorrow, o'ercasting my soul.

I seemed to ascend like a bird in the air,
And the pinions that bore me, amazed me the more;
I gazed on the plumage of beauty so rare,
As they waved in the sun, at each effort to soar.

My spirit aspired to a happier sphere,
The buoyancy even of youth was surpassed;
One effort at flight not divested of fear,
And the flutter ensued, was successful at last.

And leaving the earth and its toils, I look down,
Or upwards I glance, and behold with surprise,

---

[1]Antonio López Prieto indicates in his *Parnaso cubano*, p. 252, that this poem was first published in *El Album* in November 1838 (pp. 115–27). The title in Spanish is "Un sueño." Also see Luis, *Juan Francisco Manzano*, 144, note 41.

The wonders of God, and the firmament strewn
With myriads of brilliants, that spangle the skies.

The ocean of ether around me, each star
Of the zodiac shining, above either pole,
Of the earth as a point in the distance afar,
And one flap of the wing, serves to traverse the whole.

The bounds which confine the wide sea, and the height
Which separates earth from the heavenly spheres;
The moon as a shield I behold in my flight,
And each spot on its surface distinctly appears.

The valley well known of Matanzas is nigh,
And trembling, my brother, I gaze on that place,
Where, cold and forgotten, the ashes now lie
Of the parents we clung to in boyhood's embrace.

How the sight of that place sent the blood to my heart,
I shudder e'en now to recall it, and yet
I'd remind you of wrongs we were wont to impart,
And to weep o'er in secret at night when we met.

I gazed on that spot, where together we played,
Our innocent pastimes came fresh to my mind;
Our mother's caresses, the fondness displayed,
In each word and each look of a parent so kind.

The ridge of that mountain, whose fastnesses wild
The fugitives seek, I beheld, and around
Plantations were scattered of late where they toiled,
And the graves of their comrades are now to be found.

The mill-house was there and its turmoil of old,
But sick of these scenes, for too well they were known;
I looked for the stream, where in childhood I strolled
By its banks when a moment of peace was my own.

But no recollections of pleasure or pain
Could drive the remembrance of thee from my core;
I sought my dear brother, embraced him again,
But found him a slave, as I left him before.

"Oh, Florence," I cried, "let us fly from this place,
The gloom of a dungeon is here to affright!

'Tis dreadful as death or its terrors to face,
And hateful itself as the scaffold to sight.

"Let us fly on the wings of the wind, let us fly,
And for ever abandon so hostile a soil
As this place of our birth, where our doom is to sigh
In hapless despair, and in bondage to toil."

To my bosom I clasped him, and winging once more
My flight in the air, I ascend with my charge,
The sultan I seem of the winds, as I soar,
A monarch whose will, sets the pris'ner at large.

Like Icarus[2] boldly ascending on high,
I laugh at the anger of Minos[3], and see
A haven of freedom aloft, where I fly,
And the place where the slave from his master is free.

The rapture which Daedalus[4] inly approved
To Athens from Crete, when pursuing his flight,
On impetuous pinions, I felt when I moved
Through an ocean of ether, so boundless and bright.

But the moment I triumphed o'er earth and its fears,
And dreamt of aspiring to heavenly joys:
Of hearing the music divine of the spheres,
And tasting of pleasure that care never cloys.

I saw in an instant, the face of the skies
So bright and serene but a moment before;
Enveloped in gloom, and there seemed to arise
The murmur preceding the tempest's wild roar.

Beneath me, the sea into fury was lashed,
Above me, the thunder rolled loudly, and now
The hurricane round me in turbulence dashed,
And the glare of the lightning e'en flashed on my brow.

---

[2]In Greek mythology, the son of Daedalus. In escaping from imprisonment, he flew too close to the sun. Its heat melted the wax of his wings, and he fell into the sea.

[3]In Greek mythology he was the son of Zeus and Europa, and after death a judge in Hades. As king of Crete, he imprisoned Daedalus and Icarus on the island.

[4]The mythological builder of the Cretan labyrinth, and father of Icarus.

The elements all seemed in warfare to be,
And succour or help there was none to be sought;
The fate of poor Icarus seemed now for me,
And my daring attempt its own punishment brought.

'Twas then, oh, my God! that a thunder-clap came,
And the noise of its crash broke the slumbers so light,
That stole o'er my senses and fettered my frame,
And the dream was soon over, of freedom's first flight.

And waking, I saw thee, my brother, once more,
The sky was serene and my terrors were past;
But doubt there was none of the tempests of yore
And the clouds that of old, our young hopes overcast.

A SPECIMEN
OF
INEDITED CUBAN POEMS,

PRESENTED TO DR. MADDEN ON HIS DEPARTURE FROM CUBA

And translated by him from the Spanish.

TO CUBA

Cuba, of what avail that thou art fair!
Pearl of the seas, the pride of the Antilles!
If thy poor sons, have still to see thee share
The pangs of bondage, and its thousand ills;
Of what avail the verdure of thy hills?
The purple bloom the coffee plain displays
Thy canes luxuriant growth; whose culture fills
More graves than famine, or the swords find ways
To glut with victims calmly as it slays.

Of what avail that thy sweet streams abound
With precious ore: if wealth there's none to buy,
Thy children's rights, and not one grain is found
For learning's shrine, or for the altar nigh,
Of poor, forsaken, downcast liberty!
Of what avail the riches of thy port,
Forests of masts, and ships from every sea,
If trade alone is free, and man the sport,
The spoil of trade, bears wrongs of ev'ry sort?

Oh, if the name of Cuban! makes my breast
Thrill with a moment's pride, that soon is o'er,
Or throb with joy to dream that thou art blest!
Thy sons were free—thy soil unstained with gore.

Reproach awakes me, to assail once more,
And taint that name, as if the loathsome pest
That spreads from slavery had seized the core,
Polluting both th'oppressor and the oppressed:—
Yet God be thanked, it has not reached my breast.

'Tis not alone the wretched negro's fate
That calls for pity, sad as it may be;
There's more to weep for in that hapless state
Of men who proudly boast that they are free,
Whose moral sense is warped to that degree,
That self-debasement seems to them unknown,
And life's sole object, is for means to play,
To roll a carriage, or to seek renown
In all the futile follies of the town.

Cuba! canst thou, my own beloved land,
Counsel thy children to withhold a curse,
And call to mind the deeds of that fell band
Whose boasted conquests, mark one frightful course
Of spoil and plunder, wrung by fraud or force;
Of human carnage in religious gear,
Of peace destroyed—defenceless people worse
Than rudely outraged, nay, reserved to wear
Their lives away in bondage and despair?

To think unmoved of millions of our race,
Swept from thy soil by cruelties prolonged,
Another clime then ravaged to replace
The wretched Indians; Africa then wronged
To fill the void where myriads lately thronged,
And add new guilt to that long list of crimes,
That cries aloud, in accents trumpet-tongued,
And shakes the cloud that gathers o'er these climes,
Portending evil and disastrous times.

Cuba, oh, Cuba, when they call thee fair!
And rich and beautiful, the Queen of isles!
Star of the West, and ocean's gem most rare!
Oh, say to them who mock thee with such wiles
Take of these flowers, and view these lifeless spoils
That wait the worm; behold the hues beneath
The pale cold cheek, and seek for living smiles,
Where beauty lies not in the arms of death,
And bondage taints not with its poisoned breath.

APPENDIX

IN RE, SLAVE-TRADE

QUESTIONS ADDRESSED TO SENOR— — OF HAVANA, BY R. R. MADDEN, AND ANSWERS THEREUNTO OF SENOR— —.

Q. When was Las Casa's[1] suggestion in favour of the importation of African slaves, first acted on in Cuba?

A. In 1523–1524 three hundred negroes were introduced into Cuba from Spain; and it is probable, that previously some had been brought in from Hayti.

Q. From that period, during the first century of slavery here, how many introduced?

A. From 1523 to 1763 sixty thousand were brought in.

Q. From that period, during the second century of slavery, how many introduced?

A. From 1764 to 1789, thirty thousand eight hundred and seventy-five.

Q. From that period, during the third century of slavery, how many introduced?

A. Through the Port of Havana from 1790 to 1821, 240,721; to which may be added, for smuggled cargoes 60,180, including omissions of entries and importations in other parts of the island.

Q. How many in all from A. D. 1523 to 1840?

A. Up to the year 1821, there were introduced 391,776, and from 1821 to 1840, calculating the imports, 20,000 negroes per annum,... 360,000,– 751,776.

Q. How many now in life, in Cuba, of the whole negro race?
A. By the census of 1827, 393,436, but it may amount to 500,000.

Q. How many then in slavery have perished in the island of Cuba?
A. 450,000, because the slaves in existence amount to 370,000, and taking from this number 80,000 which may be calculated as the number of Creoles, there remain 290,000, which sum deducted from the total importations 751,776, according to Senor Arrango's[2] authority, the mortality amounts to 460,776 negroes.

Q. How many slaves in Cuba, and by what census determined?[3]
A. By the census in 1827, 286,942; by the estimate of Saco[4], 350,000.

Q. How many free-coloured people in Cuba, by the same census?
A. 106,494, but according to Saco, 140,000.

Q. If the slave-trade were stopped, in how many years would the slave-population be extinct, provided the system of management remained unaltered?
A. In twenty years, or thereabouts; but the ordinary mortality is calculated at 5 per cent., although it is certain that on the sugar plantations the mortality is much greater; while in the towns, on coffee properties, and other farms, the deaths are much less[5].

Q. In what proportion on sugar estates are males to females?
A. Three to one, that is to say, three men to one female.

Q. Ditto on coffee estates?
A. One and a-half, or three males to two females.

Q. What is the average mortality of slaves on a sugar estate?
A. Eight per cent.

Q. What is the average mortality on a coffee estate?
A. Two per cent.

Q. Do the births exceed the deaths on sugar estates?
A. Oh, no!

Q. Do the births exceed the deaths on coffee estates?
A. On many coffee plantations they do.

Q. What is the current market price of an adult bozal male negro?
A. From 350 to 400 dollars.

Q. What is the current market price of an adult bozal female negro?

A. Rather less, from seventeen doubloons to twenty-one.

Q. What is the current market price of an adult Creole male negro?

A. If he has no trade the same as a bozal, but less if he is a native of a town, and is destined for field labour; but if he is a Creole praedial slave, and is destined for agriculture, then he is worth more than a bozal.

Q. What is the current market price of an adult Creole Female negro?

A. Rather less than that of the male.

Q. What is the current market price of a child of ten years of age?

A. From 150 to 200 dollars.

Q. What is the current market price of a Creole child before birth?

A. Twenty-five dollars, or fifty dollars eight days after birth.

Q. At what price can the slave-mother purchase the unborn child's freedom?

A. Twenty-five dollars.

Q. How are negroes paid for in general, in cash or by bills?

A. In both ways; generally by the latter, together with interest at five per cent a month.

Q. What is a negro now worth on the Gold Coast?

A. He would cost from 60 to 68 dollars.

Q. How do the slave-factors and captains pay for the negroes?

A. One negro with another, the slaves stand them in from 50 to 60 dollars a head, buying by the lot in Africa, but the price varies according the place where they are bought and the state of the market.

Q. What kind of goods are sent from Cuba to Africa in exchange for negroes?

A. Both goods and money are sent. Doubloons, dollars, aguardiente[6], powder, guns, copper vessels, all classes of cotton goods.

Q. Are these chiefly of British manufacture?

A. Almost all.

Q. How are these British goods called?

A. As specified in answer 27.

Q. Where do the shackles come from, used in this trade?

A. The chains, manacles, and other fetters must be of English manufacture, of which class all descriptions of iron ware brought here, are known to be.

Q. To what amount are goods sent from Cuba to Africa in exchange for slaves a-year?

A. To answer this question it is essential to know the number of slave-ships, and of that we are ignorant.

Q. To what amount is money sent for the same purpose?

A. See the preceding answer.

Q. What number of ships may be employed in this trade between Cuba and Africa?

A. We yet are not in possession of sufficient data to answer this question with respect to the Havana, but as to Matanzas we can declare with certainty, that from fifteen to twenty ships are annually dispatched for Africa by various Catalans.

Q. Under what flags do they chiefly sail?

A. Almost all under the Portuguese flag; and those which proceed from Havana with the Spanish flag or American, change again in the Portuguese islands of Cape de Verds.

Q. Where are they built?

A. The greater part in the United States, chiefly in Baltimore; even some are constructed in the Havana; some likewise in Matanzas; we know of a schooner built in Matanzas, by a company of Catalans, which the curate baptized, as if its mission was for the redemption of captives, and its people a band of brothers of the order of mercy.

Q. Where are they insured, what is the insurance now on slave cargoes?

A. They were insured formerly by the Insurance company of Havana from 25 to 38 per cent. This company has now ceased to insure vessels from Africa. Certain individuals here now insure them at prices extremely high.

Q. What number of slaves, one vessel with another, do they carry?

A. The greater part of the vessels sent from here are schooners and pilot-boats from 70 to 100 tons; these carry from 200 to 400 negroes. Ships and brigs also are employed in this trade, which go very far to the south; the first-named ships carrying 800 negroes, and the others 500 and 550.

Q. Do the slaves suffer more or less on the Middle Passage than before?

A. Perhaps less, but not on account of any decrease in the trade, but on account of the imperceptible progress of civilization.[7]

Q. Have you heard of any instances of half the cargo perishing on the voyage?

A. Yes; and even more than half.

Q. What is the average loss on the passage?

A. A loss of one-fifth part of the cargo may be calculated on.

Q. What ought to be the clear gain on a cargo of 500 slaves landed at Havana?

A. From 120,000 to 130,000 dollars.

Q. If a slave-trade merchant has five vessels in the trade, and four are captured, if one arrives safe does he lose or gain?

A. He loses the expense of an expedition to the coast amounting to 40,000 dollars for 500 slaves, these cost 175,000 or 200,000 dollars, and the gain on one cargo is what we have stated above.

Q. Does the wealth acquired in this trade remain in Cuba, or benefit the legal trade of the island?

A. Yes; it does.

Q. What punishment is inflicted on those found on board captured slave-ships?

A. The Spanish government reserved to itself the right of framing a penal law, at the time of concluding the last treaty, to punish persons employed in the trade in slaves, but it never has been promulgated.

Q. Would the punishment of death for this crime tend to suppress it?

A. No; the penalty of death inflicted in this case (similia similibus)[8] would be only one atrocity opposed to another.

Q. Has the government of Cuba instructions to suppress it?

A. Yes; and it would be well if the Captain-general[9] had only the inclination to suppress it.

Q. Has it the desire to suppress it?

A. None whatever; because the authorities believe that on it depends the material prosperity of the island, from which the mother-country draws three or four millions of dollars a-year in contributions.

Q. Have the Spanish governors of Cuba instructions to suppress it?

A. Yes; they have public instructions, wrung from the government when the English cabinet is importunate with that of Madrid.

Q. Did the late Governor-general Tacon endeavour to suppress it?

A. No; it was he who protected it.

Q. Do the Captain-generals receive a sum of ten dollars a-head for permission to land the slaves?

A. Before Tacon's time, the subordinate authorities received this money, but it is not known if the Captain-generals were privy to it;

but Tacon organized the plan of this contribution so, that the whole of it went into his hands, that is to say, eight and a-half dollars, not ten.

Q. What other authorities receive money for the same purpose?

A. In the capital, no others; but in the other chief ports of the island, all the authorities, especially of the marine, participate in it.

Q. What amount of money did General Tacon receive during the four years he was in Cuba, in this way?

A. The amount of 450,000 dollars, and this fact is known and given from documents with the precise data on this point.

Q. How was that money applied?

A. It was invested in bills of exchange, on Paris and London.

Q. For what service did the eminent slave-dealer, Joaquin Gomez, get the title of Excellentissimo?

A. We cannot tell.

Q. Was this Excellentissimo Senor a confidential adviser of Tacon?

A. We have reason to believe so.

Q. Was this person appointed by Tacon to the office of protector of the emancipated slaves?

A. We are ignorant who the protector of slaves is, but certain it is, that he was charged by Tacon with the distribution of the emancipated negroes, and the realization of the funds which their sale produced.

Q. Was Senor Gomez a fit person for that office?

A. See the former reply.

Q. Has he duly performed the duties of his office?

A. The duties of distributor and disposer of the emancipadoes, perfectly.

Q. Is there any other person associated with Gomez in the office of protector of emancipated slaves?

A. For that of protector—No; but for that of distributor and disposer, there were associated with him, the Most Excellent the Count of the Reunion, and a member of the Municipal Council, Senor Cabrera.

Q. Has that person been engaged in the slave-trade?

A. Yes; he has been, and is, like the greater part of the capitalists of the Havana.

Q. What was the price of an emancipated negro, in Tacon's time?

A. From six to nine doubloons each.

Q. What may be the number living of emancipated slaves, (emancipadoes?)

A. We do not know.

Q. Has a single one of these emancipadoes ever acquired his liberty?

A. We believe not; but it has been said, that one did get his liberty lately, through the interference of one of the officers employed in the commission.

Q. Is it likely that the emancipadoes ever will be liberated?

A. Most certainly not, the government refuses to liberate them. On one occasion, some of these emancipadoes having sought their liberty, offering for it, the price that any person would have given to retain them in their service; the government refused, stating that if they did, they might escape from the island—this was in the time of Tacon.

Q. Was it the custom in Tacon's time to sell them for terms of seven and ten years?

A. Yes; for seven years.

Q. To what class of persons was it customary to sell them, and under what names was the price paid?

A. To all who sought for them—whose money was received as a compensation for the labour of the emancipado, who was already destined to be employed on the public works, as in the mending of roads, reparation of bridges, construction of prisons, laying out of gardens.

Q. Have these emancipadoes, to your knowledge, been sold twice over?

A. Yes.

Q. Are these emancipadoes better or worse off than the slaves?

A. They are in a worse condition.

Q. How may they be worse off?

A. Because even offering the price of their liberty, the government refuses to receive it, they are considered as slaves for life.

Q. Do they receive any moral or religious instruction?

A. No; except the few who find themselves in the hands of some woman of piety or individual in some obscure station.

Q. Do they receive any wages for themselves?

A. None.

Q. Are the intentions of the British government fulfilled with respect to them?

A. From what has been said it may be judged.

Q. Is it desirable that the British government should apply for their removal from slavery here?

A. Yes; and very expedient too.

Q. If the British government offered to remove them free of all cost to the authorities, would they be given up?

A. We believe they would.

Q. Was it one of the original stipulations that they should not be removed out of the district of Havana?

A. It was.

Q. Have they been distributed over the island?

A. They have.

Q. Have many of them been sold by Tacon to the Agent of any British Mining Company at St. Jago de Cuba?

A. We do not know.

Q. Have you heard wherever one of them was on an estate, it was customary when the death of a slave occurred to represent the death as being that of an emancipado?

A. We have heard a great many cases of the kind.

Q. And did the emancipadoes thus pass into slavery?

A. They did.

Q. Have you any idea of the number of them that died of the cholera?

A. It is difficult to know.

Q. May I ask your opinion of the conduct of General Tacon with respect to the emancipadoes?

A. With respect to the emancipadoes, his conduct was infamous, because he reduced them to a state of misery, worse than the condition of the slaves.

Q. Are the emancipadoes in reality slaves or freemen?

A. Slaves!!!

Q. Should not General Tacon be impeached in Spain for selling and re-selling these freemen, under the pretext of his voluntary contributions?

A. General Tacon has not been badly thought of in Spain, and none of his measures have been disapproved of by the Spanish government.

Q. What agent of General Tacon's received for him the ten dollars a-head importation fee on the negroes?

A. An adventurer who was his "major domo," Senor Luanco.

Q. Did General Tacon, on his arrival here, make any avowal of his sentiments with respect to the slave-trade?

A. None.

Q. Within what distance of General Tacon's country-house were the principal bozal negro barricones situated?

A. About 100 or 150 yards from his gardens, they exist still in the sight of all the world, the railway passes in front of them.

(Signed)

R.R. Madden,

Havana, July lst, 1839.

Notes

1. Bartolomé de las Casas (1474–1565).
2. Probably Francisco de Arango y Parreño (1765–1830), author of *Discurso sobre la agricultura de la isla de Cuba y los medios de fomentarla* (1792).
3. Madden noted: "Saco's estimate was made, about four years previously; there is reason to believe in that period the actual number of slaves in Cuba has increased to 430,000."
4. José Antonio Saco (1797–1879), Cuban historian and authority on slavery who wrote the important *Historia de la esclavitud de la Indias en el Nuevo Mundo* (1883).
5. Madden noted: "The mortality is, I think, under-rated that on sugar estates being about 10 per cent, and on coffee estates 5 per cent."
6. Whiskey.
7. Madden noted: "I doubt the correctness of this answer."
8. Similar things for similar things; an eye for an eye.
9. Miguel Tacón (1777–1854).

QUESTIONS RESPECTING THE STATE OF RELIGION IN CUBA, ADDRESSED TO SENOR * * * OF THE HAVANA, BY R. R. M. AND THE ANSWERS GIVEN TO THEM.

Q. How many bishoprics in the Island of Cuba?

A. Two; one in the Havana, and an archbishopric in St. Jago[1] de Cuba.

Q. Is that of St. Jago de Cuba superior in rank to that of the Havana?

A. It is, being the metropolitan, but its revenue is smaller; in matters of dispute the appeals are reciprocal from one bishopric to another.

Q. How is that of the Havana administered?

A. By the archbishop of Guatemala residing at the Havana, who was exiled from the former place by the government; and shortly after his arrival here, he received from Rome, faculties to administer the affairs of this diocese as its bishop.

Q. How is that of Cuba administered?

A. Its archbishop being absent, in spiritual matters, it is governed by a parish priest; in secular matters by a curate, both supposed to have been appointed by the Spanish government.

Q. With whom does the nomination rest?

A. The Court of Spain have the privilege of nominating bishops, which nomination is subject to the sanction of the Pope.

Q. What is the revenue of the archbishop of Cuba?

A. Not known.

Q. What is the revenue of the archbishop of Havana?

A. It formerly amounted to 80,000 dollars, now it amounts to 50,000; the revenues have diminished, with the falling off in the tithes.

Q. When the See of either is vacant, who receives the revenue?
A. The Crown.

Q. What portion of that of Havana does the State receive?
A. The revenues of the bishopric are composed, first, of a part of the tithes; and, secondly, of the church revenues, furnished by the parish dues, for births, deaths, marriages, &c.; of which the State takes no part.

(Note, it is the general opinion, however, that the present bishop receives only a small portion of the revenues of the See, the State receiving a considerable portion of them.—R.R.M.)

Q. What is the number of parishes in the Island?
A. In St. Jago de Cuba, 38; in the Havana district, 117.

Q. What is the number of friars or monks in the island?
A. In July, 1837, there were 150 monks (priests), 15 choristers and 65 lay-brothers.

Q. Does the State give any stipend to the monks and friars?
A. None; they support themselves out of their own means.

Q. Are tithes still a legal impost?
A. They are.

Q. Have they been abolished by the Cortes,[2] and when?
A. Their abolition had been warmly contended for in the Cortes in 1838; however it has been determined they should be collected the present year.

Q. Does the abolition extend to this island?
A. We imagine if they were even definitively abolished in Spain, the abolition would not extend to this island.

Q. What is the gross value of the tithes of Cuba?
A. The tithes of Cuba amount to 416,000 dollars; the ninth part goes for the support of the public hospitals, to the Royal Treasury (Real Hacienda), which is also entitled to the tithes of the best property (finca) of the parish, which is called "Casa escusada," the remainder into equal portions; one goes to the treasury, and the other to the bishop, canons, and parish priests.

Q. Do they extend to all kinds of agricultural products?
A. They do not.

Q. How many cathedrals in the Island?
A. Two; one at St. Jago de Cuba, and another at Havana.

Q. Do the clergy receive dues for christenings, burials, and marriages?

A. They do.

Q. What is the amount for a christening?

A. Six reals (de plata) or three-quarters of a dollar.

Q. What is the amount for a burial?

A. Seven dollars and a-half.

Q. What is the amount for a marriage?

A. From five to forty, or fifty dollars, according to the means of the parties.[3]

Q. What portion of these go to the Parish priest?

A. The fourth part.

Q. How is the rest disposed of?

A. Divided between the Bishop, the Curate or "Sacristian Mayor", and a church fund.

Q. Can one priest hold two parishes?

A. Yes, "ad interim."

Q. With whom does the appointment to a parish rest?

A. The bishop—who nominates after the candidate has sustained a public theological discussion.

Q. How are the religious houses maintained?

A. In the convents all who wish to enter are received, if the applicants are favourably known:—Bastardy is no hinderance, neither is obscurity of birth. The nuns require applicants for admission into their communities—to be persons of good origin—they require "liempieza de sangre."[4] The stipend of a monk varies from 250 to 600 dollars a year, according to the revenues of his convent.

Q. What is the average income of a secular priest of Cuba?

A. According to the capital of his "capellania," from the income of which he is bound to maintain himself; as no priest can be ordained who does not possess a certain capital, and this is called his "capellania," unless he is sent as a curate to some other parish, his stipend then would average 25 or 30 dollars a month. The parish priest receives from 800 to 1000 dollars a year, the canons 4000 dollars, the inferior prebends 2000, and the superior prebends 3000 dollars—the dignitaries (los dignidades) 4500, and deans 6000 dollars.

Q. What sort of influence recommends a priest for a curacy?

A. Their favour or influence with the bishop.

Q. Are the clergy amenable to the common civil tribunals?

A. They are not, they are subject to the ecclesiastical tribunals during their lives.

Q. Have any recent laws in Spain affected their privileges?

A. In Spain they have been deprived of the privilege of being elected deputies of the Cortes.

Q. Are any ecclesiastical offences punishable by civil law?

A. Ecclesiastical offences are taken cognizance of by ecclesiastical courts, but crimes committed by priests, as citizens, are taken cognizance of by the civil tribunals.

Q. Is it lawful for ecclesiastics to follow the profession of the law?

A. It is; but they cannot plead in criminal causes in the civil courts: but they can plead in these causes in the ecclesiastical courts.

Q. To what extent are the monasteries endowed with lands?

A. The territorial property in the towns and in the country of the convents, of the monks, and of the nunneries, amounts to 3,652,685 dollars by their own estimate, of the 11th of July, 1837; besides the other property of the convents which may safely be estimated at 3,500,000 dollars more—in all, 7,152,685 dollars.[5]

Q. Do they possess much property in slaves?

A. The convent of Bethlehem is the only one which possesses a considerable number of slaves. The richest order in Cuba is that of Bethlehem.

Q. Are the libraries of the convents valuable?

A. Yes; in books of scholastic theology.

Q. Has any order been received for their suppression?

A. Yes, on their suppression in Spain; but General Tacon opposed the suppression, considering them to have great influence in the country, which is false.[6]

Q. Has it been acted on?

A. The property of the convents has been put up to sale to the amount of 2,000,000 of dollars to meet the war subsidy for Spain.

(But no sale was effected up to October 1839, R.R.M.)

Q. Has their property been sequestered?

A. All their property has been sequestered by a royal order of Dec. 2nd, 1836, promulgated in February 1837.

Q. Has the state made any provision for them?

A. Notwithstanding the order, as they yet receive their revenues, the state has had no necessity of assigning any stipends for them.

Q. Does the Franciscan order hold property in land?

A. It does not. Its means consist of capital invested for its use, as pious bequests for funeral masses, and the service of religion on certain festivals, besides they seek eleemosynary assistance all over the island.

(Note—This order especially at Guanabacoa[7] is deservedly the most respected of all in the island. R.R.M.)

Q. To what authority or tribunal are the friars amenable?

A. To their respective conventual superiors.

Q. How many nunneries in the island?

A. Four in Havana, and one in Puerto Principe.[8]

Q. What is the number of religious women in them?

A. One hundred and twenty-six nuns professed, and nine novices, in July 1837.

Q. Are the nuns allowed to leave their convents?

A. Once received they are not allowed to leave their convents.

(Note—Except in cases of extreme illness. R.R.M.)

Q. Is there any fixed sum for entrance into them?

A. The sum of 300 dollars for each, some are admitted gratis.

Q. Are the women who take the veil of the higher class?

A. Generally they are—but now not so much so, as at former periods.

Q. Are there female schools attached to the nunneries?

A. By the royal orders of 1824 and 1826, schools were directed to be established, but now these exist only in the Ursuline Convent by its institute.

Q. Is there any convent of the sisters of charity here?

A. No.

Q. Are these convents possessed of much property?

A. Yes; for the dowers received, go on increasing. The convent of Santa Clara[9] is the richest.

Q. Are they possessed of property in slaves?

A. Some nuns, such as the rich chiefly, hold domestic slaves.

Q. Which of the convents possess most property?

A. Santa Clara.

Q. Have any of the nunneries been suppressed?

A. None.

Q. Is any portion of the tithes applicable to educational purposes?

A. Not any.

Q. Have the poor, the sick, and the aged, any claim on them?

A. The revenues of the bishop are supposed to be held in stewardship for these persons, and according as the ideas of such a responsibility are, on the part of a prelate, so are his duties well or ill performed.

Q. Are there any poor schools supported by the clergy?

A. Not one.

Q. What is the number of churches in this island?

A. One hundred and seventy-one in all—of which 155 are parochial, five monasterial, and eleven conventual.

Q. What is the number of priests of all denominations in this island?

A. Four hundred and twenty-five in all, of which in the diocese of Havana there are 150 exclusive of parish priests, and in St. Jago de Cuba 50. In that of Havana 117 parish priests, and 38 in that of Cuba; 55 curates in the former and 15 in Cuba.

Q. What is the total population of Cuba of blacks and whites?

A. Total population of the island, according to the official statistics of 1830 was 775,195 souls; and now 1839, it may be estimated at one million.

Q. What is the proportion of the clergy to the population?

A. About one priest for every 2000 souls.

Q. Is it incumbent on country pastors to visit slave plantations?

A. They go there only when they are sent for to baptize or to marry slaves.

(Note—For the latter purpose they are hardly ever sent for to the estates. R.R.M.)

Q. Are such plantations usually far distant from a church?

A. Yes, there are parishes whose jurisdiction extends as far as eight leagues.

Q. Is it usual for the slaves to attend divine worship?

A. On the sugar estates it is not, on the coffee estates in a very few, on the smaller farms which are situated near a church the slaves are permitted to go to church on Sundays.

Q. Is there any instruction in the doctrines of christianity on estates?

A. When the time of making sugar is over during crop time, it is customary to repeat the rosary on the estates, this is the only religious practice; as to instruction in the morals or in the dogma of religion, the masters themselves are not conversant with them "esta es la unica practica religiosa que tienen, en cuanto a instruction de la moral y de los dogmas—ni los amos la tienen."

Q. Is free access afforded to the clergy on the estates?

A. The parish priests are privileged to reprove the masters for neglecting the due instruction of their slaves in the doctrine and precepts of the church; but none of them avail themselves of their privilege.

Q. Are the country clergy usually slave-holders themselves?

A. Yes; the most of them hold landed property, "fincas rurales," with the slaves which correspond to their farms, which they treat in the same way as the other inhabitants of the Island.

Q. Had Las Casas any ecclesiastical sanction for the first slave importations?

A. For the answer to this question, see the life of Las Casas, by Quintana,[10] in his 3rd vol. of Espanoles celebres—here you will find that far from considering he had any sanction of the kind for the error he had fallen into, he had soon become convinced of it, and heartily repented of it.

Q. Has the slave-trade ever had any sanction from Rome?

A. My opinion is, that no council ever sanctioned the slavery of the negroes, and most assuredly the Council of Trent[11] does not. On this point, the opinions of the learned divines in Spain, in the 16th century, may be collected from the writings of Dom. de Sota, professor of Jurisprudence in Salamanca, and confessor of Charles the Fifth, who sent him as theologian to the Council of Trent; he expresses himself thus, in his work de "Justitia et Jure," printed at Salamanca, 1540—"If what is told of the Portuguese traders, be true, that they entrap unfortunate negroes on the coasts, then embark them as slaves; it is my opinion that neither those who take them—nor those who buy them—nor those who possess them, can be said to have clear consciences, while they do not manumit them; when these slaves are not able to redeem themselves."

Q. Are the clergy generally advocates of slavery in Cuba?

A. The clergy here follow blindly the impulse of those moral causes which warp the public mind, and debase it to the point of defending the injustice of slavery.

Q. Can the state of religious opinion be much lower, short of general indifference or disbelief?

A. To me it seems it can not.

Q. Is indifference or unbelief the prevailing evil?

A. Indifference is much more common than incredulity among the lower orders and the uneducated higher classes, which are the most numerous here. On the contrary, the lawyers, physicians, official persons, and in fine the gentry, who have any pretence to intelligence, it is amongst these that incredulity prevails.

Q. In what class has religion most votaries?

A. Amongst the free negroes and coloured people, and also in many of the old families in the principal towns, and amongst those in the suburbs of the Havana.

Q. Does infidelity arise here, from ill-directed studies or philosophical research?

A. Nothing of the kind; in part it arises from the profoundest ignorance of everything relative to metaphysics; and in part from the reading of those books of the infidel French philosophers of the last age.

Q. Does it allow any serious inquiries into the nature of revealed religion?

A. Much less—here no other inquiries are made, except about the price of sugar and coffee.

Q. Does it arise from the intolerance here of any other form of worship than that of the Roman Catholic?

A. Neither is that the case, notwithstanding in these latter times, there have not been wanting men of intelligence, who seeing the corruption of the clergy, as they imagined the chief cause of the deplorable state in which religion is found here, have desired to see tolerated the free exercise of all forms of christian worship.

Q. Do you consider the abuses of religion arise from the influence of its connexion with the state?

A. The demoralization that prevails here is a complex fact, whose causes are various—viz., political despotism, domestic slavery, and ignorance.

Q. What influence has slavery on the religious sentiments of the people?

A. The influence which it ever has produced in every community where slavery exists: see the profound treatise on "Legislation," by Mons. Charles Comte, liv. 5, on the subject of slavery.

Q. Is the laxity of discipline in the church of Cuba so great as to need reformation, and is that reformation to be expected for the revival of religion in the land?

A. The church of Spain has produced learned theologians, who respecting the evangelical doctrines have criticised with sufficient freedom, the abuses in the discipline of our church, which have frequently destroyed the spirit of the dogma, and discredited the doctrines of our religion.

Q. How is the laxity of discipline to be remedied?

A. In the state of prostration in which we find the heads of the church here, I see no other remedy than to preach the faith in the periodical publications of the day.[12]

Q. By what means are the removal of these evils, and the rescue of the people from infidelity, to be expected?

A. It is to be observed, our clergy are, generally speaking, neither enlightened nor moral men, they are devoid of zeal for their holy mission, and unworthy of it—exceptions there are, but they are very few.

Q. If the clergy do not call for the removal of these scandals, and the people do not think of the necessity, ought not the literary men of Cuba to originate the demand for the convocation of a council for this purpose?

A. It is to public opinion, and not to our rulers or authorities, we must look for these reforms.

Q. Is it not incumbent on the intelligence of your community, on your men of letters, to come forward and help to remove these evils?

A. In this community, there are not above three or four men of letters, by profession, and of this number, one or two who are believers in christianity.

Q. Is the gospel at present preached in the churches—or practised in the cloisters?

A. No; it is neither preached in the churches—nor read nor meditated on in families, which are denominated christian. In the pulpit, they preach panegyrics, in the houses they repeat devotional words, but they do not pray, they mechanically move their lips—and this is all their homage to the Almighty, while in the cloisters, which already begin to be deserts, the precepts of the gospel have been brought into contempt.[13]

Signed, _____

Havana, Sept., 1839.   R.R.M.

Notes

1. Probably a reference to Jagua, a municipality in Havana province.
2. The Spanish parliament.

3. Madden noted: "This evidently applies to towns. In the country, where the priest has to come from a distant part of his parish, I have known as much as six doubloons or 102 dollars, demanded for the marriage ceremony by the clergyman."
4. Purity of blood.
5. Madden noted: "In English money, say £1,430,537 sterling."
6. Madden noted: "If General Tacon opposed their suppression 'without desiring or contributing to their reformation, then indeed his view of their influence was false.'"
7. Municipality in the province of Havana.
8. The original name of the present-day Province of Camagüey in central Cuba.
9. The capital city of the Province of Las Villas.
10. Manuel José Quintana (1772–1857), Spanish writer, politician, and author of *Vidas de españoles célebres* (1807).
11. The nineteenth ecumenical council of the Roman Catholic Church (1545–1563).
12. Madden noted: "This opinion I cannot coincide in—the remedy would never reach the evil that preys upon the morals of the land."
13. Madden noted: "From this censure, I grieve to say but too well founded, there are two convents that are entirely exempt, one of Franciscans at Guanabucoa, and another of the order of St. Philip of Neri at Havana; and from my own knowledge of both, I can say with truth, that the service of the church, and the rites of religion, are most piously performed and observed, and the ministers of both establishments are most highly respected by those who attend their churches."

NECESSITY OF SEPARATING
THE IRISH IN AMERICA
FROM THE SIN OF SLAVERY

There is one subject which peculiarly demands the attention of the people and clergy of Ireland. The evils connected with it, no effort of the government can reach, but the subject is one, to which attention may be directed with great advantage. I allude to the use that is made in America of the extraordinary political influence of the poor people of Ireland who emigrate to that country, and to the efforts that ought to be made to give them right and wholesome feelings on the subject of slavery, and a just understanding of the value of those efforts that are made to right the wronged; although the persons that are injured, and whose rights are outraged, are men of a different complexion to their own. It is impossible for any one who had not visited America, to conceive what an extraordinary influence on the government of that country the votes of the Irish people have, or how little beneficial use they make of the power they possess and exercise at the hustings with such extraordinary effect.

With regard to the opinions of the Irish settlers in America on the question of slavery, I speak from my own experience of this matter; and, I may truly add, I speak of it with regret, and have witnessed it with feelings of surprise and sorrow. Surely they have been "as strangers" themselves in their own land, "and should know the hearts of strangers." The truth ought to be known, and the evil that exists of the ignorance of our countrymen abroad—of the national rights of men of all classes, creeds, and colours, should be remedied by all speedy and seasonable means. They should not be left to depart from our own shores, ignorant that there does not exist in nature, in religion, or in civil polity, a reason for robbing any man of his liberty, be he black or white—that there is neither truth, justice, nor humanity in the declarations they hear, that slavery is consonant to the condition of negro men, has a sanction in nature, or is sanctified by the permission of any christian church. The fact must be forced on their attention—that slavery has no sanction from their church—that to devote one-fourth part of the habitable globe to perpetual bloodshed and warfare—to give up the vast continent of Africa to the ravages of the man-robbers who deal in flesh and blood—the marauders who sack the towns and villages—the merchant murderers who ply the odious trade, who separate the child from the mother, the husband from the wife, father from the son, is a monstrous system of cruelty that, in any of its forms, is intolerable and unjust. The state of things of which I speak I have myself seen; and the experience I have alluded to, is the result of what I have observed on three occasions that I have visited the United States during the last six years. Of the necessity that exists for diffusing sounder opinions on the subject of slavery, I am sure I need bring forward no other argument than this—that if the political influence of the Irish settlers and emigrants of America were exerted in favour of the cause of the abolition of slavery in the United States, that system could not possibly endure! That the Irish in America exert an extraordinary political influence—that they have it in their power to decide the great political interests of the republic, and to give the preponderance to the party which actually returns the President of the United States, cannot be denied by any one conversant with the political struggles of America; and with regard to the great question of slavery, I grieve to be obliged to state, that they are not only apathetic and indifferent on the subject of the emancipation of the slaves, but that they are even strenuously opposed to the efforts of those who labour in behalf of this cause of justice and humanity in the United States. They have mistaken views of the men who are interested in it, and of the object, for which their exertions are made. But from my own knowledge of such men as Garrison, Tappan, Birney, Levitt, Jay, and Smyth,[1] I am so fully convinced of their singleness of purpose, genuine philanthropy, and the heroic fortitude and truly Christian forbearance of those men, I can safely state, that never were the efforts of good men more needlessly suspected or more entirely misunderstood.

I therefore consider it of the utmost moment that the persons interested in this cause in Ireland, and the clergy of the Roman Catholic church especially, should labour to inculcate sounder opinions on the subject of slavery amongst the lower classes of our countrymen; and particularly that their opinions in reprobation of this accursed system of slavery should be made known as extensively as possible, through the Catholic priesthood in America, to the Irish emigrants in that country. There can be no doubt on the mind of any person who has recently visited America that great ignorance prevails on this subject; and that the grossest prejudices are entertained against the slaves by our countrymen; and in fact, that they look upon all those who differ from them in complexion as inferior to them in every moral attribute. It is a melancholy fact that, such is the evil influence of slavery in every country where it exists, that the notions of the best men become perverted, and that men are let down by such easy stages from crime to crime, that even the ministers of the gospel, of all persuasions, fall insensibly from the contemplation and intoleration of slavery into the practice of it. When I have argued with gentlemen of this class, holding slave property in Cuba, against the system, as incompatible with that of christianity, I have been told that slavery was not only compatible with it, but had the positive sanction of the church for its support. I was not satisfied that such was the fact, and on anxiously inquiring, myself, into the truth of those statements, no doubt whatever was left on my mind that the religion they professed had been maligned. The result of these inquiries I now lay before you, and the authorities adduced will enable you to judge, whether religion is responsible for the atrocities which are committed in Cuba and elsewhere, and even the tolerated by some other wise good men, who, not knowing the tenets of their religion, and being left in ignorance of its express ordinances and obligations, believe that slavery and the slave-trade are actually sanctioned by their creed, and not opposed to it either in letter or in spirit:—

AUTHORITIES FROM THE FATHERS, THE DOCTRINES OF THE CHURCH, AND THE DECREES OF THE POPES, AGAINST SLAVERY, AND HISTORICAL, ECCLESIASTICAL REFERENCES TO THE CONDUCT OF THE CLERGY.

"St. Anselm, in 1102, held a national council in St. Peter's church at Westminster, in which, among other things, it was forbid to sell men like cattle, which had till then been practised in England."— Butler's Lives.

"In the great provincial council of all the bishops subject to the see of Canterbury, presided over by Archbishop Walfred, in presence of Kenulf, King of Mercia, it was enacted, on the death of a bishop, that, three slaves should be set at liberty, and three shillings be given to each."—Life of St. Willibrord.

"The great synod of Armaghat a period of general consternation declared 'that the public calamities were to be held as an infliction of divine justice on account of the sins of the Irish people, and more especially because that in former times they used to make bond-slaves of the English, whom they had purchased as well from merchants as from robbers and pirates—a crime for which God now took vengeance upon them by delivering them into like bondage themselves. For the English people,' it was added, 'while yet their kingdom was in a state of security, were accustomed, through a common vice of the nation, to expose their children for sale. And,' adds the historian, 'acting upon the spirit of these humane and Christian views, the synod unanimously decreed and ordered' that all the English throughout the island who were in a state of slavery should be restored to their former freedom."—Moore's History of Ireland, vol. ii. p. 232.

(This general act of emancipation of slaves, it is worthy of notice, is the first on record in any European country.)

The Northumbrians, according to Malmesbury, sold their own children for slaves, and the pious author of the life of St. Augustine, the apostle of England, reprobating slavery, says these slave-traders of Northumbria "surpassed in barbarism and ferocity the negroes of this day."—Life of St. Augustine.

"St. Raymond, of Pennafort, concerted with St. Peter Nolasco the foundation of the order of mercy, for the redemption of captives."—Life of St. Raymond of Pennafort.

"St. John the Almoner (Patriarch) sent two bishops and an abbot to ransom captives."—St. John's Life.

"St. Sulpicius Severus set at liberty several of his slaves, and admitted them and some of his old stewards to familiar intercourse and conversation."—St. Sepulicius Severus.

"St. Elegius, Bishop of Noyan, was particularly zealous to ransom captives. When a slave was to be sold in any neighbouring place he hastened thither, and sometimes ransomed fifty or a hundred at a time, especially Saxons, who were sold in great numbers."—Life of St. Elegius.

"St. Francis Xavier walked through the streets of Goa with a bell in his hand, summoning all masters, for the love of God, to send their children and slaves to catechism; and such was the effect of his preaching, restitution was made of unjust gains, slaves who had been unjustly acquired were set at liberty."—Life of St. Francis Xavier.

"St. Bathildes, Queen of France, forbade christians to be made slaves, gave great numbers their liberty, and declared all capable of property. The Franks still retained slaves, with this condition, attached to certain manors or farms, and bound to certain particular kinds of servitude. The kings of the second race often set great numbers free, and were imitated by other lords. Queen Blanche and St. Lewis contributed more than any others to ease the condition of the vassals; and Lewis Huttin abolished slavery in France, declaring all men free who live in that kingdom, according to the spirit of christianity, which teaches us to treat all men as our brethren."—Butler's Lives.

"In 1610, the pious Father Claver was sent to preach the faith to the infidels at Carthage and the neighboring country in Africa. At the first sight of the poor negro slaves he was moved with the strongest sentiments of compassion, tenderness, and zeal, which never forsook him, and it was his constant study to afford them all the temporal comfort in his power. The title in which he gloried was that of the slave of slaves."—Hist. de Eccles. de Berrault.

"St. Gregory the Great (Pope) happened one day to be walking through the market, and here taking notice that certain youths of fine features and complexions were exposed for sale, he inquired what countrymen they were? and was answered they came from Britain."—Life of St. Gregory. To this circumstance is due the mission of St. Augustine to England.

St. Euphrasia on renouncing the world, writes to her friends:—"For the sake of my parents be pleased to distribute their estates among the poor, the orphans, and the church. Set all my slaves at liberty, and discharge my vassals and servants, giving them whatever is their due."—Life of St. Euphras.

"Genseric, the Arian king of the Vandals, plundered Rome and brought innumerable captives from Italy, Sicily, Sardinia, and Corsica, into Africa, whom the Moors and Vandals shared among them on the shore, separating, without any regard or compassion, weeping wives from their husbands, and children from their parents; St. Deogratias sold everything, even the gold and silver vessels of the church to redeem as many as possible; he provided lodgings and beds, and furnished them with all succours, and though in a decrepit old age, visited them that were sick every day and often in the night."—Life of St. Deogratias.

"After the departure of the Vandals with their captives and an immense booty, St. Leo sent zealous Catholic priests and alms for the relief of the captives in Africa."—Life of St. Leo the Great (Pope.)

"St. Thomas of Jesus, a most holy man, in 1532, caused the money that was sent him for his own use by his sister, the Countess of Linares, and by kings Henry and Philip II., to be employed in ransoming slaves, and chose to stay, though no longer a prisoner, at the Sagena, or prison, where were detained above two thousand christian slaves, of different nations, whom he never ceased to comfort and assist with heavenly exhortations, and the functions of his sacred ministry."— Life of St. Augustin.

"St. Augustin sometimes melted down part of the sacred vessels to redeem captives, in which he was authorized by the example of St. Ambrose. He reproved one Romulus for the oppression of his poor vassals."—Ibid.

"St. Raymond Nonatus took the new Order of Mercy for redemption of captives. In the discharge of his office of ransomer, he purchased at Algiers the liberty of a great number of slaves. When all his means were laid out in that charitable way, he voluntarily gave himself up as a ransom for the hostage of certain others whose situation was hardest, and whose faith seemed exposed to imminent danger. It was a saying of his, 'that a man is more precious than the whole world.' St. Raymond was loaded with chains and iron bolts, and cast into a dungeon where he lay full eight months, till his ransom was brought by some religious men of his order."—Butler's Lives.

As to the character of slavery in every age, and the similarity of the outrages inflicted, whether on christians or pagans, we have but to read the brief account of its horrors, given in the history of the martyrdom of St. Nemsianus and others:—

"When the President of Numidia proceeded, with renewed severity, against the christians, tortured many, and afterwards put several to barbarous deaths, and sent others to work in the mines or quarries, whilst others continued their lingering martyrdom in hunger, nakedness, and filth, exhausted with hard labour, and tormented with daily stripes and perpetual reproaches and insults—in the words of Nemsianus, 'though they had manacled their feet with fetters, marked their bodies with infamy, they could not reach their souls.'"— St. Nemsianus.

"A number of christians being taken into captivity, of both sexes, eight bishops wrote to St. Cyprian, imploring his assistance for the redemption of the prisoners. St. Cyprian shed many tears upon reading these letters, and at his recommendation the clergy and the people of Carthage raised a sum amounting to one hundred thousand sestertii—that is about seven hundred and eighty-one pounds, English—for the redemption of the saves."—St. Cyprian.

In 506, St. Remigius wrote to Clovis,—"Let the gate of your palace be open to all, that every one may have recourse to you for justice. Employ your great revenues in redeeming slaves."

"Clovis sent a circular letter to all the bishops in his dominions, in which he allowed them to give liberty to any of the captives he had taken, but desired them to make use of that privilege in favour of persons of whom they had some knowledge."—St. Remigius.

"St. Hilary, to redeem captives, caused the church plate to be sold, not excepting the sacred vessels, making use of paters and chalices of glass in the celebration of the divine mysteries."—Butler's Lives.

"In the reign of Pope Pius V., fifteen thousand slaves that were found on board the galleys of the Turkish fleet were set at liberty."—St. Pius V. (Pope.)

"St. John de Prado being sent by the authority of the Congregation de Propaganda Fide, to preach the faith in the kingdom of Fez and Morocco, he discharged himself with so great zeal, that the Mahomedans cast him into a dungeon, loaded with chains."—Ibid.

"St. Margaret devoted her extensive alms to restore to foreign nations, especially the English, their captives, and was solicitous to ransom those especially, who fell into the hands of harsh masters."—Ibid.

"St. Vincent, of Paul, when taken prisoner by the Mahomedans, with some others, states that they gave to every slave a pair of loose trowsers, a linen jerkin, and a bonnet. In this garb they were led five or six times through the city of Tunis to be shown, after which they were brought back to their vessel, where the merchants came to see them, as men do at the sale of a horse or an ox. They examined who could eat well, felt their sides, looked at their teeth to see who were likely for very long life, they probed their wounds, and made them walk and run in all paces, lift up burdens and wrestle, to judge of their strength."—Life of St. Vincent of Paul.

St. Vincent, like St. Patrick, was a runaway slave. The fact of their flight is a sufficient condemnation of slavery.

"The French and Burgundians laid siege to Aries in 508, and a great number of captives were brought into the city. St. Cesarius furnished them with clothes and victuals, and employed in relieving them the whole treasury of the church. He stripped the pillars and rails of the silver with which they were adorned, and melted down, and gave away the very censers, chalices, and paters, saying, 'Our Lord celebrated his last supper in mean earthen dishes, not in plate, and we need not scruple to part with his vessels to ransom those whom He has redeemed with His life. I would fain know if those who censure what we do, would not be glad to be ransomed themselves in like manner, were the same misfortune to befall them.'"—Life of St. Cesarius.

Lactantius says, "that the redeeming of captives enters not less into the obligations of justice and tender charity, which I rank even above the gifts of munificence. The exercise of the latter requires riches, it does not always pretend to the pure sentiment of justice. It is only the just, properly so called, who make it a duty to feed the poor, to redeem prisoners."

"Beneficence is exercised towards a relation, towards a friend; is there so much merit in that? It is only acquitting a rigorous debt imposed by nature, by decorum, by interest in one's reputation, and fear of blame; but to be generous to a stranger, to an unknown one, that is true merit, because humanity alone has been the mover of it; but to deliver captives, to assist the widow and the orphan, to succour the sick, to bury the dead to whom their family have not been able to render that office, it is not only following a natural sentiment—it is obeying the law of God—it is offering one's-self as a victim to the Lord, and preparing for one's-self a magnificent reward."—Lactantius Divine Institutions, p. 587, &c.

"Give for the redeeming of captives this gold that you destine for the buying of animals."—Ibid. p. 587. &c.

"You expect from your slave that he be devoted to you, man of a day! Is this slave less a man than you? He came into the world on the same conditions, your equal by his birth, by his death, provided with the same organs, endowed as well as you with a reasoning soul, called to the same hopes, subject to the same laws, as well for the present life as for the time to come; you oblige him to obey you and to be subject to you, and if he happen to forget for one moment the right you have to command him, if he neglects to execute your orders with a rigorous precision—misfortune to him! Imperious master, unpitiable executor of the rights of your domination, you spare neither blows, nor whips, nor privations; you chastise him by the punishment of hunger and thirst, you strip him, often you load him with chains and shut him up in a dungeon. Miserable man! While you know so well how to maintain your quality of master over a man, you are not willing to recognise the Master and Lord of all men!"—St. Cyprian. Treatise against Demetrius.

"Justice teaches men to know God and to love men, to love and support one another, being all equally the children of God."—Lactantius on Justice.

"Both religion and humanity make it a duty for us to work for the deliverance of the captive. They are sanctuaries of Jesus Christ, who have fallen into the hands of the infidel. It is Jesus Christ himself whom we ought to consider it our captive brothers; it is him whom we should deliver from captivity—him who has delivered us from death. We must redeem with a little money him, who has redeemed us with all his blood. Can we, no matter how little humanity we possess, believe that these captives are strangers to any one of us, who altogether form but one family?"—St. Cyprian to the Bishops of Numidia.

"Of evils similar to slavery Tertullian says—One cannot argue from scripture that it condemns such practices, but will it be argued from its silence that it does not condemn them?"— Tertull. Lib. Cor., p. 121.

St. Ambrose orders that, for the redeeming of captives, the priests sell if necessary, even the sacred vases. "The God who had not a piece of gold to give to his apostles, when he sent them to preach the gospel, had not more to give to his churches when he founded them. The church has gold, not to keep it, but to distribute it to the indigent in their necessities. To what good is it to keep that of which we do not make use? Do we not know of all the gold and silver, that the Assyrians found in the Temple of Jerusalem? Is it not better for the priest to make sure of the riches of the sanctuary, by placing them in the hands of the poor, than to expose them to become the prey of our insolent enemy? The Lord will say to us, 'Why, under your eye, do the poor die with hunger? With the gold that you have, you could give alms. Why are so many unfortunate beings subject to slavery, even to death, for want of being redeemed with gold? Men are better worth preserving than metals.' What have you to reply? 'Must we deprive the temple of its ornaments?' But the Lord will reply, 'It is not necessary that the sacred things be clothed in gold.'"—St. Ambrose. Treatise de Officiis, p. 103.

As to the express doctrines of the Catholic church on the subject of slavery, I find them laid down in terms that cannot be misunderstood in "The Catechism of the Council of Trent," written under the direction, and with the sanction, of Pope Pius V., under the head, "Seventh Commandment," it is laid down:—

The unjust possession and use of what belongs to another are expressed by different names. To take anything from a private individual is called theft; from the public, peculation; to enslave and appropriate the freeman or servant of another, is called 'man-stealing.'—Catechism of the Council of Trent. Ed. Ang., p. 47.

And then, at p. 420, the doctrine is further explained—"That those who pay not the labourer his hire are guilty of rapine, and are exhorted to repentance." In the words of Scripture: "Behold the hire of the labourers who have reaped down your fields, which by fraud has been kept back by you, crieth aloud, and the cry of them hath entered into the ears of the Lord of Sabaoth."

In Bancroft's recent History of the United States, a work written in no very favourable spirit to the Roman Catholic religion, the writer acknowledges that "the slave-trade between Africa and America was never sanctioned by the See of Rome; the spirit of the Roman church was against it."

"The Cardinal Ximenes, the gifted coadjutor of Ferdinand and Isabella, the stern grand inquisitor, the austere but ambitious Franciscan, saw in advance the danger which it required centuries to reveal, and refused to sanction the introduction of negroes into Hispaniola, believing that the favourable climate would increase their numbers, and infallibly lead them to revolt."—Bancroft, vol. i.

With respect to the part which the benevolent Las Casas[2] had in the introduction of negroes into the West Indies and America, Bancroft states, (what is, indeed, to be collected from the best of the old Spanish historians), that "it was not Las Casas who first suggested the plan of transporting African slaves to Hisbaniola."—Bancroft, vol. i. p. 169.

But what Bancroft did not know, and what the earlier historians have not noticed, has been brought to light by the researches of the recent historians of the apostle of the Indians. In the last document existing in the handwriting of Las Casas, Quintana[3] informs us that Las Casas expresses himself in the most contrite terms for having been instrumental to the introduction of African negroes, with a view of preventing the utter extinction of the Indian race; because in Las Casas' own words, "la misma razon es de ellos que de los Indios." The one had the same privileges and rights as the other; and, therefore, "he repented, judging himself (in his own words) guilty by inadvertence, and trusting that this plea would hold him excused before the Divine Judge of all." And well may his historian say, "Esta confession de su error, tan severa como candoroso, debe desarmar el rigor de la philosophia, y absolverte adelante de la posteridad."[4]

PAPAL SANCTION WITHHELD FROM SLAVERY IN ANY FORM.

Pope Leo the Tenth declared that "not the Christian religion only but nature herself, cries out against the state of slavery." —Vide Bancroft's History of the United States, vol. i. p. 172.

Pope Paul the Third, in two separate briefs, imprecated a curse on the Europeans who should enslave Indians or any other class of men. 1537. (See the brief in Remusal, Hist. de Chiappa, book 3, chap. 16.)

Pope Urban the Eighth issued another bull, still more expressly condemnatory of the slave-trade, east or west, dated 1639, and addressed to the Apostolic Chamber in Portugal.

Pope Benedict the Fourteenth confirmed these decrees by a new bull, addressed to the government authorities of the Brazils, in 1741.

Pope Zachary, on certain Venetian merchants having bought at Rome many slaves, to sell to the Moors in Africa, promptly forbade such an iniquitous traffic, and, paying the merchants their price, gave these slaves their liberty.—Vide Butler's Life of Zachary.

Pope Pius the Second, even earlier, in 1402, when Portuguese dominion was extended into Guinea, wrote letters to the Portuguese bishop proceeding thither, gravely animadverting on those Christians who carried away people into slavery.

Pius the Seventh, moved by the same spirit, concerted with the European government the means of suppressing this odious trade.

And finally, I refer to the recent bull of Gregory the Sixteenth for the abolition of slavery and the negro slave-trade—a document which must be considered calculated to effect much good in Cuba and other slave countries; and also to a memorial addressed to the Roman Catholic prelates on the subject of the communication of this express denunciation of the traffic in slaves, and the holding of those in bondage wrongfully and illegally enslaved.[5]

ON THE THIRD OF DECEMBER, 1839,

BULL OF POPE GREGORY I. FOR THE
ABOLITION OF THE SLAVE-TRADE,
THE NINTH YEAR OF THE PONTIFICATE.

Placed as we are on the supreme seat of the apostles, and acting, though
by no merits of our own, as the viceregent of Jesus Christ, the Son of
God, who, through his great mercy condescended to make himself
man and to die for the redemption of the world, we regard as a duty
devolving on our pastoral functions that we endeavour to turn aside
our faithful flocks entirely from the inhuman traffic in negroes, or
any other human beings whatsoever. Beyond a doubt, when the light
of the Gospel first began to diffuse itself, those unhappy persons who
were plunged into the severest condition of slavery, in consequence
of the numerous wars at that time, found their condition alleviated
among the christians. For the apostles, inspired by the Divine Spirit,
taught even their slaves to obey their carnal masters as Christ, and to
do the will of God heartily. They also taught their masters that they
should act well to their slaves, and do unto them what was just and
equitable, and to abstain from threats, knowing that the God, both
of them and of their slaves, dwells in heaven, and that with Him there
is no acceptance of persons. But while a sincere and universal spirit of
charity is especially enjoined by the law of the Gospel, and our Lord
himself said that he would consider any act of benevolence and mercy
done to the least or poorest, or denied, as done or denied to himself,
it readily followed, that the christians not only considered their slaves,
especially such as were christians, in the light of brothers, but were
even very prone to endow with liberty such as deserved it. Indeed
Gregorious Nissenas informs us, that such liberation of slaves was customary on the occasion of the paschal solemnities. Nor were there
christians wanting who, stirred up by a more burning zeal, subjected
themselves to slavery to redeem others, many of whom, that apostolic
personage, our predecessor, Clement I., testifies that he knew. Hence,
in the progress of time, as the clouds of heathen superstition became
gradually dispersed, circumstances reached that point that during several centuries there were no slaves allowed amongst the great major-
ity of the christian nations; but with grief we are compelled to add,
that there afterwards arose, even among the faithful, a race of men
who, basely blinded by the appetite and desire of sordid lucre, did not
hesitate to reduce in remote regions of the earth, Indian negroes, and
other wretched beings, to the misery of slavery; or finding the trade
established and augmented, to assist the shameful crime of the others.

Nor did many of the most glorious of the Roman Pontiffs omit severely
to reprove their conduct as injurious to their soul's health, and disgraceful to the christian name. Among these may be especially quoted
the bull of Paul III., which bears the date of the 29th of May, 1537,
addressed to the cardinal archbishop of Toledo; and another, still more
comprehensive, by Urban VIII., dated the 22nd of April, 1639, to the
Collector Jurium of the Apostolic Chamber in Portugal, most severely
castigating by name those who presumed to subject either East or
West Indians to slavery. Pope Benedict XIV. subsequently confirmed
these decrees of those distinguished Pontiffs by a new bull, addressed
to the heads of the governing authorities of Brazil, and other regions,
on the 17th of December, 1741. Even before another predecessor of
ours, more ancient than these, Pius II., in whose age the dominion of
Portugal was extended to Guinea, wrote on the 7th of October, 1642,
to the Portuguese bishop who was about to repair thither, a letter, in
which he not only gives to that high functionary, powers to exercise
with greater success his sacred ministry in those parts, but gravely
animadverted on the same occasion upon those christians who carried
away youths into slavery. And in our time, Pius VII., moved by the
same spirit of religion and charity as those who had gone before him,
seduously interposed his good offices with the men in power, that the
trade in blacks should at length be put an end to entirely amongst the
christians. These injunctions, and these good offices of our predecessors, served not a little, with the help of God, towards protecting
the Indians, and the other aforesaid races, both from the cruelty of
their invaders, and from the cupidity of the christian merchants; not to
such an extent, however, that the Holy See can have to rejoice at their
flocks having totally abandoned such practices, since on the contrary,
the trade in blacks, though diminished to some extent, is still carried
on by many christians; wherefore, we, desiring to avert this disgrace
from the whole confines of christianity, having summoned several of
our reverend brothers, their eminences the cardinals, to our counsel,
and, having maturely deliberated on the whole matter, pursuing the
footsteps of our predecessors, admonish by our apostolical authority,
and urgently invoke, in the name of God, all christians, of whatever
condition, that none henceforth dare to subject to slavery, unjustly
persecute, or despoil of their goods, Indian negroes or other classes of
men, or be accessories to others, or furnish their aid or assistance in so
doing; and on no account henceforth to exercise that inhuman traffic
by which negroes are reduced to slavery, as if they were not men, but
automata or chattels, and are sold in defiance of all the laws of justice and humanity, and devoted to severe and intolerable labours. We

further reprobate by our apostolical authority, all the above described offences as utterly unworthy of the christian name; and by the same authority we rigidly prohibit and interdict all and every individual, whether ecclesiastical or laical, from presuming to defend that commerce in negro slaves under any pretence or borrowed colour, or to teach or publish in any manner, publicly or privately, things contrary to the admonitions which we have given in those letters.

And finally, that this our bull may be rendered more apparent to all, and that no person may allege any ignorance thereof, we decree and order that it shall be published according to custom, and copies thereof be properly affixed to the gates of St. Peter, and of the apostolic chancel, every and in like manner to the General Court on Mount Pitatonio, and in the field of the Campus Florae, and also through the city, by one of our heralds, according to aforesaid custom.

Given at Rome, at the palace of Santa Maria Major, under the seal of the fishermen, (sub annulo piscatoris) on the 3rd day of December, 1839, and in the ninth year of our pontificate.

(Counter-signed by)

CARDINAL A. LAMBROSCHINI.

Notes

1. Prominent American abolitionists.
2. Bartolomé de las Casas (1474–1565).
3. Manuel José Quintana (1772–1857).
4. "This confession of your errors, as severe as it is candid, ought to assuage the rigor of the philosophy, and absolve you before posterity."
5. Madden noted: "The following is a copy of the memorial addressed to the Catholic Archbishops and Bishops in Ireland, in Synod assembled:

> My Lords,—The subject on which I presume to address your lordships, is one of great interest to religion and to humanity; and the expression of your lordships' opinion on it of vast importance at the present juncture. The advantage can hardly be overrated of giving the effect of a general publicity to the late rescript of his holiness the Pope for the suppression of the odious traffic in human beings, and the unhallowed system of slavery that has grown out of it.
>
> I humbly trust, that your lordships will consider less the insignificance of the person who addresses you, than the great necessity of adopting the course he has ventured to suggest. In the opinion of some of the best and ablest supporters of this cause, your lordships' publication and interpretation of this rescript, would be most eminently serviceable to the interests of humanity, which its object is to promote and to protect. The necessity of taking some step for the purpose of making

our countrymen in America acquainted with the obligation which this bull so forcibly points out, is universally felt by the advocates of this cause.

My Lords, in venturing to lay before your lordships a document containing a report of an address lately delivered in this city, on this subject, and making use of arguments founded on the opinions of its divines, and the decrees of its councils—the apparent presumption of one like me referring to such authorities, I trust, will be overlooked, and the object I had in view alone considered, that of taking away a plea, or a pretence, for the continuance of an evil that only wants the more recent condemnation of our ecclesiastical authorities for its universal reprobation. And thus a scandal to our people, and a pretext for censure, would be removed. In those distant lands to which I have referred, my official station affords me the means of knowing the ignorance that remains to be dispelled, and the calumnies to be refuted on this subject, as connected with the sanction which slavery has the audacity to derive from religion.

My Lords, it may seem an astounding paradox, that the very poverty of our country should raise up a power in a foreign land, potent enough to influence any question of political moment that rises in it, and to turn the scale, whatever way its feelings tend. Such is the political influence of the Irish emigrants settled in America, and such over them is the authority of the prelates of their native land, that were your lordships' public response to the recent decree of his Holiness communicated generally to our countrymen, the knowledge of its existence would probably not only be due to that publication, but, I might add, the question even of its very authenticity would be determined by your lordships' publication of it.

My Lords, deeply interested in a subject which I am practically acquainted with, in a Catholic country, where slavery unfortunately exists, in all the magnitude of its frightful evils, I address myself to your lordships under a less painful sense, if it be possible, of the terrible outrages offered to humanity by the trade in stolen men, and the system that grows out of it, the injustice of which transcends all the other oppressions that are done under the sun, than I feel for the desecration of our religion and the scandals to it which slavery and its demoralising effects are the fruitful source of, in those Spanish colonies, where that religion is in name the religion of the land, and where this contaminating influence is extended even over sacred things, and comes within the precincts of sacred places.

My Lords, even in those countries it is in the power of your lordships' opinion on this subject of slavery, to deal a heavy blow and great discouragement to it by the bare expression of your lordships' concurrence with the enlightened views that are taken of slavery in all its cruel forms, in the late decree.

I therefore, most humbly and respectfully beg to direct your lordships' attention to the advantages that would arise from giving publicity to the recent rescript condemnatory of the crime of slavery.

I have the honour to be, my Lords, with the most profound respect, your Lordships' most obedient humble servant,

R. R. Madden."

BARTHOLOMEW LAS CASAS

Several documents of the time of the "Conquistadors" recently brought to light by the researches of the excellent historian of Las Casas, Quintana,[1] present the character and proceedings of that benevolent man, in their true colours, and without concealing his errors, do ample justice to his noble virtues. He was born in the year 1474. Having accompanied his father to Cuba, and joined Narvaes[2] in his exploring expedition in 1514, he remained at a place where it was determined to found the city, now called Trinidad; and on the customary distribution of the Indians and the lands "Repartimientos de los Indios y las tierras,"[3] Las Casas was rewarded with a large allotment, both of slaves and land in this neighbourhood, and he commenced life thus as a planter and slave-master, in company with a good man, of the name of Pedro de Renteria, who, subsequently, from conscientious motives, abandoned his slave property. Las Casas in his own history says, he prosecuted his new pursuit with extreme energy (for he could enter into no pursuit without energy),, and it must be inferred that his slaves were severely worked "both in the mines and in the fields," for he says himself, he was perfectly unconscious of any criminality in holding these unfortunate people in slavery, in his own words, "en aquella materia tan ciego estaba por aquel tiempo el buen padre como los seculares todos que tenia por hijos."[4]

But at the feast of Pentecost, having to preach at Baracoa,[5] and referring to the Scriptures for a text, he happened to read the 34th chapter of Ecclesiasticus, and on coming to the words, "The most High approveth not the gifts of the wicked, neither hath he respect to the oblations of the unjust, nor will he be pacified by the multiplicity of their sacrifices." "He that offereth sacrifice of the goods of the poor is as one that sacrificeth the son in the presence of his father." "The bread of the needy is the life of the poor, he that defraudeth them thereof is a man of blood." "He that sheddeth blood, and he that defraudeth the labourer of his hire are brothers."

An immediate reformation was effected in his sentiments, he determined from that moment to abandon his pursuits, to renounce his share of the "Repartimientos," and to dedicate his life to the advocacy of the rights of the poor and oppressed. From this time, he inveighed against the slavery of the Indians from the pulpit; but the Spaniards heard him as they would now hear a man who would dare to preach against the evils of negro slavery. In the words of Las Casas, to say, that they could not hold the Indians in servitude, was the same as to say, that they could not make use of the beasts of the field. "El decir que no podian tenir los Indios en su servicio, era la misma que decir que los bestios del campo no podian servirse."

The word "Encomiendas" given to the Repartimientos, originated in a slight variation of the form used by Columbus, made by Ovando,[6] which ran thus. To you, so and so, so many Indians are allotted in such a district, to be instructed in our holy religion. "A vos Fulano se os encomiendan tantos Indios en tal cacique, y ensenales las cosas de nuestra Sante Fé Catolica." The abominable pretext of making the Indians slaves in order that they might be instructed in the faith, "que pudiesen ser doctrinada in la fé," from the beginning of the conquest to the period of the extermination of the whole race was never forgotten; and now for negro slavery the same impious and hypocritical apology continues to scandalize christianity in this Spanish colony.

In 1517, Las Casas, having visited San Domingo, returned to Spain, and was ordered by the king to send in a memorial of the remedy he proposed for the disorders in the West Indies, and for the protection of the Indians. The memorial was sent in, and a minute of it is still extant; amongst the various remedies he proposed was one that he had before less distinctly intimated, "to send to the West India islands labourers from Spain, and also to accord the privilege for the inhabitants of the West Indies, to carry away negroes, ("la libre saca de negros,") and to bring them to the islands to be employed on the sugar estates, and in the mines, ("que llevados alla se empleason en los ingenios del azucar y en el laboreo de las minas,") vide Quintanas Vidas Espanoles celebres, 3 tome, page 304, and the reason given for their importation is, that the labour was insupportable to the weak Indians. It is in vain to deny that Las Casas committed this most lamentable error, as many have asserted, and amongst others, the Abbé Gregoire,[7] Quintana has produced the original documents in which this suggestion is made by Las Casas. But they who claim Las Casas for an advocate of the slave-trade, are little aware that he himself heartily repenting of his proposal, condemns it in his own history, lib. iii, chap. 101, and in his own words, "Because they (the negroes) had the same rights as the Indians"—"porque la misma rozon es de ellos que de los Indios."

The government immediately put the proposal in execution. The privilege of stealing away the negroes from Africa, for the shortsighted benevolent project of alleviating the hardships of the Indians in Cuba and San Domingo, was sold to a courtier, the Baron de Bressa. This worthy Baron sold it to the Geneose, and eventually it proved abortive, so that Las Casas was obliged to go through the provinces of Spain, soliciting the labouring people to accompany him to the colonies, and after collecting a vast number, and obtaining the sanction of the court, and making a great outlay for the voyage, the people abandoned him, and returned to their homes. It seemed as if thus by not prospering his undertaking in either instance, it was designed to show that God had a controversy with him. When the episcopal dignity was conferred on him, on reaching his see, the first use he made of his pastoral power was to deny the sacraments to all those who held slaves and refused to give them up, and those who bought and sold them, "y que se compran y venden publicamente en este cuidad."

At Gracias Adios, on his way from Guatemala, the corporation received him in their assembly with the most outrageous injuries; the president, Maldanato, reviled him in the grossest terms, calling him the most opprobrious names, "Bellaco, mal hombre, mal fraile, mal obispo," to all which the venerable prelate, with his hand extended on his breast, his head bowed down, replied with humility, "I merit truly all that you say of me," yo lo merezco muy bien todo eso que U.S. dice Senor Licenciado Alonso Maldonado; while the other magistrates cried out, "Echad de ahi à ese loco," "Away with this madman from this place." On reaching Chiapa, however, in the midst of his enemies, at his entrance into the city when the streets were filled with people who had been lately clamorous for his destruction, the majesty of virtue and religion regained their empire, and as he passed on, the cry was general, "this is the holy prelate, the venerable protector and the father of the Indians;" "este es el Santo obispo, el venerable protector y padre de los Indios!" But in Spain, his character and principles were attacked with the greatest rancour, Dr. Juan Gines de Sepulveda,[8] a great theologian, a distinguished historian, and chaplain of Charles V., took up the advocacy of slavery and the slave-trade in opposition to Las Casas, in a work called Democritus the Second, he propounded the monstrous doctrine, that the Indians, and all barbarous people like them, were naturally slaves, and might lawfully be held in slavery, that it was lawful to make war on savages and to reduce them into servitude;—"que se subjugan a aquellos que por su suerte y condicion necessariamente han, de obdecer a otros no tenia nada de injusta, (y por consequencia)—que siendo las Indios naturalemcntc siervos, barbaros, incultos e inhumanas de se negaban solea suceden, a obdecer a atros hombres mas perfect as era justo sujetarlas por la fuerza y por la guerra a la manera que la Materia se sujeta a la forma, el cuerpo al alma, al apetito a la razon, lo peor a lo mejor."[9]

This work, which is still held in the highest estimation by Spanish slave-traders and slave-holders, was most ably and warmly refuted by Las Casas. At his departure from the West Indies the sinfulness of slavery was boldly denounced from the pulpit, by the father Montesino, a Dominican; but this good man was driven from the island, and had to plead his cause before the Emperor for preaching against the slavery of the Indians.

There are incontestible proofs given in Quintana. vol. iii. p. 467, that the introduction and commerce of negroes in America existed previously to the suggestions and recommendations made by Las Casas to the Spanish government. Besides Herrera's authority on this point, there are several others, and especially the inedited papers called "Extractos de Munos en la collection de Senor Iguina." By them we learn that a caravel was sent to Ovanda, by the government, with various classes of merchandise, stores, and seventeen negro slaves, "esclavos negros por sacar cobre de las minas y de este metal en la Espanola,"[10] long before Las Casas's recommendation.

In 1510, Diego de Nicuesa, in his ship Trinidad, by order and on account of the government, carried to San Domingo, thirty-six negro slaves.

1513. The treasury began to issue licenses for the slave-trade at two ducats each.

1514. Certain Portuguese were captured off San Domingo, and deprived of their bozal negroes. They memorialized their government complaining of this outrage, and ended by saying, that they had been deprived of "ciertos negros que llenaban hurlados de la costa de Guinea."[11]

As to the Abbe Gregoire's denial of Herrera's statement of Las Casas's proposal for Negro slavery, the documents brought to light by Quintana, leave no doubt whatever on the subject. Las Casas himself, in various of his works, refers to it, and in his memorial in 1516, presented to Cardinal Cisneros,[12] he suggests, que cada communidad mantenga algunos negros, "that every district should maintain a certain number of negroes." Vide Extractos de Munos. Previous to this memorial, when the government ordered him to propose some remedies for the state of things in "Tierra firma," he presented a memorial, and the third remedy proposed in it was, "que llevan francamente los negros y las negras."[13] Idem. In his contract with the government for his Cumana expedition, he stipulates for the privilege, for himself and his companions, of three negro slaves each, half the number males, half females. Even ten years after this period, in 1531, he maintained the same opinion and acted on it; and in the representation which he made to the council of the Indies,[14] bearing date 20th January, 1531. He says: "The remedy for the christians is certainly this, that your Majesty should be pleased to grant to each of the Islands 500 or 600 negroes, to be placed in the hands of fit persons for distribution among the planters, who now have only Indians." "El remedio de los christianos es este muy cierto, que S.M. tenga por bien aprestar a cada una de estas Islas 500 ó 600 negros, a los que pareciere que el presente bastaren para que se distribuyen por los vecinos que hoy no tienen otra cosa sino Indios." And in the same document he complains of the grandees throwing difficulties in the way of the Negro slave-traders, "no conceden libremente a todos cuantos quieran traer las licencias de los negros, lo cual yo pedire alcance de S.M."—Collection del Senor Iguina.[15]

But fortunately this good man at length discovered the signal error he had fallen into, and his consciousness of this error, and his repentance are fully detailed in his general history of the Indies.[16] Wherein speaking of himself and his former opinion, he condemns the error he had fallen into, and thus speaks of it:—

"And because certain Spaniards of this island, (San Domingo), said to the priest Las Casas, after their manner of viewing things, that the Dominican friars refused absolving those who held Indians, if they did not relinquish them, and therefore if a license was obtained from the king, if they might not carry hither from Spain a dozen of negro slaves, who would assist the Indians. The priest according with this proposition, stated in his memorials, that it would be an act of grace to the Spaniards in these islands, to permit them to bring from Spain a dozen of negro slaves, more or less. This advice that license should be granted to bring negro slaves into these lands, the priest Las Casas first gave, not considering the injustice with which the Portuguese had taken and made them slaves." Speaking of the representatives made to him by the Spaniards of San Domingo, he says, "they informed the priest Las Casas—suiting their statements to their views, that the clergy refused them the sacraments if they would not abandon their Indians, therefore they sought a license from the king to introduce about a dozen more or less of negro slaves, to enable them to relax the severity of the labour of the Indians. And the priest

Las Casas consenting to this proposal in his memorials, asked this favour for these Spaniards, to bring from Spain the dozen or so of negroes, to relieve the Indians." "Este aviso de que se diese licencia para traer esclavos negros en estas tierras dio primero el clerigo Casas no advirtiendo la injusticia con que los Portugueses, los toman y haren esclavos." Las Casas evidently speaks here of the first recommendation for the introduction of negroes into which he had been entrapped.

In the latest production from the pen of Las Casas, he confesses the grievous fault he had fallen into, and begs for the forgiveness of God in the most contrite terms, for the misfortunes he had brought on the poor people of Africa, by the inadvertence of his counsel, "and this confession," says his historian, "of his error, so full of candour and contrition—should disarm the rigour of philosophy, and hold his benevolent disposition absolved before posterity."

Let him, whose philanthropy is without fault, and whose nature is superior to error, cast the first stone at the memory of the venerable Las Casas.

Notes

1. Manuel José Quintana (1772–1857).
2. Pánfilo de Narváez (1470–1528), Spanish conquistador who participated in the conquests of Cuba and Mexico.
3. Land and slaves bequeathed by the Spanish government to settlers in the New World.
4. "The good Father was just as blind in those matters as were the lay people whom he treated as his own."
5. A city in eastern Cuba founded in 1512 by Diego Velázquez.
6. Nicolás Ovando (1460–1518), first royal governor of Hispaniola. He ruled from 1502 – 1509.
7. Henri Gregoire (1750–1831), French priest who fought for the rights of slaves.
8. Juan Ginés de Sepulveda (1490?–1573), Spanish humanist who challenged Las Casas's reformist views concerning the Indians.
9. "That one ought to subjugate those who by their natural condition ought to obey others. The Indians are by their very nature, barbarous uncultured, servile, and subhuman. It is natural thus that they should obey men who are better than they are and it was just, indeed, to control them, by force."
10. "Black slaves to take copper from the mines for Spain."
11. "Certain blacks who were snatched away from the Coast of Guinea."
12. Francisco Jiménez de Cisneros (1436–1517), confessor to Isabel I and founder of the University of Alcalá.

13. "Freely take black men and women away."
14. A council organized in 1509 by Ferdinand I of Spain to administer the crown's holdings in the New World.
15. "They don't freely grant permission to bring blacks, something I shall ask your majesty to do."
16. The reference is to Las Casas's ponderous *Historias de Indias*, which was begun in 1520 and finished in 1561.

EVILS OF THE CUBAN SLAVE-TRADE

I am well persuaded that, difficult as it may be to exaggerate the evils
of slavery, it is possible to damage the best cause by a foolish effort to
promote its interest at the expense of truth. And surely, a cause like
this whose efforts are directed to the removal of ills, terrible beyond
all other evils, that involves the question of life and death—that treats,
not of the doom of one man, or ten thousand, but of the destiny of
the whole people of a quarter of the globe—whose business is with
the wrongs and sufferings of stolen men, and whose denunciations
are for the atrocious deeds of christian brokers in the trade of blood,
who roll in riches and move in the goodly circles of Cuban society—
surely it requires no exaggeration of the evils of Cuban slavery. They
are great, indeed, beyond the power of imagination to picture to
itself. All that I have ever seen of slavery—and I have seen some of its
horrors in various countries—in Africa itself, in Asia likewise, and in
America, even in as bad a form as in either of these regions—all that
Clarkson[1] ever penned of the magnitude of its evils, when this trade
was at its height, or that Sturge[2] or Scoble[3] recently witnessed of its
mitigated atrocities, in the transition from slavery to freedom, in the
British colonies—and mitigated as they were, God knows they were
bad enough to be witnessed even by those already acquainted with all
the evils of this system, but still worse to be seen by persons whose
eyes were not accustomed to the practical horrors of slavery; yet all
that these gentlemen witnessed or described in our colonies, or that I
have myself seen there of cruelties inflicted or endured, falls infinitely
short of the terrible evils of the slave-trade, that is now carried on in
Cuba.

It is little to say, that 25,000 human beings are annually carried
into Cuban slavery; that at the expiration of thirty years from the date
of the abolition of the slave-trade on the part of Great Britain, the
odious traffic continues in full force; that no small amount of foreign
capital is invested in this trade; that British subjects, now that slavery

is put down in our colonies, are embarking their means with impunity in slave properties in Cuba, are buying their slaves of necessity in the slave market, for there is no natural increase of the slave population of Cuba, but a terrible decrease by deaths; which, at the ordinary mortality on the sugar plantations, would sweep away the race in slavery, in ten years, and, according to Humboldt's calculation, in much less, for he states this mortality to vary from ten to eighteen per cent per annum.

It is little to say that the mortality on the middle passage from Africa to Cuba is very great, that it averages at the very lowest computation, twenty-five per cent.: that I have known a single slaver to lose one hundred out of three hundred, nay, two hundred and fifty, out of seven hundred; that between the wars that are made to spoil a village and steal its people, the slaughter in the strife, the spearing of the old and infirm, the morality of the slave coffle on the frightful journey to the coast, often a distance of thirty days from the interior, through a wilderness, where the land-marks are the heaps of human bones bleaching in the sun, the remains of the victims of former slave-trading adventures, the resting place of former coffles, the final place here of rest indeed for thousands upon thousands of human beings, who sank under fatigue, and whom God mercifully saved from the slow death of Spanish slavery; the further mortality on board the slaver from the sweeping pestilence of small-pox and dysentery, from the baneful effects of the contaminated atmosphere of a crowded slave-ship. From all the sufferings, terrible beyond any idea I ever formed of misery, till I saw that human hell, a slave-ship, crammed with chained men, cramped, crowded together, worn with suffering—spectres of men, breathing an atmosphere that came steaming up from the hot hold, with such horrible effluvia, that to me, somewhat acquainted as a medical man with the effects of the contaminated air of crowded places in gaols and hospitals, in countries too where the pestilence that walks by noon day, lives, moves, and probably has its being—it seemed to me astonishing that life could be maintained in so foul an atmosphere, or under so frightful an amount of pain and suffering as I had witnessed in those slave-ships that had fallen under my observation. The further mortality from the loss of the mutilated negroes on board the slavers, when from ophthalmia they become blind, or from scrofulous ulcers they become so maimed in their members as to be unfit for sale, at the sale marts of Cuba; and to save the provisions, these worthless and exhausted slaves are slipped over the side; the further mortality from the waste of life after the landing of the slaves during the first six months of acclimation, as it is called, consequent upon the hardships they have endured—when all these sources of misery are traced and the several amounts of mortality summed up, it will be found that for every stolen man, carried away from Africa, and who is alive in Cuban slavery at the end of six months, two human beings must have necessarily perished.

It is nothing to say this traffic is nefarious and appalling: why even the miscreants in Cuba, who are steeped to the very lips in slave-trade interests, foreigners and Spaniards, admit that the traffic is wholly unjustifiable—they condemn it freely, but they pray you to acquit their honour because the interests of the country require it to be carried on, and they have a very favourable opinion of the profitableness of it. It is useless even, perhaps, to enter into general details of the sufferings of these victims of the fell spirit of avarice that reigns in Cuba; you hear occasionally, perhaps, of 400 or 500 naked savages having been captured in a small slave-schooner; that every man, woman and child on board the captured vessel was brought into port, bare and naked; that the men were chained, and the children were sickly and exhausted, that the women were haggard, emaciated, miserably attenuated creatures. The mind either recoils from the painful impression of so much misery or the picture is one of such general suffering, that no adequate idea of the particular wrongs of the wretched negroes is conveyed to the mind. The portraiture of a battle affects us less than that of a single captive such as Sterne depicted; we see "the iron entering into his soul," and, yet we know we are but gazing on an imaginary sufferer.

Let me present to the imagination a real captive—one that has recently fallen under my own observation, and, I may add, under my own charge—one into whose soul the iron of affliction had verily and indeed entered—a single sufferer, a negress, taken out of a captured slaver, a wan, emaciated, listless, silent woman, a sullen savage, in the phraseology of Cuba, in cases of anguish and despair—a person who neither spoke nor moved from the place where she sat rocking her naked body to and fro all day long. There was a calm settled look of deep, unspeakable wretchedness in her regard, which made me dissatisfied with the explanation I received of the strangeness of her conduct, that she was a sulky negress, and showed no thankfulness for anything that was done for her, like the other women. The others were dressed in the new apparel which had been just given them, enjoying the good fare now provided for them, and celebrating with songs and dances the happy change in their lot. I thought she must have great reason for such dejection; the poor thing left the food untouched that was brought to her at each meal; her new clothing lay folded up beside her; when she was asked through the interpreter to tell what ailed her, she gave no reply; day after day she was questioned, and deep sighs were the only answers that could be got from her.

Negroes are said by planters to be insensible to kindness; they, no doubt, have so many benefits to be grateful for, that any thanklessness, on their parts, is too glaring a defect to pass unnoticed. The kindness that was shown to this poor creature was appparently thrown away, but apparently only, for by little and little it subdued the sternness of her grief; and what grief could surpass her affliction—for hers was that of a mother robbed of her infant child? One day I stooped down to speak to her, and endeavoured to ascertain the cause of her trouble, while I was offering her some beads, such as I had given to some of her companions, she burst out crying. It seemed at last as if she had found ease, in giving vent to one loud outbreak of sobs and sighs. She wept bitterly, put her hands to her breast, then stretched out her arms, started up on her feet, and, looking wildly over the side of the vessel, cried out for her child—and over and over again she repeated the words—in fact this was her cry the live-long day. Ask her what you would, "the cry of the heart," continually was—"for her child." It was long before this tempest of sorrow was assuaged sufficiently to obtain from her any collected account of the loss of her infant. It appeared that when the slaver was chased by our cruiser, fifty of the negroes were thrown overboard (twenty-four of whom were picked up by the cruiser's boats) with the view of detaining the latter vessel, and of thus eluding the pursuit; and this part of the story was confirmed by the account of the humane and resolute captor himself, by the account given to me by Captain Hollond, of the whole affair, off the Isle of Pines. And during this commotion on board the slaver, and the mortal terror at seeing their comrades flung overboard, this unfortunate woman lost her infant, but how, at what period it was taken from her, she could not tell. No creature could seem more sensible of the sympathy that was felt for her than this poor woman. But how often have I been told these people are savages—they have no natural affections—the separation of families is nothing to them— the sundering of the ties that "bind mothers to children, and children to parents, is nothing to negroes?" They do admit that even the she-bear will pine after her lost cubs; but the grief of a negro mother for her child is only a gust of passion that proceeds, not from any emotions of the heart, but from the violence of the irascible temper of negro women. Oh! how often have I heard this language, and how often have I known these sentiments adopted by men—aye, even by ministers of religion, who tell you, in Cuba, as well as in America, they see no hardships in slavery—that the slaves are kindly treated, are well fed, and decently clad, and have nothing to complain of! What do these gentlemen know of slavery? They eat and drink, no doubt, in the houses of the opulent planters in the towns, and they reason on the strength of the goodness of their entertainments, that the slaves of their hosts are treated like their guests.

If I ask one of those reverend gentlemen at Havana or Charleston, how are the poor slaves treated in those places—They see nothing in the houses they visit to shock humanity. There is no scourging of men or women inflicted in their presence— the child is not torn from the mother's breast in the presence of the reverend gentlemen—they hear no howlings of grief or pain in these well-regulated families. No doubt of it; these planters of the towns whom they visit are men of honour and respectability, and therefore it follows, that "they are all honourable men;" all the tribe are necessarily humane, and every master is, by parity of reasoning, a kind owner, a merciful proprietor, and a considerate employer. I am sick of this language. I have heard it from intelligent, nay, even from "religious" men, and sometimes confounded, sometimes grieved, sometimes angered at such folly, falsehood I must not call it, I have asked these gentlemen, how often had they judged of the condition of the negroes, not in the houses, but on the sugar properties? Had they seen these properties in the absence of their friends, the planters?—Did they know how many hours the slaves worked?—How great is the mortality on their estates?—What is the proportion of the sexes?—What modes of punishment are in use?—but I have never received any satisfactory reply, and generally speaking, these are matters of which our tourists are left in total ignorance.

Notes

1. Thomas Clarkson (1760–1846), British abolitionist. He wrote *History of the Abolition of the Slave Trade* (1808).
2. Joseph Sturge (1793–1859), British abolitionist.
3. John Scoble, first secretary the British and Foreign Anti-Slavery Society.

CONDITION OF SLAVES IN CUBA

If it be true that negro slaves have always been treated with peculiar mildness in the Spanish colonies, it follows, that the slaves of the island of Cuba, for example, are a contented race, that they are not overworked, nor underfed, nor ill-clad; that the sexes are equalized, that the mortality is small, and the increase by births considerable; that the amount of produce obtained by the labour of a given number of slaves is less than it has been in former years in the British colonies—that there is a considerable number of aged slaves on the estates—that the pregnant women are allowed exemption from hard field-labour in the last six or eight weeks of their pregnancy—that the females are not usually flogged—that the children are instructed in the elements of the christian faith—that the negroes on the estates are married by ministers of religion—that they are suffered to attend a place of worship on the Sabbath-day—that it is not lawful to hunt them down by dogs when they are fugitives from the estates—that when they are scourged to death or killed by violence, the white man, who is their murderer, may be brought to justice, and punished with the utmost rigour of the law—but not one of these measures of justice, or means of protection for the praedial slaves are known to exist in Cuba—not a single one of these I have pointed out is to be looked for, to the law, and yet the law allows these things, and solemnly condemns every withdrawal of them. But the law was never framed with any reasonable prospect of being enforced, it never has been enforced, and, what is more, it never can be enforced against the planters, who are the transgressors of it, because in fact, these are the men who are entrusted with the execution of it. In the towns and cities, the case, is indeed, different with the domestic slaves; but what a small portion do these form of the number of slaves in Cuba! These domestic slaves, especially those of the opulent proprietors, comparing their condition with that of the praedial slaves, may be said to be fortunately circumstanced. They have the power, in the large towns and cities, of availing themselves of the privileges the law accords them. If they have a harsh owner, they may demand permission to seek another master, and it is compulsory on that master to sell them, either for the sum he paid for them, or at such a rate as the Sindico, or the special protector of the slaves, and the judges may determine, in consideration of any reasonable increase in their value, or in consequence of their having been taught a trade or calling. But how is the praedial slave to avail himself of these legal privileges? The officers of justice in the country-towns are usually slave-holders themselves; the estate may be ten, nay twenty miles distant from a town; the Sindicos, the Alcaldis, the Capitanos de parudos, all are planters. The idea of a praedial slave going to the mayoral or overseer, and telling him he wants a "paper,"— a permission for two or three days to seek another master, (buscar amo) would be laughed at in Cuba; the unfortunate negro who would make so daring an attempt to obtain his rights, would, in all probability, be flogged on the spot; he dare not leave the estate to seek the Sindico in any adjoining town; and, no matter what injustice may be done him, were he to pass his master's gate, he would be subjected to punishment, "bocco abajo,"[1] without appeal as a fugitive, and if he still presumed to talk of the law, and to insist on being taken before a magistrate to claim the privileges which that law gave him, he would then be treated with a degree of rigour beyond the law, as an insolent and rebellious slave. But granting that he succeeded in getting to the Sindico, the Alcaldi, or the Capitano de partidos, what chance of justice has an unfortunate slave in Cuba against the powerful influence of a rich, and perhaps a titled, owner? The planter is the friend of the authorities of his district, they dare not disoblige him, and if they dared, they are at last to be gained over by a bribe, or got rid of, by a remonstrance to the govemor, and a suitable present to the assessor of the governor, who is one of the great law-officers of the crown. How in the name of common sense is the law to be looked to, in a Spanish colony for the mitigation of the evils of slavery, or the protection of the slave? The excellence of the Spanish civil law is admitted by every one, yet the iniquity of Spanish tribunals, the corruption of Spanish judges, and the incomparable villainy of the Spanish lawyers, is proverbial in all the colonies of Spain. Justice is bought and sold in Cuba with as scandalous publicity as the bozal slaves are bought and sold in the barracones. Is there a man in Cuba who had suffered wrong in property or in person who would be mad enough to go for redress into a court of law, and expect to obtain it by trusting solely to the merits of his case? How then are we to expect from any code, for the regulation of negro slavery, justice for the slave who has not the means to buy the judge? How are we to expect to restrain the cruelty, or to control the cupidity of men, who have the means to bribe the bench of every tribunal in the land, to make "impegnos," as these solicitations are called, with the sons, and servants, the cousins, and the familiars of the judges in their cause? Is it then to cedulas and laws, to parchment justice, or to statute book benevolence, we are to look for that peculiar character of mildness, which we are told, is the characteristic of slavery in Spanish colonies? Surely what we know of slavery in every country where it has existed, should be sufficient to satisfy every enlightened person, that bondage is an evil that cannot be mitigated by any partial measures of reform, so as essentially to serve the slave, to improve the system, to humanise the master, and thus to benefit society at large. But in Cuba it is not that I have heard or read of the atrocities of Spanish slavery, but I saw them with my own eyes. I lived for a whole year at the Havana, before I could so far disembarrass myself of the merchant-planter influence of that place (that deadening influence of slavery which steals so imperceptibly over the feelings of strangers in the West Indies), as to form an opinion for myself, and to trust to my own senses alone for a knowledge of the condition of the praedial slaves. It was only when I visited estates, not as a guest of the proprietors, seeing through the eyes of my hospitable hosts, thinking as they thought, and believing as they saw fit to administer to my credulity, the customary after-dinner dose of the felicity of slaves —it was only when I went alone, and unknown and unexpected, on their estates, that the terrible atrocities of Spanish slavery became known to me. I have already said, and I repeat the words, so terrible were these atrocities, so murderous the system of slavery, so transcendent the evils I witnessed, over all I had ever heard or seen of the rigour of slavery elsewhere, that at first I could hardly believe the evidence of my senses. Nay, I have known men of great intelligence, whom I myself accompanied over estates in various parts of the country; and here in Cuba, so terrible were the admissions made by the mayorals or overseers on the estates we visited, that they could not believe they heard correctly the accounts that were given to us, even by the managers themselves, of the frightful rigour of the treatment they described. Till we made partially known at the Havana the evils that had come to our knowledge, on the sugar estates especially, there were persons who had resided there for years, who said they were utterly ignorant of these evils, but, who having read certain laws for the protection of slaves, and seen certain cedulas for the nominal mitigation of the cruelties of slavery, had actually imagined that the laws were enforced, and the negroes happy and humanely treated.

With respect to my own experience, it is not by particular instances of cruelty or oppressions the fact is to be established that slavery in Cuba is more destructive to human life, more pernicious to society, degrading to the slave, and debasing to the master, more fatal to health and happiness, than in any other slave-holding country on the face of the habitable globe. Instances of cruelty enough no doubt have come to my knowledge, of the murder of negroes, perpetrated with impunity, of men literally scourged to death, of women torn from their children, and separated for ever from them; of estates where an aged negro is not to be seen—where the females do not form a third part of the slave population, nay, of estates where there is not a single female; of labour in the time of crop on the sugar properties being twenty consecutive hours, frequently, for upwards of six months in the year, seldom or never under five, and of the general impression prevailing on this subject, and generally acted on by the proprietors, that four hours sleep is sufficient for a slave. These cases, were I to describe without a shade of colouring to heighten the effect of the naked outline of so frightful a detail, I am persuaded it would seem marvellous that such things could take place in a christian land—could occur in the present age—could be done by men who move in society, who are tolerated in it, and bear the name and wear the garb of gentlemen. There is an argument stated and restated hundreds of times in answer to the ordinary charges of ill-treatment brought against slave-owners, namely, that it is the interest of a man to give good treatment to the beast and "pari passu,"[2] to the slave he keeps for use, or sale, or hire. No doubt it is his duty, but is it his interest, according to his ideas, to do this? Is it the supposed interest of the owners of our miserable hacks to treat the animals thus which they let on hire, or use daily, or rather, can you persuade these people it is their interest to do this? Unquestionably you cannot. They act on the principle that a quick return of the money outlaid on horse-flesh, no matter how great the wear and tear of the animal, that is worked or hired, is better than moderate work with small gain, and a longer use of the means from which that return is derived. These persons deny it is their interest to spare their horses, and admit it is their interest to get the greatest possible quantity of work in the shortest space of time, from their hacks, and when they are worked off their legs to purchase new ones. In fact, it is on this very principle the fast mail coaches are horsed and run. But I have heard it said, however they may work them, it surely is their interest to feed them well. To this I answer, the universal feeling of the tribe is this, their true interest is to keep them cheaply. True it is, if they gave them treble the quantity of good hard provender, they would last much longer; but you cannot persuade these men you understand their interests better than they do, you may indeed easily persuade the owner of a stud of race-horses of the soundness of your opinion, but the high-blood racers that belong in England to gentlemen on the turf, in proportion to the hacks and state-horses, are about in the same ratio, as the slaves in Cuba, belonging to intelligent, considerate, humane proprietors, are to the wretched negroes in the hands of unreflecting, grasping owners.

The murder of a slave by a white man, in no case whatever, is punished with death. During my residence in Cuba, some of the most atrocious murders that I ever heard of, came to my own immediate knowledge, the murders of slaves by their masters or mayorals, and not in any one instance was the murderer punished, except by imprisonment or the payment of the costs of suit. During General Tacon's administration of the government in the latter part of the year 1837, in the village of Guanabacoa, a league from the Havana, where I was then residing, the murder of a slave was perpetrated by his master, a well known lawyer of the Havana. The name of the murderer is well known, and he moves without reproach in the goodly circles of genteel society at Havana, in that society where the capitalist who has acquired his riches in the abominable slave-trade, by the especial favour of his sovereign, bears the title of "Excellentissimo," where the prosperous dealer in human flesh now retired from the trade, is a noble of the land, where the foreign merchant who still pursues the profitable traffic on the coast is the boon companion of the commercial magistrates of the place, and where the agents of foreign governments themselves are hailed as the private protectors and avowed well-wishers of the interests of the trade. The murdered slave of the Cuban lawyer was suspected of stealing some plated ornaments belonging to the harness of his master; the man denied the charge; the customary process in such matters to extort a confession from a suspected slave was had recourse to. He was put down and flogged in the presence of his master. The flogging it appeared by the sworn testimony of the witnesses who were present, given before the commandant of Guanabacoa, a colonel in the army, a gentleman of the highest character, commenced at three o'clock, it ceased at six, the man having literally died under the lash; a little time before the man expired, he had strength enough left to cry out, he would confess if they flogged him no more. The master immediately sent for the commissary of police to receive his confession; this officer came, and stooping down to speak to the man, he found him motionless; he said the man had fainted. The brutal master kicked the lifeless body, saying, "the dog was in no faint, he was shamming." The commissary stooped down again, examined the body, and replied "the man is dead." The master hereupon called in two physicians of Guanabacoa, and rightly counting on the sympathies of his professional attendants, he obtained a certificate, solemnly declaring that the negro had laboured under hernia, and had died of that disease. In the meantime, the atrocity had reached the ears of the Captain-General Tacon, the Alcaldis of Guanabacoa were ordered to inquire into the matter; they did so, and the result of the inquiry was, of course, the exculpation of the murderer. General Tacon, dissatisfied with the decision immediately ordered the military officer commanding at Guanabacoa to proceed to a strict investigation, de novo, without reference to the decision of the civil authorities, and this gentleman, with whom I was well acquainted, proceeded with all the energy and integrity belonging to him, to the inquiry. The result of this inquiry was an able report, wherein the commandant declared that the testimony adduced, plainly proved that the negro had died under the lash in presence of his master, in consequence of the severity of the punishment he received during three hours. I have entered at large into this case, because I speak from actual knowledge of the judicial proceedings, and on the authority of the judge in the cause. Now what was the result in this case, why, in due time, the Captain-General communicated to the commandant the law opinion of the assessor or legal adviser of his administration, to the effect that the report was evidently erroneous; inasmuch as the commandant had examined negro witnesses in the investigation, when their masters were not present, which was illegal, and consequently all the proceedings were vitiated. In plain English, the murderer was acquitted, and the upright officer who declared him guilty was rebuked, nay, more he was ultimately removed from his post at Guanabacoa. The folly of talking about illegality in the proceedings is evident, when it is considered that the setting aside the civil authorities, and putting the cause in the hands of the military tribunal was a course obviously illegal, but rendered necessary in the mind of the governor by the base corruption of the civil tribunal, and the iniquity of its decision. On inquiry into the amount of money paid by the murderer in the way of bribes to obtain the decision in his favour, and the costs of suit, I found that the expenses amounted to 4000 dollars.

The next case I have to direct attention to, has been given to the world in the recent admirable work of Mr. Turnbull[3] on Cuba, a work which it required more honesty, closer observation, and a higher spirit of humanity to produce, than any work on the West Indies that has been given to the public. I happened to be with Mr. Turnbull, on the journey of which he speaks in reference to this case, when a person who accompanied us on our return from a sugar estate in the vicinity of Guines, informed us that the estate in question was the terror of all the negroes in the vicinity. Of this fact, what we had ourselves witnessed of the management of the property, and what we had heard from the mayoral himself, left but little cause to doubt, but it was not without surprise we learnt that this very overseer, who was still left in charge of the estate, had recently been brought before the authorities of Guines on the charge of flogging one of the slaves of the estate to death, and that the result of this investigation, was similar to that of the case at Guanabacoa; the body of the murdered slave was examined by medical men, and the usual certificate was given in all due form, satisfactorily accounting for the death of the negro, and in the eye of the law of Cuba, the slave that was murdered by a white man and expired under the lash of legitimate authority, died a natural death. The wretch who committed this act left the court, of course, without a blemish on his character, and the employer of this man, who had taken him back into his service, to the terror of every negro on his estate, this respectable planter was living at ease, fifty miles from the scene where the blood of his murdered negro was shed with impunity, enjoying the pleasures of the Havana, and perhaps, by the urbanity of his manners, and the hospitality of his house, and the indulgent treatment of his domestic slaves, convincing the passing tourist, who was fortunate enough to be his guest, of "the peculiar mildness of slavery in the Spanish colonies."

The next case of negro murder committed by a mayoral, of which I have to speak, came to my knowledge in the autumn of 1839. I was travelling in the vicinity of Matanzas, accompanied by a gentleman who resided in that district. I was informed by my companion that he had just received very unpleasant intelligence of an acquaintance of his, a mayoral of an estate on the Pan of Matanzas, who had unfortunately flogged a worthless negro, and the worthless negro had unfortunately died, and the soldiers had just been sent down to arrest the mayoral, and they did not find him. The misfortune of the mayoral touched me indeed less than the murder of the slave; but if my sympathies had been ever so strongly directed to the inconvenience the mayoral had been put to, by his flight, I might have been comforted by the assurance that he had only to keep out of the way for some time, and the thing would pass over; or, if he were taken, at the worst, he had only to suffer in purse, and perhaps in person, by imprisonment for some time, if he was a poor and friendless mayoral. This was only another vacancy in the negro gang to be filled up by the purchase of a new bozal—another life taken away under the lash to be added to the list of Cuban crimes—another item in the long account that slavery has to settle with a just God.

The last case of murder perpetrated on a slave by a white person, to which I will refer, took place at the Havana in the year 1839. This crime was commiteed by an American woman on a poor negro girl, under such horrible circumstances of cold-blooded cruelty, that I doubt if there is any parallel to be found to it in the records of crime in Cuba. The girl that was murdered belonged to a Spaniard of the Havana, who was the paramour of the American. This woman was possessed of property to a considerable amount. She had been long resident in Havana, and was somewhat remarkable for her personal attractions. Her friend, the Spaniard, had sent to her house one of his slaves to assist her, and this girl became the victim of her jealousy, it is supposed—for no other adequate reason, has been assigned for the cruelties practised on her. The cries of the unfortunate girl had been heard in the adjoining houses: at length the usual screams were heard no longer, but night after night the sounds of continued moaning were noticed by the neighbours, and at length they gave information of the matter to the police. The commissary of police proceeded to the house of the American woman. On searching the outhouses in the yard, in one of these offices, converted into a dungeon, they found a dying negro girl, chained by the middle to the wall, in a state that shocked the senses of all who were present, so loathsome a sight, so pitiful an object, the persons who discovered this unfortunate girl never beheld. On releasing her from this dreadful dungeon, where she had been, she could not tell how long, it was found that the chain round her body had eaten into the flesh, and the ulcers in it, were in a state of gangrene. She was taken to the hospital, and she died there in two or three days' time.

The monster who committed this murder, when I left the Havana, in October last year, was alive and well; in prison, indeed, but in one of the halls of distinction (salas de distinction), where the prisoner who has money, no matter what his crime, may always obtain superior accommodation. She was visited there by persons of my acquaintance. She did not admit, that she had committed any crime, and she had no fear for the result of the process that was going on, except on the score of its expense. She looked on her imprisonment as a conspiracy only of the Spanish lawyers to get money from her, because they knew she was rich; and in this she probably was not much mistaken.

The teniente Gobernador, one of the principal officers of state, was in the habit of visiting her in prison, and encouraging her with the assurance that her suit would speedily be terminated, and that she had nothing worse than banishment to fear. A lawyer of the name of Garcia had defended her some short time before her committal on the present charge, in another case of cruelty practised by her on a slave, and he publicly boasted that if she had come forward in the present case, with a sufficient sum, he would have brought her through her present difficulty, without any more inconvenience than in the former instance. Such is the administration of justice in the island of Cuba, and the execution of those laws which are thought, so mild in their character, and benevolent in their principles, that the slave who lives under them, is protected from injustice, and in consequence of their excellence, that the slaves in Spanish colonies are comparatively happy. It was said by the late Mr. Canning[4] that all laws for the partial amelioration of the condition of slaves, were necessarily defective, because such laws had no executive principle, inasmuch as the persons who were expected to carry them into operation, were interested in defeating them: My experience entirely bears out the assertion of Mr. Canning; and both, I am sorry to say, are at variance with the common opinion entertained even by well-informed persons in this country, on the subject of Spanish slavery.

R.R.M.

Notes

1. Face down.
2. With equal step, likewise.
3. David Turnbull (1811–1863), British abolitionist and author of *Travels in the West: Cuba with Notices of Porto Rico and the Slave Trade* (1840).
4. George Canning (1770–1827), British statesman.

LAWS FOR THE PROTECTION
OF SLAVES IN CUBA

In the report presented by Mons. A. de Tocqueville[1] to the Chamber of Deputies on the 23rd of July, 1839, in the name of the commission charged with the examination of the proposition, relative to the slaves of the French colonies, I find very important errors, on the subject of the laws for the protection of negroes held in bondage in the Spanish colonies. At p. 17 of the published report, I find it stated, that "it is of public notoriety in the New World, that slavery has always had with the Spaniards a peculiar character of mildness; one can convince himself of this in reading over the ordinances made by the kings of Spain, at an epoch when, amongst the other nations of Europe, the laws for the government of slaves were so strongly tinctured with barbarity. The Spaniards who showed themselves so cruel towards the Indians, have always ruled their slaves with a singular humanity. In their colonies, the distinction between blacks and whites was less than in all the others, and the authority of the owner resembled more that of a father of a family, than of a master. The slave, better treated in these colonies, sighed less after liberty, which ought to be preceded by arduous exertion; hence the legislator accorded him a right, which he very seldom wished to avail himself of." Now in the above statement, there are six distinct propositions, and five of them are entirely erroneous; namely these—1st. That negro slavery has always had in the Spanish dominions "a peculiar character of mildness."[2] 2nd. That any sufficient proof of such a character could be fairly drawn, from the ordinances of the kings of Spain for the government of their distinct colonies. 3rd. That the Spaniards who had been such cruel masters to the Indians, had always "treated their slaves with singular humanity." 4th. That the authority of the master resembles that of a father of a family. 5th. That in consequence of good and humane treatment, the slaves seldom desired to avail themselves of the privilege of claiming their freedom by purchase; and the only statement that is really correct in the whole passage, is contained in these words; "In these colonies the distinction between blacks and whites was less than in all the others,"—presuming the meaning of the observation to be, that among the Spaniards, the prejudice against the stolen people of Africa, on account of their complexion, is less than amongst the colonists of other European States. Such unquestionably is the fact, and there is too much Moorish blood in the veins of the descendants of the old "Conquestadors," for the feeling to be otherwise. Tolerably well acquainted with some of the British West India islands, with one of them, both previously and subsequently to the act of emancipation,[3] and having seen something of slavery in many eastern countries, I brought perhaps some little knowledge of the condition of men held in slavery to the subject, which has been the object of anxious inquiry with me, during a residence of upwards of three years in a Spanish colony, where slavery flourishes, and where upwards of four hundred thousand human beings, exist in that condition. Perhaps this extensive acquaintance with slavery in various countries during the last ten years, may have qualified me to form some opinion of the relative evils or advantages of slavery in a Spanish colony.

The first proposition—"That slavery has always had with the Spaniards a peculiar character of mildness," is one that I have seen stated in books so often, and heard laid down so frequently by merchants who have resided in Cuba—by naval officers who have visited the shores and harbours of that island; and by transient visitors who have made tours of pleasure, or winter journeys, in pursuit of health, from one large town on the coast to another; and seen the interior economy of one of two estates of opulent proprietors, what in our colonies would be called "crack plantations," that I really feel astonished at the amount of error that prevails on this subject—error so great, and held by men entitled to credit, that I have sometimes felt absolutely doubtful of the evidence my own senses, and when the irresistible conviction of the excessive rigour of slavery in Cuba has been forced on my mind, and then I have dwelt on the appalling scenes I have witnessed, it often seemed hopeless to me, and even imprudent for me, to attempt to disabuse the public mind, and to set my experience against the opinions of many people, whose sentiments on any other subject I considered entitled to respect. But on a question of such vast importance and where erroneous sentiments are calculated to do so much injury to the objects of the solicitude of anti-slavery exertion, it would be an act of cowardice to suppress the truth, or at least one's strong persuasion of it, in deference to error, however generally diffused, or honestly adhered to, it may be. These erroneous conclusions, that Spanish slavery is of a peculiarly mild character, are arrived at by four ways of viewing this question; they may be briefly stated as follows: —1st. It is concluded, that because the laws for the government of slaves in the Spanish colonies are mild, that these laws are executed, and the slaves are happy. 2nd. It is considered by some who visit the large sea-port towns, that the condition of the praedial slaves is similar to that of the domestic servants, and that because the latter are lazy, well-fed, and decently clad, and lightly worked negroes, the poor field slaves are likewise idle and indulged, kindly treated and contented slaves. 3rd. The condition of the slaves is judged of, by men who have no immediate interest in slavery, but who have long resided in slave-countries, or been in places where opportunities of visiting these colonies, have made them acquainted with the proprietors of estates, and in course of time, familiar with their views, then favourable to their interests, and at length accustomed to the evils of slavery, and insensible to the sufferings of its victims. 4th. The treatment of slaves in general, in Cuba and elsewhere is inquired into, by transient visitors and tourists at the tables of the planters, over the wine of the slave-holders—and where truth is drowned in hospitality, and the legitimate inquisitiveness of a stranger's curiosity is merged in a courteous acquiescence in the sentiments, or at least the statements of a liberal entertainer, and a gentlemanlike host. Now, of these different ways of coming towards conclusions, it is evident that it is to the first the signal error of this Report is to be attributed. In fact, it is admitted that the opinion of the mildness of Spanish slavery is derived from the royal ordinances and laws made for the regulation of it.

I freely grant that the spirit of these laws and ordinances is humane, but the great question is, are such laws compatible with the interests of the slave-owners? Are they put in execution? Negro slavery, as it ever has existed in the West India colonies, has been a condition in which the profitableness to the master of unpaid labour, for the time being, has always rendered the happiness of the labourer, a question of comparative unimportance. What, one might call humanity to the negro, there is not a proprietor in Cuba who would not deem injustice to the planter. You cannot legislate partially, humanely, and yet efficiently, for any slave colony in a prosperous condition—you may pass measures of general effect for the total abolition of slavery, but you can carry none into execution for effectually modifying its nature, and leaving unpaid labour to be wrung out of its victims, while a show is made of surrounding its compulsion, with humane arrangements, duly detailed in royal cedulas, and set forth in legal books with all the solemn mockery of Spanish law. This report states as a curious anomaly in the history of Spanish slaves, that while the Indians were treated by the Spaniards with such terrible cruelty, the negroes, on the contrary, have always been treated with peculiar mildness. I need hardly observe, that while the poor Indians were writhing under the lash of the most unmitigated cruelty the world up to that period ever saw; while the Spanish colonies were exterminating the whole race of their victims, by the astounding rigour of their slavery; the kings of Spain were dictating benevolent cedulas, and humane ordinances for the treatment of the unfortunate slaves; while the council of the Indies was continually framing laws for the better regulation of the repartimientos, or distributions of the natives; while the heads of the Spanish church, the mitred politicians of the day; half statesmen, half churchmen—were constantly sending out missions and commissions to co-operate with the illustrious apostle of the Indies,[4] the protector of the slaves—in fact, while all the machinery of the government that was four thousand miles off, was brought to bear on this question of the amelioration of slavery in the Spanish colonies, yet the Indians perished in the mines, they died under the lash, sunk under famine in caves, or sought in voluntary death, a final refuge from Spanish cruelty. Yes, the whole race perished, while the kings of Spain and its ministers were framing laws, impracticable, because they were partial, measures of relief for the preservation of their Indian subjects. The same terrible system of cruelty is going on this day in the Spanish colonies—the same terrible evils are silently in operation. Change the term Indians for negroes, the word mines for plantations, and in every other respect the same bloody tragedy is acting over again— the same frightful work of extermination, the same cruel mockery of staying the evil by laws without enforcement, cedulas, without a hope being entertained of their being carried into effect, is now practising in Cuba, and the awful waste of human life, that in the time of the Indians was, for a limited period made up by the ravages of the man-robbers on the coasts of the New World, has for three centuries been filled up in Cuba alone, by an annual importation that has now reached to the amount of twenty-five thousand stolen men from the shores of Africa. To understand thoroughly the subject of the laws in the Spanish colonies for the protection of slaves, it is necessary to refer to a work not easily to be met with, being only to be found in the hands of the Syndics, which is entitled, "Espocion sobre el origen, utilidad prerogativas, derechos y deberes de los sindicos, pro-curadores generales do los pueblas por D. Jose Serapio Majorrietta, abogada de la real audiencia." This book, it is to be noted, is printed at Puerto Principe, in Cuba, by royal authority, by command and at the expense of the real Audiencia, the highest law tribunal in the island; and it is the legal guide of the Syndics, or protectors of slaves, in the administration of justice between master and slave over the whole island, and by which they are bound to act. The work begins by stating that the Supreme Court, in the year 1766 created the office of Syndic; every town was placed under the legal protection of one of these officers; its rights were to be defended by them; and, in the words of the cedulas, "When there was any grave or important matter, it should be treated by them, joining themselves with some of the neighbours (juntandose con los vecinos) for the consideration of it. Now here is a most important regulation for the due administration of justice; in fact one giving to the accused the advantages, to a certain extent, of a jury. And now let us see how the law authorities of Cuba, as represented in this work, interpret these words. The treatise in question says—"These words are not to be understood in their literal sense; this method is contrary to the nature of our government, and for this reason, so responsible is the post of a Syndic, that he is appointed, not by an open meeting (cabildo abierto) of the corporation (aguntamiento), but by the votes of the judicial body, or the regidores. Their duties in the rural districts are to watch over the order and maintenance of the public markets, the prevention of monopolies in corn, meat, &c., inspecting the accounts of overseers, agents, &c., protecting the interests of proprietors of estates before the tribunals of the district, by all the legal privileges accorded them, even to the point of demanding the suspension of the royal laws or ordinances in which they may hurt or harm some private person (hasta el punto de poder pedir la suspencion, de las cedulas y reales rescriptos, en qui se donon a algun particular). Behold the value of all the royal laws for the protection of slaves. The Syndic, their protector, is likewise the legal defender of his master; and the suspension of every law that is distasteful to the latter, it is in the power of this officer to demand of the higher tribunals of the law. In fact, the whole secret of the conduct of the Cuban government, with respect to the fulfilment of the treaties with England for the suppression of the slave-trade, and the laws which enforce them, is here let out, and the shameful duplicity of the government of Spain, with respect to these royal orders, is disclosed, for at page 10 of the treatise in question, the opinion of the legal authorities of the island, is laid down as to the proper mode of interpretation, of the royal cedulas, when these are opposed to Creole interests, or supposed to be so, in these words—"It has been laid down by his Majesty, that his sovereign will is, with respect to these laws, that they be obeyed and not fulfilled;" and reference is made to lib.16, Now. Recap. (que se tienne manifestado que su soberano voluntad es, que se obedezcan y no se cumplan.) This seems to me to be the very acme, indeed, of public immorality; and there is no reason to doubt, the duplicity of the conduct here ascribed to the framer of these laws, and the weakness of his sovereign will, and that these things are done for the purposes of delusion, to throw dust in the eyes of foreign powers, by the enactment of laws which are to be received and not executed. Now with respect to the jurisdiction of the Syndics in the case of slaves, and the mode of interpreting the law for their defence, this treatise lays down very minute rules, and points out a course of proceeding which is universally acted on in Cuba, for it is to be remembered this treatise is published with the express sanction and approbation of the judges of the highest tribunal of the land, of the Real Audiencia. "It is to be observed," says the author, "either the rights which slaves complain of being infringed, are violated by their masters or a third person."

"In the last case, their complaint is to be preferred by their masters—by the general rules of right, which subjects them entirely to those who exercise dominion over them; but if the slaves attempt to complain (intentan presentarse) against their masters, then comes the authority of the Syndics, because by no other mode, can there be made a true decision, there being no legitimate litigation of parties, which consists in this, that the plaintiff and the criminal should be different persons. But supposing this distinction to be made in such a case (as perhaps some one might say it ought to be), it appears the slave ought to have the right of naming an attorney or agent (personero), and the law, that so much protects the natural defence of the slave, should leave in his power the exercise of this precious right. But how many inconveniences would not this measure cause? In the first place, slaves have no proper person (los esclavos no tienen persona), they have no representation in society, they are considered as things subject to the dominion of man, and ill could such beings name agents or attorneys, who cannot appear in their own character in our courts. And yet, if abating the rigour of fixed principles, we chose to leave to slaves, the free election of which we treat—how many and how expensive would be the insubordination alone of this class of domestics, when unfortunately interested men are not wanted to derive the advantage of lucre from such miserable discord. The Syndics, however, as chosen by the corporation, should be adorned with all the fine qualities we have already stated, and in the degree that they may undertake to protect the rights of these unfortunates, they will take care to beware of encouraging unjust complaints, by maintaining the slaves under due submission and respect, which system is certainly the most happy that can be adopted to conciliate the private interests of the slaves with those of the owners of them."

Now the next interpretation of the royal law, or cedula of 1789, which at p. 3, ordains the regulation of the daily labour of slaves "so that it should begin and conclude from sunrise till sunset," and moreover should leave them two hours of the intermediate time for their own use and benefit, is given in these terms—terms, indeed, most worthy of profound attention:—"But this is not observed, and neither the magistrates regulate the time of labour, nor do the slaves cease to serve their masters at all hours of the day;" (Esto nose observa y ni las justitias, regolan el tiempo de labor ni los esclavos dejan de servir a sus duenos en todas las horas del dia). Well may the expounder of the sentiments of the Royal Tribunal of the Audiencia of Cuba say, the laws are not observed, "the slaves cease not at all hours of the day to work for their masters." But this second Daniel, this Cuban commentator on Spanish law, rigidly, indeed, as he sticks to the sense of the colonial judges, tells but half the truth, when he says, that "the slaves cease not to work for their masters at all hours of the day;" he should have said on the sugar estates during the time of the crop, for upwards of six months in the year, at all hours of the night, with the exception of four for sleep. It did not suit the purpose of the Royal Audiencia to startle the ears or astonish the weak minds of the people in the towns with the frightful announcement of the appalling fact that the wretched negroes, in spite of the express terms of the royal law for the regulation of slave labour, were worked to death on these estates for twenty continuous hours, twelve in the field and eight in the boiling-house or at the mill, and that even on the coffee estates, where the necessity for hard labour is so much less, that at certain times of the year, it is a common practice during the bright moonlight nights to work the slaves at fieldwork, for four or five hours by the "Clara de la luna," as it is called. But what are the sentiments of the Royal Audiencia on the subject of that great privilege on paper, conferred by the laws on the slave, in the power nominally given him of purchasing his freedom, or portions of it, by the payment at once, or at different periods, of the price his master paid for him. It is to be observed that the payment of a part of this sum to the master gives the negro the legal right of having that sum deducted from his price, whenever he happens to be sold, and entitles him, as it is most erroneously but generally believed, to an immediate reduction of labour, in proportion to the sum paid.

The paying a sum of money to a master on the part of slaves towards the purchase of his liberty renders the payer what is called "coartado," the meaning of which is, in part manumitted. The word is derived from coartar, to cut or separate, and not from quartear, to divide into four parts, as is commonly supposed. "Some Syndics," says the law treatise in question, "have attempted to alleviate slavery, so as to pretend to concede a half of their time to slaves who are bound in service to their masters" (when they have paid half of their value to their owners); "but this opinion is not in conformity with the law, and the Syndics should respect the rights of the proprietary power without allowing themselves to be led astray by a notion of equity badly understood. The coartacion (or part payment made to a master by a slave towards the attainment of freedom) was not established to reduce slavery into halves, but only to prevent any alteration in the price to the slaves. A slave who, being worth 500 dollars, gives to his master 400 by way of coartacion, remains as subject to servitude as any slave who is so entirely. The master cannot be deprived of the proper rights of his authority, and the slave is under the obligation of devoting all his service to him; for such reasons the Syndics ought to avoid the wish to establish such demands." Then comes the interpretation of the law in Cuba as laid down in this treatise on that most important privilege of all to the negroes in Spanish colonies, the power nominally given by the law to the slave who is ill-treated or discontented with good cause with his master, to seek another owner on payment of the price at which he might be valued by the judicial authorities.

Now hear the mouth-piece of the Real Audiencia of Cuba on this subject. "The question may also be asked if slaves (coartados) have the right to go out of the power of their masters whenever they desire, and the answer is not difficult, if we consider that the slaves (enteros) entirely so are obliged to allege some great reason to compel their masters to sell them. And what difference can there be between one and the other, when we see that the yoke of slavery on all is the same? If the slaves (coartados) do not enjoy the rights of freemen, on what principle can they claim the right of changing masters at their pleasure? Is it for some light correction? This is not sufficient to enable them to use this privilege. And then, could the masters exercise their authority with the due severity which is necessary? By no means, and hence we have seen that the Real Audiencia has always repelled similar demands in all the suits that have been promoted on this point and brought for their superior decision. But some persons desire, notwithstanding, founding their opinion on the Royal Cedula of the 8th of April, 1779, that slaves (coartados) should be left in possession of the privilege in question. In answer to this, let us refer to the terms of the cedula. We declare, it says, that the masters of slaves (not coartados) have the liberty to sell them for whatsoever price they agree on with the buyers, according to their actual worth, that when masters for just reasons are obliged by the judicial authority to sell their slaves (those so entirely) it shall be for the price at which they shall be valued by those authorities; but if the buyer wishes to take the slave without valuation, agreeing thereon with the master, they can arrange between them the price, and the authorities have no power to prevent it, although the master is compelled to sell, except that in order to diminish the amount of the alcabala duty (or tax on the sale of property) some collusion between the parties be suspected; further, that for slaves who are 'coartado,' or have paid that portion remaining of it, the same obligation is binding on the buyer; that in all cases the seller shall pay the alcabala tax according to the price paid; further, that if the slave 'coartado' by bad conduct gives a reasonable motive for selling him, however slight his crime, the addition to the price be made of the alcabala tax on his sale; and finally, that no slaves of any kind, entire or coartados, who redeem themselves by their lawful earnings, ought to pay this tax. The masters shall be obliged, conformable to the custom, to give them their liberty the moment they bring the due price for it."

Now to any ordinary capacity, the plain meaning of the terms of this beneficient law of 1778, is that slaves have the power of demanding to be sold to another master, if another master can be procured to pay the price fixed on by the judges to the actual owner. In fact, the slave by this means puts himself in the position of a coartado, one who has the right to demand his freedom whenever a price has been agreed on, or fixed by judicial valuation; and having procured a person to advance the money, he is content to have his liberty sold again in consideration of the change of masters. But mark the chicanery by which every practical utility of this benevolent law is frittered away by the interpretation of the judicial authorities of Cuba. The slave who would change owners is first called on to produce a reasonable cause for this application. He alleges severe punishment or harsh treatment, who is to decide whether the slave has been maltreated or not. The Syndic. Who is the Syndic? A planter himself. And who is the master? The neighbour of the Syndic. But what says the Real Audiencia exposition of the law for the regulation of the practice of these Syndics? Why, that the due severity of the discipline of the proprietary power towards the slaves is not a sufficient cause for a slave's application to be sold, and that the only sufficient causes are insufficient nourishment, scarcity of clothing, and dearth of instruction in the christian religion. Now what does the last obligation on the planters amount to in Cuba?—to the christening of the slave, and to the burial of him, with the ordinary rights of the church. This is the whole amount in Cuba of religious assistance, save and except the teaching of the newly imported pagans to repeat, like parrots on certain feasts, the Lord's Prayer, the confiteor, and the decades of the rosary; but as for having the slightest conception of the meaning of the words they repeat by rote, it would be a folly to expect it, for they are never instructed in religion by priest or layman, except on the estate of (a rare phenomenon in Cuba) a pious planter, a scrupulous master, and a christian man. As to the complaint of insufficiency of food, the Syndic of course acts on the general opinion, that it is the interest of an owner to feed his slaves well, and to clothe them also for the sake of the preservation of their health and strength.

And now for their moral condition and the administration of the laws affecting it, on the high authority of the work published with the sanction and at the expense of the Real Audiencia of Cuba. "As amongst the Romans (says the author) there could be no marriage solemnized except among citizens, the union of the slaves was accomplished by concubinage, and the children followed the condition of the mother; our district law has adopted the same system (nuestra ley de partida ha adoptado la misma disposicion), and when recently coartacion was established, the question was discussed if the infant of a slave coartado should enjoy the same privileges as the mother, but the doubt has ceased since the publication of the Royal Cedula of the 10th February, 1789[5] in which we find the point in question definitely settled."

There can be no doubt of the express meaning of the Royal law on this subject being what it is described, and there is unfortunately no doubt that the slaves of Cuba have none of the rights of citizens, that they are not suffered to marry, and that a general system of concubinage is that which the christian law of the Partida sanctions in Cuba, and to which it condemns nearly half a million of human beings. Here I take leave of the Cuban exposition of the Spanish laws for the amelioration of slavery. No one can dispute the authority of the treatise I have referred to, for the express sanction of the Real Audiencia is prefixed to it. It was with no little difficulty I procured a copy of that work, for I have already stated it is not allowed to fall into the hands of strangers. Such is the specious benevolence of the Spanish laws, that have never been carried into execution, and are incapable of enforcement in any country where slavery exists, and where the interests arising from it are prosperous and powerful.

R.R.M.

Notes

1. Alexis Charles Henri Maurice Clérel de Tocqueville (1805–1859), French statesman and author.
2. Curiously enough this same idea is still held. See, for example, Hortensia Ruiz del Vizo, *Black Poetry of the Americas* (Miami: Ediciones Universal, 1972), pp. 9–17.
3. British Act of Emancipation of 1833.
4. Bartolomé de las Casas.
5. The Royal Cédula of February 1789 permitted Spaniards and foreigners to introduce slaves into certain ports free of all charges for two years.

EMANCIPATION OF SLAVES IN CUBA

In the year 1824, Mr. Secretary Canning[1] addressed a despatch to the Chief Commissioner at the Havana, desiring to be furnished with information on the subject of the manumission of slaves in the Spanish colonies, and enclosing a memorandum which had been presented to our government at that period, when the question of gradual emancipation in our colonies was attracting attention. The document enclosed is to the following effect:—

"That slaves, (namely those in the Spanish colonies,) are generally appraised at four hundred dollars; that a slave paying down the fourth part of his value, or one hundred dollars, immediately acquires a right to be coartado—that is, that he can work out, paying his master three reals de vellon or bits a-day, until he can make a further deposit; or, if the master requires his service, he can oblige the man to work for him, paying the slave one real; thus a deposit of two hundred dollars gives the slave a right to two reals daily; of three hundred, three reals, and thus till the completion of the payment of the whole sum in which he had been appraised. A dollar is worth eight reals or bits."— (Vide Slave-trade Reports, 1824–1825, Class A., page 63.) In the first place, the common error with respect to the meaning of the term of coartacion, which I have already referred to, is pointed out in the reference, made to the question of paying down one-fourth part of the value of the slave. The next error is in the statement that a slave coartado has the right to work out or to leave his master's service, paying him wages in a certain proportion to the sum still due for his liberty, the law treatise I have so largely quoted explicitly denying that the slave has any such right against the consent of his master. The Chief Commissioner replied to Mr. Canning's inquiry, October 9th, 1824, stating that he had consulted the most able lawyers and government authorities on the subject of manumission, and encloses a memorandum—a most valuable paper—though by no means to be considered as practically applicable to the attainable privileges of praedial slaves, and that distinction is not sufficiently drawn in the document, but only slightly alluded to at the end of the memorandum.

The commissioner, informs Mr. Canning that he has been wrongly informed that slaves are valued at any fixed price for "coartacion;" that he has known one sell for 1000 dollars, but that the tribunals discountenance excessive valuation; that the average valuation of full-grown negroes on estates is 500 dollars; that house-slaves are valued at six, and mechanics at still higher prices; that the statement is incorrect in asserting, "if the master require the service of his coartado slave, he can oblige the man to work, paying the slave a certain sum," the fact being, that in all cases the master is entitled to the service of his slave, whether coartado or not, without any remuneration whatever. That the wages of a common field labourer is about four reals a day, (there being eight reals "de plata,"[2] and twenty reals "de vellon"[3] to the dollar, the writer of the memorandum previously referred to having confounded these) and, moreover, that the negro is fed and clothed, and that as mechanics earn from a dollar-and-a-quarter to three dollars a-day, consequently, a coartado slave, who works out is able to pay his master the daily quota proportioned to his price, and to lay by something towards the further attainment of his liberty. That the regulations for ameliorating the condition of slaves are founded principally on custom which has acquired the force of law, many of which are confirmed by royal decrees. That when a slave applies to purchase his liberty, the master is not allowed to fix an arbitrary price, but if he and the slave cannot agree upon it, two appraisers are named, one by the master and another by the Syndic on the part of the slave, and if they differ the judge names an umpire, and in these cases the slave is exempt from the payment of the Alcabala duty, which is six per cent on the sale of slaves sold in venta real or by public auction. That a master will be compelled to sell a slave if a purchaser is found to engage to emancipate the slave at the end of any reasonable time. That ill usage justifies an application for change of masters. That a slave once emancipated cannot again be reduced to slavery. That the master having once given an "escritura de coartacion," binds himself never to demand more than a stipulated sum, though less than the actual value, and has no relation to the actual price originally paid for him. That the coartado slave, when his master allows him to work out on hire, is only bound to pay his master one real a day for every hundred dollars in which he is coartado (thus if his appraised price was four hundred dollars, and he had paid one hundred towards his liberty, he would only have to pay three reals a day to his master). That a pregnant negress may emancipate her child even when in the womb at the fixed price of twenty-five dollars, and from the time of its birth, till it be baptized for fifty dollars. That the system respecting the manumission of slaves, although in the country parts where there are few magistrates, there may be, and undoubtedly there are, many abuses, yet in the Havana, and other large towns and in other populous districts, it is efficiently observed.

I have already stated how far these nominal advantages are admitted by the expounders of the law, and shown that the system of manumission, and the regulations in force for ameliorating the condition of the slave in the Spanish colonies, honourable as these are to the apparent intentions of the Spanish government, are of little real benefit to the praedial slaves, that is, to the great body of the slave population in these colonies. There are exceptions, that are instances where slavery has not rendered masters heedless of all laws human and divine, even where their pecuniary interests are concerned. But these are few on the estates. There are instances where the owners and persons of high rank, and wealth, and standing in society—noblemen like the Count Fernandina, and a few others of his order, where the rights and privileges of the slaves are in some degree respected. These men, however, live not on their properties, and it is only to their occasional visits the slaves on their properties have to look for justice. It is, as I have said before, in the large towns alone, and for the nonpraedial slaves, that the privileges in question can be said to be available, and where manumission can be hoped for, the means acquired of obtaining it, and the opportunity given of applying for it, and for the redress of any wrong suffered by a slave.

R.R.M.

Notes

1. George Canning (1770–1827), British statesman.
2. of silver.
3. of copper.

GLOSSARY* OF CREOLE TERMS IN COMMON USE IN CUBA, AND OF THOSE RELATIVE TO SLAVERY AND THE TRADE IN SLAVES

AGIACO— A mess corresponding to the pepper-pot of Jamaica. It is composed of pork, sliced plantains, calabash, seasoned with red pepper and lemon-juice, in common use at planters' and overseers' tables.

AGUACERO— The small fire-fly, smaller and less brilliant than the Cucuyo or common fire-fly.

AGUARDIENTE— The spirits distilled from the sugar-cane.

ALMA EN BOCA Y HUESOS EN COSTAL— Term of the limited warranty, given with newly imported negroes. It signifies that the vendor will not answer for blemishes or diseases that may appear after the sale.

ARRENQUIN— In a team of oxen, the first or favourite leader.

AVENTADOR— A kind of winnowing machine for cleaning coffee.

AY— A common ballad, each line of which begins with this word, and is sung, or rather roared out, by the "monteros," or country people on their journeys, and at their labours in the field. The dance to this tune is called the "Zapateo."

ADMINISTRADOR— Attorney on an estate.

ALAMBIQUE— The still-house on a sugar estate.

AURA TENOSA— Equivalent to the John Crows of Jamaica.

BANCA FALLUSTA— A common gambling game.

BARRACON— A species of barracks where the newly imported slaves are kept till they are sold. The yard surrounded with sheds or huts on estates in which the slaves are shut up every night, are called barracones.

* This follows the alphabetization of the 1840 edition.

BEMBO— A negro with thick heavy lips.

BIBI— Negroes of the Carabali race.

BOBA— A game of cards.

BOCOY— A puncheon, when used for Molasses contains 110 gallons, when used for sugar from 50 to 54 arrobas, the arroba is about twenty-five pounds weight.

BOLAS— A game played by the negroes with small round stones.

BOLANCHERA— A dance in a circle, performed by men and women in alternate rounds.

BOMBA— The ladle used in the boiling houses. A term also for the toasts or "brindas," at convivial parties.

BOZAL— The African negro recently brought from his country into Cuba or Puerto Rico and newly stolen, and recently sold or exposed for sale there.

BRICAMOS— African negroes from a district of that name.

BRICHE— Negroes from the Carabali country.

BROCHA— A game of chance.

BUTACA— A large lounging elbow-chair.

CABILDO— The re-unions of Bozal negroes on festival days, in common use at the Havana, in which dancing, singing, and playing on rude instruments (ataboles) great clamour and confusion are the chief amusements. Each nation has its own Cabildo, and these orgios are called Cabildo Arara, Cabildo Congo, &c. &c.

CACHAZA— The scum of the boiled cane juice, or guarasso, of which all cattle are fond, and it is said to fatten them.

CAFETAL— Coffee estate.

CASA DE CALDERAS— Boiling house.

COGOLLOS, (de la cana,)— Cane tops.

CASA DE PURGA— Curing house.

CONTRA-MAYORAL— Driver who superintends, whip in hand, the field labour of the slaves.

CUADRILLA— That part of the negro gang that is worked by spells, and relieved at stated times.

CAPITAN DE PAPELLAS— Generally the mates of American vessels, with ship's papers fraudulently obtained at the American consulates, to enable the Spanish and Portuguese slavers to pass for American vessels.

CAPITAN DE PARTIDO— A district magistrate.

CARABOLI— Negroes from that part of Africa; they are accounted wild and rebellious; their front teeth are generally sharpened to a point.

CONUCO— The negro grounds or garden.

CEIBA— The giant cotton tree.

CIMARRON— A runaway negro in the country, in contra-distinction to HUIDO the runaway slaves in towns.

COARTADO— A slave the price of whose freedom is fixed, either in consideration of past service, or on account of his having paid a sum of money to his master towards the purchase of his freedom, and which sum is deducted from the price fixed on his manumission whenever he is sold, or buys his freedom.

CUCUYO— The fire-fly, or Elater Noctilucus, the fields of Cuba are peopled with these flying insects. In the darkest room it is possible to read by holding one of these insects along the line; there are two lights in the head and one in the belly. In the spring, the fields at night are illuminated with them; children delight to chase them, and the Creole girls adorn their hair with them, or keep them in cages and feed them on cane and sugar.

CONGO— African slaves from the country of this name, the most esteemed in Cuba for their fidelity and vigour.

CORRAL— An estate which consists of a league of land in circuit, used for the breeding of cattle.

CRIOLLO— All persons, whether white or black, born in the island, are called Creoles.

CUADRO DE CAFE— A piece of land, the fourth of a "caballeria" in extent, and generally with 10,000 coffee plants on it, are thus called.

CUERO— The whip used by the overseer on estates to flog the slaves, the handle short, of hard wood, the lash generally of a single thong, made of cow hide, the toughest that can be obtained, from a yard and a-half to two yards long; the knots on it are humorously called "Pajeulos." Da Cuero signifies to flog. Tocar el cuero, to crack the whip to call the slaves to work, or to their meals.

CUNA— An assemblage of people of colour for diversion.

CHARANGO— A game of chance in use in the country among the lower orders.

CHATA— Negroes with very flat noses.

CHINO or CHINA— The child of a mulatto and negro.

CHUCHO— The common house-whip, which every lady has at hand, for household use. It resembles our riding whip, the thong is made of twisted leather, and is generally painted green or red.

ENVASE or CAJA— The box in which the sugar is exported. It contains from 15 to 20 arrobas of sugar, or from 375 to 500 lbs. weight.

ESTANCIA— A small farm where fruit trees, vegetables, grain, &c. are cultivated.

FAENA— Extra hours of labour on feast days, on sugar estates, &c.

FUETE— A whip of any kind.

FUFU— A dish composed of plantains, yams, or calabash, beaten into a mass.

FINCA— A country place, a house with lands.

GENTE DE COLOR— Negroes, mulattoes, &c.

GUARDO RAYA— The walks in coffee grounds between the plots called in Jamaica intervals.

GUARAPPO— The juice of the cane extracted by the compression of the rollers of the mill.

HACENDADO— A country gentleman.

HATO— Breeding farm consisting of two leagues of land in circuit.

INFIERNO— A game at cards.

INGENIO— Sugar estate.

LADINO— In contra-distinction to Bozal, a negro born in Africa, but acclimated in Cuba, able to speak in Spanish, and supposed to be introduced before the slave-trade was prohibited.

LOANGO— A negro of the Congo country.

LUCUMI— A negro of the Lucumese country.

MACUA— A negro of the country of this nation.

MACHETO— A sword which the country people and overseers on estates wear.

MAESTRO ASSUCAR— A white man on the sugar estate, who superintends the making of sugar.

MANDINGO— A negro from the country of his name, the most civilised of the African nations.

MAREMBA— A musical instrument of the Bozals.

MAYORAL— The overseer of an estate. All the mayorals of Cuba are natives of Spain.

MAJOR DOMO— The book and account keeper on an estate.

MINA— A negro from the country of his name.

MONTE— A game of chance in general use amongst the gentry, and is forbidden by the laws. The word Monte also signifies the country generally, and Montero a countryman or small farmer.

NEGRERO— A slave ship.

NINO or NINA— The way of addressing young masters or mistresses on the part of slaves, and free coloured people.

PALENQUE— A place of resort in the woods and mountains for the fugitive slaves.

PANCHO— The pet name of children called Francisco.

PICA PLEITOS— Pettyfogging attorneys, who foment lawsuits.

PARDO, or PARDA— Mulatto man or woman, the term Moreno is more complimentary to them.

POTRERO— A farm laid out in pasturage, and for the breeding of stock.

QUITRIN— A two-wheeled carriage in common use, differing from the volante, the head being made of flexible leather, which may be lowered at pleasure, while the top of the volante is immoveable.

ROMPER MOLIENDA— To commence grinding sugar-cane.

SAFRA— Crop time, from the cutting of the cane to the packing of the sugar. On coffee estates, the crop time is called cosecha.

SAMBOMBIA— A negro drink, made of treacle and water.

SITIO— A farm being part of a hato or corral, having a house and offices for stalling cattle. A hato consists of several sitios. A sitio de labor is the same as estancia.

TERTULLIA— An evening party.

TACHO— Tache, or boiler.

TRECILLO— A fashionable game at cards.

TANGO— A festive re-union of Bozal negroes.

TASAGO— Coarse dried beef, brought from Tampico, of a very offensive smell; it is given to the slaves on estates in small quantities, and with yams and plantains, constitutes their diet.

TRAPICHE— The mill that grinds the cane.

VOLANTE— The chaise in common use in Cuba. An equipage in the keeping of which, the luxuriousness of the owner's taste in the large towns is chiefly shown.

ZAPATEE— See Ay, a vulgar dance.

ZUMZUM— The humming bird. The smallest and most beautiful of the feathered tribe. It cannot live except in liberty. If caught and put into a cage, it droops and dies in two or three days.

MANZANO'S POEMS IN THE ORIGINAL SPANISH

MIS TREINTA AÑOS

Cuando miro el espacio que he corrido
desde la cuna hasta el presente dia,
tiemblo y saludo á la fortuna mia
más de terror que de atención movido.
Sorpréndeme la lucha que he podido
sostener contra suerte tan impía,
si tal llamarse puede la porfía
de mi infelice sér al mal nacido.
Treinta años ha que conocí la tierra;
treinta años ha que en gemidor estado
triste infortunio por doquier me asalta;
mas nada es para mi la cruda guerra
que en vano suspirar he soportado,
si la comparo, ¡oh Dios!, con lo que falta.

EL RELOX ADELANTADO

En vano, relox mio
Te aceleras y afanas.
Marcando silencioso
Las horas que no pasan;
Si, aunque veloz el tiempo
Como el viento se escapa.
Jamás el sol brillante
De sus límites pasa
Él con dedo de fuego
Las verdades señala,
Y en las reglas que fija
ni un solo punto falla.
Si, hurtando los momentos,
A mis ojos engañas,
No por eso este dia
Más brevemente pasa.
   Pero si un mal interno,
O de tus ruedas varias
Los aguzados dientes
Te muerden las entrañas;
Aprende de mi pecho,
Que en tal fatal desgracia.
Por ser igual al tiempo
De lágrimas se baña.
Mas ¡ay! que no me entiendes,
Ni en tu carrera paras,
Tal vez horas buscando
Ménos duras y amargas
Tus pasos desmedidos,
Tu acelerada marcha,
Todo sigue, y demuestras
Una ofensiva causa;
Y en tan discorde curso
Y á mi dolor igualas.
Que con el largo tiempo
Siempre más se adelanta.

LA COCUYERA

Un incauto cocuyo
Revolaba brillando
Ya del prado á la selva.
Ya de la selva al prado.
Libre cual mariposa
Hendiendo el aire vago,
Liba en vírgenes flores
Jugos almibarados
Ora esplende, ora oculta
Del fósforo inflamado
La luz á que no cabe
Color acomodado.
¡Cómo vuela invisible!
Lucero es ya bien claro:
Si puesto se oscurece,
Presto ilumina el campo
En vano los mancebos
Le siguen anhelando.
Con teas encendidas.
El placer de tomarlo.
Pues revolando en torno
Al silbo suave y blando,
Vuelve la luz en niebla,
Se pierde entre las manos:
Y en la frondosa capa
De un florido naranjo,
Opaca luz despide
Dejándolos burlados
    Entónces Niña bella,
Gloria y honor del campo,
Envidia de las flores,
Delicia de su amado,
Toma la cocuyera,
Que con curiosas manos
Labró en felices dias
Su tierno enamorado,
Y en alto suspendiendo
Tan bellisimo encanto,
La mueve, y mil cocuyos
Alumbran encerrados.
    "Baja, le dice, baja,
Que en mi amante regazo
Cañas dulces te ofrezco,
De cañutos dorados:

Dormirás en mi alcoba
Mi aliento respirando;
Serás de mis amores
Confidente sagrado."
  El fúlgido cocuyo
Plácido susurrando,
Vuela, desciende y toca
Sobre sus mismos labios;
Probó la miel hiblea,
Con que amor ha endulzado
Los divinos claveles,
Honor del cútis blanco
Del nuevo prisionero
Celébrase el hallazgo,
Y en la prisión contento
Brilla que es un regalo...

Bibliography

Aimes, Hubert H. S. *A History of Slavery in Cuba, 1511 to 1868.* New York: G. P. Putnam, 1907.

Almeida, Joselyn. "Translating a Slave's Life: Richard Robert Madden and the Post-Abolition Trafficking of Juan Manzano's *Poems by a Slave in the Island of Cuba.*" In *Circulations: Romanticism and the Black Atlantic,* ed. Paul Youngquist and Frances Botkin (October 2011): 2. Web.

Arrom, José Juan. *Historia de la literatura dramática cubana.* New Haven, CT: Yale University Press, 1944.

———. "La poesía afrocubana." *Revista Iberoamericana* 4 (1942): 379–411.

Arrufat, Antón. "Cirilo Villaverde: Excursión a Vueltabajo." *Casa de las Américas* 2.10 (1962): 133–40.

Autobiography of a Slave/Autobiografía de un esclavo. Edited by Ivan A. Schulman. Translated by Evelyn Picon Garfield. Detroit: Wayne State University Press, 1996.

Azougarh, Abdeslam. *Juan Francisco Manzano: esclavo poeta en la isla de Cuba.* Valencia: Episteme, 2000.

Baker, Houston A., Jr. "Balancing the Perspective: A Look at Early Black American Literary Artistry." *Negro American Literature Forum* 6 (1972): 65–70.

Ballagas, Emilio. "Situación de la poesía afroamericana." *Revista Cubana* 21 (1946): 5–60.

Barnes, Gilbert Hobbs. *The Antislavery Impulse: 1830–1844.* New York: Appleton, 1933.

Barreda, Pedro. *The Black Protagonist in the Cuban Novel.* Amherst: University of Massachusetts Press, 1979.

Bayliss, John F., ed. *Black Slave Narratives.* New York: Macmillan, 1970.

Bergero, Adriana J. "Escritura, vida cotidiana y resignificaciones en La Habana de Juan Francisco Manzano." *Afro-Hispanic Review* 24.2 (2005): 7–32.

Blassingame, John W. "Black Autobiographies as History and Literature." *Black Scholar* 5 (December 1973–January 1974): 2–9.

———. *The Slave Community: Plantation Life in the Antebellum South.* New York: Oxford University Press, 1972.

Blassingame, John W. *Slave Testimony: Two Centuries of Letters, Speeches, Interviews, and Autobiographies.* Baton Rouge: Louisiana State University Press, 1977.

Bontemps, Arna, ed. *Great Slave Narratives.* Boston: Beacon Press, 1969.

Boti, Regino E. "La poesía cubana de Nicolás Guillén." *Revista Bimestre Cubana* 29 (mayo–junio 1932): 343–53.

Botkin, Benjamin A. "The Slave as His Own Interpreter." *Library of Congress Quarterly Journal* 2 (1944): 37–45.

———. "We Called It Living Lore." *New York Folklore Quarterly* 14 (1968): 189–201.

Branche, Jerome. *Colonialism and Race in Luso-Hispanic Literature.* Columbia and London: University of Missouri Press, 2006.

———. "*Mulato entre negros (y blancos)*: Writing, Race, the Antislavery Question, and Juan Francisco Manzano's *Autobiografía.*" *Bulletin of Latin American Research* 20.1 (2001): 63–87.

Bremer, Thomas. "The Slave Who Wrote Poetry: Comments on the Literary Works and the Autobiography of Juan Francisco Manzano." In *Slavery in the Americas,* ed. Wolfgang Binder, 487–501. Würzburg: Königshausen and Neumann, 1993.

Brickhouse, Anna. "Manzano, Madden, 'El Negro Mártir,' and the Revisionist Geographies of Abolitionism." In *American Literary Geographies: Spatial Practice and Cultural Production, 1500–1900,* ed. Martin Brückner and Hsuan L. Hsu, 209–35. Newark: University of Delaware Press, 2007.

Brown, Henry Box. *Narrative of Henry Box Brown.* Boston: Brown and Stearns, 1849.

Brown, John. *Slave Life in Georgia: A Narrative of the Life of John Brown, a Fugitive Slave,*ed. L. A. Chamerovzow. London: British and Foreign Anti-Slavery Society, 1855.

Brown, Sterling. *The Negro in American Fiction.* Washington, DC: Associates in Negro Folk Education, 1937.

Brown, William Wells. *Narrative of William Wells Brown, a Fugitive Slave. Written by Himself.* Boston: Anti-Slavery Office, 1847.

Buckmaster, Henrietta. *Let My People Go: The Story of the Underground Railroad and the Growth of the Abolition Movement.* Boston: Beacon Press, 1959.

Bueno, Salvador. *Historia de la literatura cubana.* Habana: Ministerio de Educación, 1963.

———. *Medio siglo de literatura cubana.* Habana: Comisión de la Unesco, 1953.

Burton, Gera. *Ambivalence and the Postcolonial Subject: The Strategic Alliance of Juan Francisco Manzano and Richard Robert Madden.* New York: Peter Lang, 2004.

Butterfield, Stephen. *Black Autobiography in America.* Amherst: University of Massachusetts Press, 1974.

Cade, John B. "Out of the Mouths of Ex-Slaves." *Journal of Negro History* 20 (1935): 294–337.

Calcagno, Francisco. *Poetas de color.* Havana: Imp. Militar de la V. Soler y Compañía, 1878.

Canaday, Nicholas. "The Antislavery Novel Prior to 1852 and Hildreth's 'The Slave' (1836)." *CLA Journal* 17 (December 1973): 175–91.

El cancionero del esclavo: Colección de poesías laureadas y recomendadas por el jurado en el certamen convocado por la sociedad abolicionista española. Madrid: La sociedad abolicionista española, 1866.

Cobb, Martha K. "An Appraisal of Latin American Slavery through Literature." *Journal of Negro History* 58 (1974): 460–69.

———. *Harlem, Haiti, and Havana: A Comparative Study of Langston Hughes, Jacques Roumain, and Nicolás Guillén.* Washington, DC: Three Continents Press, 1979.

———. "The Slave Narrative and the Black Literary Tradition." In *The Art of Slave Narrative: Original Essays in Criticism and Theory,* ed. John Sekora and Darwin Turner, 36–44. Macomb: Western Illinois University Press, 1982.

Corbitt, Roberta Day. "A Survey of Cuban Costumbrismo." *Hispania* 33.1 (February 1950): 41–45.

Corwin, Arthur F. *Spain and the Abolition of Slavery in Cuba, 1817–1886.* Austin: University of Texas Press, 1967.

Coulthard, G. R. *Race and Colour in Caribbean Literature.* London: Oxford University Press, 1962.

Coupland, Sir Reginald. *The British Anti-Slavery Movement.* New York: Barnes and Noble, 1933.

Curtin, Philip D. *The Atlantic Slave Trade (A Census).* Madison: University of Wisconsin Press, 1969.

———. *The Image of Africa: British Ideas and Action, 1780–1850.* 2 vols. Madison: University of Wisconsin Press, 1964.

Curtin, Philip D. and Jan Vansina. "Sources of the Nineteenth Century Atlantic Slave Trade." *Journal of African History* 5 (1964): 185–206.

DeCosta, Miriam. "Social Lyricism and the Caribbean Poet/Rebel." *CLA Journal* 15.4 (1972): 441–51.

———, ed. *Blacks in Hispanic Literature: Critical Essays.* Port Washington, NY: Kennikat Press, 1977.

DeCosta-Willis, Miriam. "Self and Society in the Afro-Cuban Slave Narrative." *Latin American Literary Review* 26.32 (1988): 6–15.

Deschamps Chapeus, Pedro. "Autenticidad de algunos negros y mulatos de *Cecilia Valdés.*" *Gaceta de Cuba* 81 (marzo 1970): 24–27.

Dizon, Alma. "Mothers, Morals, and Power in the Autobiography of Juan Francisco Manzano."*Revista de Estudios Hispánicos* (Río Piedras, Puerto Rico) 21 (1994): 109–17.

Douglass, Frederick. *Narrative of the Life of Frederick Douglass, an American Slave. Written by Himself.* Boston: Anti-Slavery Office, 1845.

Draper, Susana. "Voluntad de intellectual: Juan Francisco Manzano entre las redes de un humanismo sin derechos." *Chasqui: Revista de Literatura Latinoamericana* 31.1 (2002): 3–17.

Duberman, Martin, ed. *The Antislavery Vanguard: New Essays on the Abolitionists*. Princeton, NJ: Princeton University Press, 1965.

Ellis, Robert Richmond. "Reading through the Veil of Juan Francisco Manzano: From Homoerotic Violence to the Dream of a Homoracial Bond." *PMLA* 113.3 (1998): 422–35.

Engle, Margarita. *The Poet Slave of Cuba. A Biography of Juan Francisco Manzano*. New York: Henry Holt, 2006.

Fernández de Castro, José A. *Esquema histórica de las letras en Cuba (1548–1902)*. Habana: Universidad de La Habana, 1949.

———. *Tema negro en las letras de Cuba, 1608–1935*. Habana: Ediciones Mirador, 1943.

Fernández de la Vega, Óscar, et al. *Iniciación a la poesía afro-americana*. Miami: Ediciones Universal, 1973.

Foley, Barbara. "History, Fiction and the Ground Between: The Use of the Documentary Made in Black Literature." *PMLA* 95 (1980): 389–403.

Foner, Laura, and Eugene D. Genovese, eds. *Slavery in the New World: A Reader in Comparative History*. Englewood-Cliffs, NJ: Prentice-Hall, 1969.

Foster, Frances Smith. *Witnessing Slavery*. Westport, CT: Greenwood Press, 1979.

Franco, José L., ed. *Autobiografía, cartas y versos de Juan Fco. Manzano*. Havana: Municipio de la Habana, 1937.

Franklin, John Hope. *From Slavery to Freedom: A History of Negro Americans*. 3rd ed. New York: Alfred A. Knopf, 1967.

Friol, Roberto. "La novela cubana en el siglo XIX." *Unión* 6.4 (1968): 179–207.

———. *Suite para Juan Francisco Manzano*. Havana: Editorial Arte y Literatura, 1977.

García-Barro, C. "The Abolitionist Novel in Cuba." *CLA Journal* 21 (December 1977): 224–37.

Gates, Henry Louis. "Editor's Introduction." In *"Race," Writing and Difference,* ed. Henry Louis Gates, 1–20. Chicago: University of Chicago Press, 1986.

Genovese, Eugene D. *The World the Slaveholders Made: Two Essays in Interpretation*. New York: Vintage, 1969.

Giacoman, Helmy F., ed. *Homenaje a Alejo Carpentier: variaciones interpretivas de su obra*. New York: Las Américas, 1970.

Gilroy, Paul. *The Black Atlantic: Modernity and Double Consciousness*. Cambridge: Harvard University Press, 1993.

Gómez de Avellaneda, Gertrudis. *Sab*, ed. Mary Cruz. Habana: Editorial Arte y Literatura, 1976.

González del Valle, Emilio Martín. *La poesía lírica en Cuba*. Barcelona: Tipo-Lit. de Celestino Verdaguer, 1884.

González del Valle, José Z. *La vida literaria en Cuba (1836–1840)*. Habana: Publicaciones de la Secretaría de Educación, 1938.

Grismer, Raymond. *Vida y obra de autores cubanos.* La Habana: Editorial Alfa, 1940.

Guirao, Ramón, ed. *Órbita de la poesía afro-cubana, 1928–37.* Havana: Ugar, García y Cia 1938.

Haberly, David T. "Poe's 'Dream-Land' in Black and White: An Approach to the Poetry of Palés Matos." *Studies in Afro-Hispanic Literature* 1 (1977): 77–88.

Hauser, Rex. "Two New World Dreamers: Manzano and Sor Juana." *Afro-Hispanic Review* 12.2 (1993): 3–11.

Henríquez Ureña, Max. *Panorama histórico de la literatura cubana.* 2 vols. Puerto Rico: Ediciones Mirador, 1963.

———. *Tablas cronológicas de la literatura cubana.* Santiago de Cuba: Ediciones Archipiélago, 1929. [Also published in the journal *Archipiélago* 1.11 (31 marzo 1929): 188; 1.12 (30 abril 1929): 204; 2.13 (31 mayo 1929): 220; and 2.14 (31 julio 1929): 246–47.]

Henson, Josiah. *Truth Stranger than Fiction: Father Henson's Story of His Own Life.* Boston: John J. Jewett, 1858.

Jackson, Richard L. *The Black Image in Latin American Literature.* Albuquerque: University of New Mexico Press, 1976.

———. *Black Writers and the Hispanic Canon.* New York: Twayne Publishers, 1997.

———. *Black Writers in Latin America.* Albuquerque: University of New Mexico Press, 1979.

———. "Racial Identity and the Terminology of Literary Blackness in Spanish America." *Revista Chicano-Riqueña* 5 (otoño 1977): 43–48.

Jahn, Janheinz. *A History of Neo-African Literature: Writings in Two Continents.* London: Faber and Faber, 1968.

James, C. L. R. "The Atlantic Slave Trade and Slavery: Some Interpretations of Their Significance in the Development of the United States and the Western World." In *Amistad I,* ed. John A. Williams and Charles F. Harris, 119–64. New York: Vintage, 1970.

———. *A History of Negro Revolt.* New York: Haskell House, 1969.

———. *A History of Pan-African Revolt.* Washington, DC: Drum and Spear Press, 1969.

Jiménez, Luis A. "Nineteenth Century Autobiography in the Afro-Americas: Frederick Douglass and Juan Francisco Manzano." *Afro-Hispanic Review* 14.2 (1995): 47–52.

Johnson, Paul. "Goodbye to Sambo: The Contribution of Slave Narratives to the Abolition Movement." *Negro American Literature Forum* 6 (1972): 79–84.

King, Lloyd, trans. *The Autobiography of a Cuban Slave.* St.Augustine, Trinidad. L. King, 1990.

———. "Nicolás Guillén and Afrocubanism." In *A Celebration of Black African Writing,* ed. Bruce King and Kolawole Ogungbesan, 30–59. New York: Oxford University Press, 1975.

Klingber, Frank J. *The Anti-Slavery Movement in England.* New Haven: Yale University Press, 1926.

Knight, Franklin W. *Slave Society in Cuba during the Nineteenth Century.* Madison: University of Wisconsin Press, 1970.

Labrador-Rodríguez, Sonia. "La intelectualidad negra en Cuba en el siglo XIX: El caso de Manzano." *Revista Iberoamericana* 62 (1996): 13–25.

Laferriere, Daniel. "Making Room for Semiotics." *Academe: Bulletin of the AAUP* 65 (November 1979): 434–40.

Lazo, Raimundo. *La literatura cubana.* México, DF: Universidad Nacional, 1965.

———. "La teoría de las generaciones y su aplicación al estudio histórico de la literatura cubana." *Universidad de la Habana* 19.112–14 (abril 1964): 30–33.

Leante, César. "Dos obras antiesclavistas cubanas." *Cuadernos Americanos* 207.4 (1976): 175–89.

Lewis Galanes, Adriana. *Poesías de J. F. Manzano, esclavo en la isla de Cuba.* Madrid: Betania, 1991.

Luis, William. "Autobiografía del esclavo Juan Francisco Manzano: Versión de Suárez y Romero." In *La Historia en la Literatura Iberoamericana. Memorias del XXVI Congreso del Instituto Internacional de Literatura Iberoamericana,* 259–68. Hanover, NH: Ediciones del Norte, 1989.

———. *Juan Francisco Manzano: Autobiografía del esclavo poeta y otros escritos.* Madrid: Iberoamerica, 2007.

———. *Literary Bondage: Slavery in Cuban Narrative.* Austin: University of Texas Press, 1990.

———. "Nicolás Azcárate's Antislavery Notebook and the Unpublished Poems of the Slave Juan Francisco Manzano." *Revista de Estudios Hispánicos* 28.3 (1994): 331–46.

Macchi, Fernanda. "Juan Francisco Manzano el dicurso abolicionoista: Una lectura enmarcada." *Revista Iberoanericana* 73. 218–19 (2007): 63–77.

———. "Richard Robert Madden y el origen de las indias." *Afro-Hispanic Review* 27.2 (2008): 71–90.

Madden, Richard Robert. *The Island of Cuba: Its Resources, Progress, and Prospects.* London: Charles Gilpin, 1849.

———. *A Letter to W. E. Channing, D.D. on the Subject of the Abuse of the Flag of the United States, in the Island of Cuba, and the Advantage Taken of Its Protection in Promoting the Slave Trade.* Boston: Ticknor, 1839.

———. *The Memoirs (Chiefly Autobiographical) from 1798 to 1886 of Richard Robert Madden; M.D., F.R.C.S.* Edited by Thomas More Madden. London: Ward and Downey, 1891.

Mansour, Mónica. *La poesía negrista.* México, DF: Ediciones Era, 1973.

Manzano, Juan Francisco. *Autobiografía, cartas y versos de Juan Fco. Manzano,* ed. José L. Franco. Habana: Municipio de la Habana, 1937.

———. *Autobiografía de un esclavo.* Edited by Ivan A. Schulman. Madrid: Ediciones Guadarrama, 1975.

———. *Obras de Juan Francisco Manzano.* Edited by Israel M. Moliner. Habana: Instituto del Libro Cubano, 1972.

McMurray, David Arthur. "Dos negros en el Nuevo Mundo: Notas sobre el 'americanismo' del Langston Hughes y la cubana de Nicolás Guillén." *Casa de las Américas* 14 (enero–febrero 1974): 122–28.

Megenney, William W. "The Black in Hispanic-Caribbean and Brazilian Poetry: A Comparative Perspective." *Revista Interamericana Review* 5 (1975): 47–66.

Miller, Marilyn. "Imitation and Improvisation in Juan Francisco Manzano's *Zafira.*" *Colonial Latin America Reviews* 17.1 (2008): 49–71.

———. "Reading Juan Francisco Manzano in the Wake of Alexander von Humbolt." *Atlantic Studies* 7.2 (2010):163–89.

———. "Rebeldía narrativa, resistencia poética y expresión 'libre' en Juan Francisco Manzano." *Revista Iberoamericana* 71.211(2005): 417–36.

Mitjans, Aurelio. *Historia de la literatura cubana.* 1890; reprint, Madrid: Editorial América, 1918.

Molloy, Sylvia. "From Serf to Self: The Autobiography of Juan Francisco Manzano." *MLN* 104.2 (1989): 394–416.

Montejo, Esteban. *The Autobiography of a Runaway Slave,* ed. Miguel Barnet. Translated by Jocasta Innes. New York: Pantheon, 1968.

Morner, Magnus. "The History of Race Relations in Latin America: Some Comments on the State of Research." *Latin American Research Review* 1 (1966): 23–44.

Mueller-Berg, Klaus. *Alejo Carpentier: Estudio biográfico-crítico.* New York: Las Américas, 1972.

Mullen, Edward J. *Afro-Cuban Literature: Critical Junctures.* Westport, CT: Greenwood, 1998.

———. "Francisco Calcagno and the Afro-Cuban Literary Canon." *PALARA* 12 (2008): 29–37.

———, ed. *The Life and Poems of a Cuban Slave: Juan Francisco Manzano, 1797–1854.* Hamden, CT: Archon Books, 1981.

Murray, David R. "Richard Robert Madden: His Career as a Slavery Abolitionist." *Studies* 61 (1972): 41–53.

Nichols, Charles H. *Many Thousand Gone: The Ex-Slaves' Account of Their Bondage and Freedom.* Leidan, Netherlands: E. J. Brill, 1963.

———. "Slave Narratives and the Plantation Legend." *Phylon* 10 (third quarter, 1949): 201–10.

———. "Who Read the Slave Narratives?" *Phylon* 20 (summer 1959): 149–62.

———, ed. *Black Men in Chains: Narratives by Escaped Slaves.* New York: Lawrence Hill, 1972.

Noble, Enrique. "Aspecos étnicos y sociales de la poesía mulata latinoameri-cana." *Revista Bimestre Cubana* 40 (1958): 166–79.

"Notes to the Text." In Martin R. Delany, *Blake or the Huts of America,*ed. Floyd J. Miller, xi–xxix. Boston: Beacon Press, 1970.

Nwankwo, Ifeoma Kiddoe. *Black Cosmopolitanism: Racial Consciousness and Transnational Identity in the Nineteenth-Century Americas*. Philadelphia: University of Pennsylvania Press, 2005.

Obras de Juan Francisco Manzano. Edited by Israel M. Moliner. Havana: Instituto del Libro Cubano, 1972.

Olivera, Otto. *Breve historia de la literatura antillana*. México, DF: Ediciones de Andrea, 1957.

Olney, James. "'I Was Born': Slave Narratives, Their Status as Autobiography and as Literature." In *The Slave's Narrative*, ed. Charles Davis and Henry Louis Gates, 148–75. Oxford: Oxford University Press, 1985.

Perada Valdés, Ildefonso. *Lo negro y lo mulato en la poesía cubana*. Montevideo: Ediciones Ciudadela, 1970.

———. "La poesía afrocubana." *Afroamérica* 2 (enero 1946): 113–19.

Piedro-Bueno, Andrés de. *Literatura cubana, síntesis histórico*. Habana: Editorial América, 1945.

Portuondo, José Antonio. *Bosquejo histórico de las letras cubanas*. Habana: Ministerio de Relaciones Exteriores, 1960.

Prieto, Antonio López. *Parnaso cubano: Colección de poesías selectas de autores cubanas desde Zequeira a nuestros días*. Havana: Miguel de Villa, 1881.

"Proceedings of the General Anti-Slavery Convention Held in London, 1840." *Eclectic Review* 8 (1841): 227–47.

Ramos, Julio. "Cuerpo, lengua, subjectividad." *Revista de Crítica Literaria* 19.38 (1993): 225–37.

———. "The Law Is Other: Literature and the Constitution of the Juridical Subject in Nineteenth Century Cuba." *Annals of Scholarship* 11.1–2 (1996): 1–35.

Rawick, George P. *From Sundown to Sunup: The Making of the Back Community*. Westport, CT: Greenwood, 1972.

Remos y Rubio, Juan J. *Historia de la literatura cubana*. 3 vols. Habana: Cárdenas y Cia, 1945.

———. *Proceso histórico de las letras cubanas*. Madrid: Editorial Guadarrama, 1958.

———. *Resumen de historia de la literatura cubana*. Habana: Molina y Cia, 1930.

"Review of New Publications." *Christian Observer* 41 (1841): 44–48.

"Richard Robert Madden, F.R.C.S.E., L.A. Lond., M.R.I.A. & c, Sc." *Dublin University Magazine* 87 (1876): 272–78.

Ruis del Vizo, Hortensia. *Black Poetry of the Americas: A Bilingual Anthology*. Miami: Ediciones Universal, 1972.

Sánchez, Reinaldo, et al. *Homenaje a Lydia Cabrera*. Miami: Ediciones Universal, 1978.

Scarry, Elaine. *The Body in Pain: The Making and the Unmaking of the World*. Oxford and New York: Oxford University Press, 1985.

Scholes, Robert, and Robert Kellogg. *The Nature of Narrative*. New York: Oxford University Press, 1966.

Schomburg, Arthur, A. *A Bibliographic Checklist of American Negro Poetry.* New York: Charles E. Hartman, 1916.

Schulman, Ivan A. "The Portrait of the Slave: Ideology and Aesthetics in the Cuban Antislavery Novel." In *Comparative Perspectives on Slavery in New World Plantation Societies,* ed. Vera Rubin and Arthur Tuden, 356–67. New York: New York Academy of Sciences, 1977.

Sommer, Doris. "Textual Conquests: On Readerly Competence and 'Minority' Literature." *Modern Language Quarterly.* 54.1 (1993): 142–53.

Souza, Raymond D. *Major Cuban Novelists: Innovation and Tradition.* Columbia: University of Missouri Press, 1976.

Spratlin, V.B. "The Negro in Spanish Literature." *The Journal of Negro History.* 19.1 (1943): 60–71.

Starling, Marion Wilson. "The Slave Narrative: Its Place in American Literary History." Ph.D. dissertation, New York University, 1946.

Stimson, Frederick S. *Cuba's Romantic Poet: The Story of Plácido.* Chapel Hill: University of North Carolina Press, 1964.

———. *Orígenes del hispanismo norteamericano.* México, DF: Ediciones de Andrea, 1961.

Stone, Albert E. "Identity and Art in Frederick Douglass's 'Narrative.'" *CLA Journal* 17 (December 1973): 192–97.

Suárez y Romero, Anselmo. *Francisco: El ingenio o las delicias del campo.* Habana: Cuadernos de cultura, 1947.

Sweeney, Fionnghuala. "Atlantic Countercultures and the Networked Text: Juan Francisco Manzano, R. R. Madden and the Cuban Slave Narrative." *Forum for Modern Language Studies* 40.4 (2004): 401–14.

Temperly, Howard R. "British and American Abolitionists." In *The Antislavery Vanguard: New Essays on the Abolitionists,* ed. Martin Duberman, 337–58. Princeton: Princeton University Press, 1965.

Trelles, Carlos M. "Bibliografía de autores de raza de color de Cuba." *Cuba Contemporáneo* 43 (1927): 1–41.

Valle, Emilio Martín González del. *La poesía lírica en Cuba.* Barcelona: Tipo-Lit. de Celestino Verdaguer, 1884.

Vera-León, Antonio. "Juan Francisco Manzano: El estilo bárbaro de la nación." *Hispamérica* 20.60 (1991): 3–22.

Vitier, Cintio. "Dos poetas cubanos: Plácido y Manzano." *Bohemia* 14 (1973): 20–21.

———. *Lo cubano en la poesía.* Habana: Universidad Central de la Villas, 1958.

Williams, Lorna. *The Representation of Slavery in Cuban Fiction.* Columbia: University of Missouri Press, 1994.

Willis, Susan. "Crushed Geraniums: Juan Francisco Manzano and the Language of Poetry." In *The Slave's Narrative,* ed. Charles T. Davis and Henry Louis Gates Jr, 199–224. New York: Oxford University Press, 1985.

Yacou, Alain. *Un esclave-poète à Cuba au temps du peril noir: autobiograhie de Juan Francisco Manzano, 1797–1851.* Paris: Karthala, 2004.

Index

Printed in the United States of America